Student Guide for Learning Macroeconomics

to accompany

Byrns/Stone
MACROECONOMICS
Sixth Edition

Student Guide for Learning Macroeconomics

to accompany

Byrns/Stone
MACROECONOMICS
Sixth Edition

Ralph T. Byrns
University of Colorado-Boulder

Gerald W. Stone
Metropolitan State College of Denver

 HarperCollins*CollegePublishers*

Student Guide for Learning Macroeconomics to accompany Byrns/Stone,
MACROECONOMICS, Sixth Edition

Copyright © 1995 HarperCollins*Publishers*

ISBN: 0-673-99345-0

94 95 96 97 98 9 8 7 6 5 4 3 2 1

Table of Contents

How to Study Economics

No doubt about it. Economics is among the most challenging topics that many of you will encounter during your college educations. This *Student Guide for Learning Macroeconomics* will help focus your study so that the time you devote to this fascinating subject is as productive as possible. Before you work on any chapter in this study guide, you should thoroughly read (and perhaps, reread) the corresponding material in our texts, *Macroeconomics* or E*conomics*. The "Contents in Brief" for this study guide provides cross-references so that you can discern which chapter here corresponds to a particular chapter from the text you are using.

Conscientious use of this study guide is the single factor that seems to differentiate students who do well in our courses from those who do poorly. This guide, instead of introducing new material, will aid you in learning and retaining the material in your text. You will find that time spent working through this study guide will pay huge dividends when you take examinations that test your mastery of economic concepts. More importantly, we hope that five years from now you remember and are able to apply economic reasoning to everyday problems. If you have any suggestions that you believe would make this guide more useful for other students, please send your comments to us, c/o HarperCollinsPublishers, 10 East 53rd Street, New York, NY 10022-5299.

A General Plan for Studying Economics

Superficial cramming is very unlikely to succeed in an macroeconomics course. Keeping up is crucial. Educational research indicates that learning is most effective when you are exposed to information and concepts in several ways over a period of time. You will learn more economics and retain it longer if you read, see, hear, communicate, and then apply economic concepts and information. This material is much more than a few facts and glib generalizations; understanding economics requires reflection. Here is one systematic study strategy that many students have found successful in economics, and have adapted for other classes.

Visual Information

Don't let the extensive graphs in economics frighten you. There is a brief review of graphical analysis at the end of Chapter 1 of your text. The introductory modules in our *MacroStudy* program and this *Student Guide for Learning Macroeconomics* also open with sets of helpful exercises. Avoid the agony of trying to memorize each graph by taking the time to learn how graphs work. Proceed to Chapter 2 of your text only after you quell your anxiety a bit. (Be sure that you also understand simple algebra. The algebra in the text is elementary, and should prove no problem if you have learned the material from a basic course.) As you become familiar with graphs, you may be surprised to find yourself mentally graphing many noneconomic relationships, and even more amazed to find this process enjoyable.

Reading

Schedule ample time to read your assignments, and try to use the same quiet and cool (but not cold) room every day. Avoid drowsiness by sitting in a hard chair in front of a desk or table. Think about the material as you read. Many students spend hours highlighting important points for later study, for which they somehow never find time. Too frequently, busy work substitutes for thinking about economics. Try to skim a chapter; then go back and really focus on five or six pages. Don't touch a pen or pencil except to make margin notes cross-referencing related materials you already know.

Writing

After a healthy dose of serious reading, close your text and outline the important points with a half-page of notes. If you cannot briefly summarize what you just read, put your pen down and re-read the material. You have not yet digested the central ideas. Don't be surprised if some concepts require several readings. Be alert for graphs and tables that recapitulate important areas. When you finish each chapter, read its Chapter Review, work through all Problems, and outline good, but brief, answers to all Questions for Thought and Discussion.

Listening

Most lectures blend your instructor's insights and examples with materials from the text, but few students conscientiously do assignments before lectures. You will have a major advantage over most of your classmates if you do, and will be able to take notes selectively. Focus on topics that your instructor stresses but which are not covered in depth in the text. Notes from lectures should supplement, not duplicate, your text.

Teaching

Your instructors know that they learn their subject in greater depth every time they teach it. Teaching exposes you to previously unfamiliar aspects of a topic because you must conceptualize and verbalize ideas so that other people can understand them. Take turns with a classmate in reading the text's Key Points (in the Chapter Review) to each other. After one person reads a Key Point aloud, the other should explain it in his or her own words. Study groups work well in this way, but you may learn economics even more thoroughly if you simply explain economic concepts to a friend who has never studied it.

Applications

Working through the material from this *Student Guide* that parallels each chapter of the text will make it easier to comprehend the economic events regularly featured in the news. When this happens, you will be among the minority who truly understand economic and financial news. Use economic reasoning to interpret your day-to-day behavior, and that of your friends and relatives. This will provide unique insights into how people function and how the world works.

Examinations

Following the preceding suggestions should prepare you for minor tests and quizzes. To prepare for major exams and finals:

1. Read the Chapter Reviews for all chapters that will be covered on the examination. Keep a record of each Key Point that you could not explain to an intelligent friend who had never taken an economics course.

2. Return to each Key Point that you have not grasped adequately. Read the text material that covers it and rework the parallel parts of the accompanying chapter from your *Student Guide*.

3. Discuss any Key Point is not clear to you with a friend.

4. Skim the Glossary included in your package for a last minute refresher before your final exam.

See if this technique works for you. We know that this is a tall order, but if you conscientiously follow these study tips, we guarantee you an enjoyable and enlightening course.

Acknowledgments

We would like to thank Professor Stephen Stageberg of *Mary Washington College* and Professor John P. David of *West Virginia Institute of Technology* for their diligent and speedy error-checking. Their corrections were greatly appreciated.

Chapter 1
Economics: The Study of Scarcity

Chapter Objectives

The economic concepts presented in this chapter provide a general framework for understanding the remainder of this book. After you have read and studied this introductory chapter you should be able to explain why scarcity is the basic economic problem; describe various kinds of productive resources and the payments to the owners of these resources; discuss a number of fundamental economic concepts, including the nature of economic prices, opportunity costs, and efficiency; discuss the nature of scientific theory, including its evolution into common sense, and the use of Occam's Razor; and distinguish normative from positive economics, and macroeconomics from microeconomics.

Chapter Review: Key Points

1. *Economics* is concerned with choices and their consequences, and focuses on ways that individuals and societies allocate their limited resources to try to satisfy relatively unlimited wants.

2. *Scarcity* occurs because our relatively unlimited wants cannot be completely met from the limited resources available. A good is scarce if people cannot freely get all they want, so that the good commands a positive price. Scarcity forces all levels of decision makers from individuals to society at large to resolve three basic economic questions:
    a. *What* will be produced?
    b. *How* will production occur?
    c. *Who* will use the goods produced?

3. *Goods* include anything that adds to human happiness, while *bads* are things that detract from it. *Economic goods* are costly; *free goods* are not.

4. *Production* occurs when knowledge or technology is used to apply energy to materials to make them more valuable.

5. The *opportunity costs* of choices are measured by the subjective values of the best alternative you sacrifice. *Absolute prices* are monetary, and are useful primarily as indicators of *relative prices*, which are the prices of goods or resources in terms of each other, and which provide information and incentives to guide our decisions.

6. *Resources* (factors of production) include:
   a. *Labor*. Productive efforts made available by human beings. Payments for labor services are called *wages*.
   b. *Land*. All natural resources. Payments for land are called *rents*.
   c. *Capital*. Improvements that increase the productive potential of other resources. Payments for the use of capital are called *interest*. When economists refer to capital, they mean physical capital rather than financial capital, which consists of paper claims to goods or resources.
   d. *Entrepreneurship*. The organizing, innovating, and risk-taking function that combines other factors to produce. Entrepreneurs are rewarded with *profits*.

7. *Economic efficiency* occurs when a given amount of resources produces the most valuable combination of outputs possible. In an efficient economy, no transactions are possible from which anyone can gain without someone else losing.
   a. *Allocative efficiency* requires production of the things people want.
   b. *Distributive efficiency* requires consumers to adjust their purchasing patterns to maximize their satisfactions from given budgets.

   c. *Productive (technical) efficiency* is obtained when a given output is produced at the lowest possible cost. Another way of looking at efficiency is that it occurs when the opportunity cost of obtaining some specific amount of a good is at its lowest.

8. *Common sense* is theory that has been tested over a long period and found useful. In general, good theory accurately predicts how the real world operates. *Occam's Razor* suggests that the simplest workable theories are the most useful or "best."

9. *Positive economics* is scientifically testable and involves value-free descriptions of economic relationships, dealing with "what is." *Normative economics* involves value judgments about economic relationships and addresses "what should be." Normative theory can be neither scientifically verified nor proven false.

10. *Macroeconomics* is concerned with aggregate (the total levels of) economic phenomena, including such items as Gross National Product, unemployment, and inflation. *Microeconomics* concentrates on individual decision making, resource allocation, and how prices and output are determined.

Matching Key Terms And Concepts

SET I

___ 1. microeconomics
___ 2. Occam's razor
___ 3. positive economics
___ 4   land
___ 5. model
___ 6. normative economics
___ 7. macroeconomics
___ 8. entrepreneurship
___ 9. financial capital
___ 10. production

a. The simplest workable theory is the best theory.
b. Economic theory that is, at least theoretically, scientifically testable and free of value judgments.
c. Securities and other paper claims to goods or resources.
d. The organizing, risk-taking, and innovating resource.
e. Contestable theories rife with value judgments.
f. Using technology to apply energy to make materials more valuable.
g. Nonhuman resources other than capital.
h. The study of individual decisions made by consumers and firms.
i. Focuses on aggregate, or economy-wide, variables.
j. A representation of a theory.

SET II

___ 1. technology
___ 2. capital
___ 3. *Homo economicus*
___ 4. labor
___ 5. rent
___ 6. scarce good
___ 7. profits
___ 8. investment
___ 9. depreciation
___ 10. wages

a. Desired amounts of a good exceed those freely available.
b. Improvements to natural resources that make them more productive.
c. The view that humans maximize their satisfaction or wealth.
d. The hours of human effort available for production.
e. Payments for labor services.
f. Physical capital accumulation.
g. Decreases in capital because of wear-and-tear.
h. Entrepreneur's reward.
i. Payment for the use of land.
j. The "recipes" used to combine resources for production.

SET III

___ 1.	interest	a.	The value foregone whenever people make choices.
___ 2.	free good	b.	Adds to human happiness, but is not scarce.
___ 3.	opportunity cost	c.	Payments to capital owners.
___ 4.	scarcity	d.	When this is reached, further gains in happiness to anyone require losses to someone else.
___ 5.	relative prices	e.	Achieving maximum satisfaction from given budgets.
___ 6.	economic efficiency	f.	The basic economic problem.
___ 7.	absolute prices	g.	Prices of goods or resources in terms of each other.
___ 8.	production efficiency	h.	Prices of goods or services in terms of some monetary unit.
___ 9.	equity	i.	Fairness.
___10.	consumption efficiency	j.	Getting maximum output from given resources.

True/False

___ 1. Economics resembles accounting or finance in being more relevant for business firms than individuals.

___ 2. Complexity is desirable in a scientific theory.

___ 3. Unlike theory, common sense emphasizes practicality.

___ 4. Normative economics is concerned with what should be, rather than what is.

___ 5. Macroeconomics focuses on aggregate variables such as national income, employment, and inflation.

___ 6. Occam's Razor is more relevant for other sciences than it is for economics.

___ 7. Economic reasoning is involved anytime people choose one thing instead of another.

___ 8. Models are less complicated and formal than theories.

___ 9. Positive economic analysis can help in determining how to reach politically-set economic goals.

___10. Positive economics specifies the value judgments used to draw inferences in economic analysis.

___11. Successful entrepreneurs combine resources productively.

___12. Financial capital refers to all improvements made to land, machinery, and equipment.

___13. Payments for the use of capital services are called profit.

___14. Deciding to take a nap is an economic decision.

___15. Self sufficiency is an efficient goal for everyone.

___16. A good is scarce if the amounts people desire exceed the amounts freely available.

___17. Prices are a meaningless concept in economies that do not use money.

___18. Economic considerations shape even such decisions as selecting a spouse or determining how many children to have.

___19. Opportunity costs are incurred while you study economics.

___20. Most of the best things in life are free.

Standard Multiple Choice

There Is One Best Answer For Each Question.

___ 1. Economics involves broadly studying how:
   a. political power is used unethically to make money.
   b. resources are allocated to satisfy human wants.
   c. proper nutrition and budgeting benefit your family.
   d. to get away with cheating the Internal Revenue Service.
   e. different species are environmentally interdependent.

___ 2. Scientific attempts to describe economic relationships are:
   a. factual and can never be wrong.
   b. accurate ways to predict political viewpoints.
   c. known as positive economics.
   d. directed at the fairness of social programs.
   e. intended to boost the egos of entrepreneurs.

___ 3. Disagreements between economists arise most commonly in:
   a. microeconomic reasoning.
   b. normative economics.
   c. positive economics.
   d. applications of common sense.
   e. macroeconomic theories.

___ 4. Economists:
   a. hardly ever agree on anything.
   b. agree on much of economic theory.
   c. never make value judgments.
   d. accurately predict the effects of all economic policies.
   e. disagree most about positive economics.

___ 5. Unnecessary complexity in a theory is a violation of:
   a. common sense.
   b. the principle of nonsatiety.
   c. the law of supply and demand.
   d. Occam's razor.
   e. the anti-parsimony corollary.

6. Which of the following LEAST explains the widespread but erroneous view that economists seldom agree?
   a. The media focus on controversy, not agreement.
   b. Politics shapes policymaking more than does economic logic.
   c. Economists who are political appointees often feel obligated to support the president even if they disagree privately.
   d. Economic policies embody controversial value judgments.
   e. Economic policy is more scientific than economic theory.

7. Macroeconomics is primarily concerned with aggregates. Which of the following is not a macroeconomic aggregate?
   a. Decisionmaking by a household.
   b. The unemployment rate, and inflation levels.
   c. National income.
   d. The supply of money.
   e. Fiscal policies of the federal government.

8. Decisions made in households, firms, and government are the focus of:
   a. positive economics.
   b. environmental economics.
   c. microeconomics.
   d. normative economics.
   e. macroeconomics.

9. When less of a good than people want is freely available, the good is:
   a. in short supply.
   b. a free good.
   c. a luxury good.
   d. scarce.
   e. a necessity.

10. Which of the following comes closest to being a free good?
    a. A wino's lunch, dug from the trash behind a restaurant.
    b. Hot lunches provided to needy students at school.
    c. Bacon and eggs bought with food stamps.
    d. A record you bought from money earned by picking up aluminum cans in your spare time.
    e. Free public education.

11. TINSTAAFL is an acronym suggesting that:
    a. tax inspectors never see the awful affects from levies.
    b. tenants in need should take all assets from landlords.
    c. there is no such thing as a free lunch.
    d. temperance in non-satiety together are adequate for life.
    e. tyrants in Nirvana seldom try avoiding acceptably full lunches.

12. Opportunity costs will always exist as long as:
    a. an economy has money
    b. relative prices are variable
    c. the opportunity to make money exists
    d. something has to be given up to get something else
    e. production is unregulated

13. Labor, land, capital, and entrepreneurship are all:
    a. examples of technology.
    b. allocative mechanisms.
    c. resources, or factors of production.
    d. tools of capitalistic exploitation.
    e. natural resources.

___14. An economy suffers from production inefficiency if:
   a. water runs off lawns and down big city streets when it is greatly needed by remote drought-stricken farmers.
   b. it operates in a region of diminishing returns.
   c. costs increase when production is expanded.
   d. a consumer could gain by buying different goods.
   e. costs could be reduced by using resources differently.

___15. Opportunity costs are the values of the:
   a. monetary costs of goods and services.
   b. best alternatives sacrificed when choices are made.
   c. minimal budgets of families on welfare.
   d. profits gained by successful entrepreneurs.
   e. freedom people enjoy in a socialist economy.

___16. Economic equity refers to the:
   a. financial settlements in civil court cases.
   b. balance of national trade.
   c. fairness of some economic arrangement.
   d. hidden costs passed on to consumers.
   e. gross value of any stocks or bonds you own.

___17. Economic efficiency for the entire economy requires that:
   a. potential gains to anyone necessitate losses to another.
   b. all goods be produced at their lowest possible opportunity costs.
   c. maximum-valued output is obtained from given resources.
   d. all benefits are obtained at the lowest possible cost.
   e. All of the above.

___18. Which of the following statements is normative?
   a. Higher oil prices will increase the inflation rate.
   b. A tariff on textiles would tend to increase the wages of domestic textile workers.
   c. Tax rates on the working poor should be reduced.
   d. Other things equal, if the price of an item is reduced, consumers will to buy more of it.
   e. If interest rates remain high this quarter, business investment will continue to be weak.

___19. Knowledge used to combine resources productively is called:
   a. entrepreneurship.
   b. capitalism.
   c. investment.
   d. technology.
   e. comparative advantage.

___20. The process by which capital becomes worn out or obsolete is known as:
   a. capital attenuation.
   b. disinvestment.
   c. bankruptcy.
   d. disinflation.
   e. depreciation.

Chapter Review (Fill-In Questions)

1. Scarcity is a result of _____ resources confronted by _____ wants.

2. Three basic economic questions are posed by scarcity and must be resolved by all economic systems: _____ economic goods will be produced, _____ will resources be utilized in production? _____ will get to consume the economic goods produced?

3. _____ is the process of using knowledge to apply energy to materials so that they are more valuable. The knowledge used to combine resources for production is referred to as _____.

4. _____ is the residual after all economic costs are paid out of a firm's revenues, and is received by _____, who organize the firm's activities, innovate new products and technologies, and take business risks.

5. People act rationally and purposefully to _____ their _____.

6. When economists say price or cost, they typically mean the value of the best _____ forgone when choices are made, rather than monetary prices. This is known as _____, or alternative cost. These costs are implicit in all choices, even when it is not obvious that conventional "economics" is involved.

7. Theory is judged by how well it _____ how the world works. _____ expresses a common preference among scientists for simple, rather than complex, workable theories.

8. _____ is the study of employment, inflation, money, the level of taxation, the relative prices of two or more countries' currencies, unemployment, national income, economic growth, and similarly aggregated variables. _____ is a more localized study of the consequences of interactive decisionmaking by individual consumers and firms.

9. _____ occurs when the opportunity cost of producing a given amount of goods is _____.

10. There is _____ efficiency if a consumer experiences maximum satisfaction from a given _____.

Unlimited Multiple Choice

Warning: Each Question Has From Zero To Four Correct Answers.

___ 1. Economics is a(n):
   a. study of decisionmaking and its consequences.
   b. mathematical and physical science, like chemistry.
   c. concern only for people who are miserly.
   d. "apparatus of the mind."

___ 2. A positive economic statement can be scientifically tested to see if it is false. Which of the following are positive economic statements?
   a. The economy will grow faster if tax rates are cut.
   b. A high tax on tobacco will severely cut cigarette smoking.
   c. People would have fewer children if their tax deductions for having them were increased.
   d. The federal budget should be balanced annually.

___ 3. Theories are:
   a. much more complicated than common sense.
   b. scientific only if based on normative value judgments.
   c. proven if only a few unimportant exceptions exist.
   d. developed when we collect data, try to explain how things work, and then test for validity.

___ 4. According to the characterization of humans as *Homo economicus*, all human behavior is:
   a. assumed to be self-interested, including charitable acts.
   b. intended to generate monetary profits.
   c. aimed at maximizing pleasure and minimizing pain.
   d. guided by an instinct to perpetuate the species.

___ 5. The basic economic questions scarcity poses for every society, and which must somehow be resolved, include:
   a. *what* quantities of which goods should be produced?
   b. *how* will the chosen goods be produced?
   c. *who* will use the goods that are produced?
   d. *which* system most efficiently distributes free goods to the needy?

Problems

1. Suppose the price of entry to your local swimming pool rises from $2 to $3 per day, while movie tickets rise from $5 to $7. Which of these forms of entertainment has become relatively more costly? _____

2. Classify the following statements as positive or normative. (CAUTION: Whether a statement is true or false has little to do with whether it is positive or normative. The possibility of testing the truth or falsity of a hypothesis (at least theoretically) distinguishes positive theories from untestable normative statements.)

   a. Relatively fewer people are poor under capitalism than under socialism. _____

   b. Higher union wages cause inflation. _____

   c. Federal budget deficits make investors pessimistic and drive up interest rates. _____

   d. American workers should not have to compete with cheap foreign labor. _____

   e. Bad weather abroad benefits most American farmers. _____

   f. Grass is pink during months that are spelled with an "r" at the end. _____

   g. It is better to be rich than to be poor. _____

   h. On average, annual income is influenced positively by education. _____

3. Fill in the table below by determining the relative price of each item in terms of all the other items.

Money Price	Item	Relative price in terms of lunches	Relative price in terms of haircuts	Relative price in terms of books	Relative price in terms of stereos	Relative price in terms of surfboards
$5	lunch	1 lunch	_____	_____	_____	_____
$10	haircut	_____	1 haircut	_____	_____	_____
$20	book	_____	_____	1 book	_____	_____
$100	stereo	_____	_____	_____	1 stereo	_____
$500	surfboard	_____	_____	_____	_____	1 surfboard

ANSWERS

	Matching		True/False		Multiple Choice		Unlimited MC
Set I	Set II	Set III					
1. h	1. j	1. c	1. F	11. T	1. b	11. c	1. ad
2. a	2. b	2. b	2. F	12. F	2. c	12. d	2. abc
3. b	3. c	3. a	3. F	13. F	3. b	13. c	3. d
4. g	4. d	4. f	4. T	14. T	4. b	14. e	4. ac
5. j	5. i	5. g	5. T	15. F	5. d	15. b	5. abc
6. e	6. a	6. d	6. F	16. T	6. e	16. c	
7. i	7. h	7. h	7. T	17. F	7. a	17. e	
8. d	8. f	8. j	8. F	18. T	8. c	18. c	
9. c	9. g	9. i	9. T	19. T	9. d	19. d	
10. f	10. e	10. e	10. F	20. F	10. a	20. e	

Chapter Review (Fill-in Questions)

1. scarce or limited; unlimited
2. What; How; Who
3. Production; technology
4. Profit; entrepreneurs
5. maximize; satisfaction or happiness
6. alternative; opportunity cost
7. predicts; Occam's Razor
8. Macroeconomics; Microeconomics
9. Productive efficiency; minimized
10. distributive (consumption); income or budget

Problems

1. The price of entry to your local swimming pool rises by 50% (($3 - $2)/$2)), while the price of movie tickets rises only 40% (($7 - $5)/$5)). Therefore , the price of a swim at your local pool has become relatively more costly.

2. a. Positive b. Positive c. Positive d. Normative e. Positive f. Positive g. Normative h. Positive

3. See the table below.

Money Price	Item	Relative Price in terms of lunches	Relative price in terms of haircuts	Relative price in terms of books	Relative price in terms of stereos	Relative price in terms of surfboards
$5	lunch	1 lunch	.5 haircuts	.25 books	.05 stereos	.01 surfboards
$10	haircut	2 lunches	1 haircut	.5 books	.10 stereos	.02 surfboards
$20	book	4 lunches	2 haircuts	1 book	.20 stereos	.04 surfboards
$100	stereo	20 lunches	10 haircuts	5 books	1 stereo	.2 surfboards
$500	surfboard	100 lunches	50 haircuts	25 books	5 stereos	1 surfboard

Optional Material: Graphical Techniques In Economics

Be sure that graphical analysis is not a mystery when you launch into economics. Take the time now to work through "Graphical Techniques in Economics" at the end of Chapter 1 of your text. That done, carefully do the following exercises, and work through the first computerized module of your copy of the Byrns & Stone *MacroStudy* or *MicroStudy* programs. The graphs that pervade economics will not appear as formidable to you as they do to the many students who suffer from "graphobia." After you have studied this material on Graphical Techniques you should be able to: (1) Plot data using the Cartesian Coordinate system. (2) Use descriptive graphs to answer questions, and (3) Measure and interpret the slopes and intercepts of lines.

Cartesian Coordinates

Problem 1

Plot the following pairs of coordinates on the figure below.

a. (1,1)
b. (-5,8)
c. (-8,-8)
d. (5,-7)
e. (3,8)
f. (9,-2)
g. (-9,2)
h. (-5,5)
i. (8,4)
j. (2,-2)
k. (-3,-4)
l. (-4,-9)

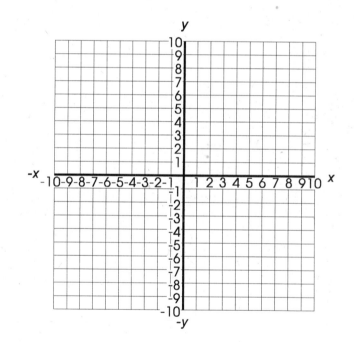

Problem 2

New "How-to-Get-Rich-Quick" books appear regularly, while old ones go out of print. Another employee at your firm (a publisher) used the letters a through l to plot monthly data for 1993 in Figure 2, showing changes in the number of "get rich" books in print and the percentage changes in worldwide sales per book.

a. You want to see if these data are related, but first you need to match the letters from the figure below with their corresponding months in the table below.

Letter	Month	Δ in # of Books	% Δ in Sales per Book
____	Jan.	-3	+2
____	Feb.	-5	+8
____	Mar.	+4	-3
____	Apr.	0	+1
____	May.	-2	0
____	Jun.	+4	-2
____	Jul.	-3	+1
____	Aug.	+7	-4
____	Sep.	+9	-3
____	Oct.	+8	-2
____	Nov.	+3	0
____	Dec.	-4	+8

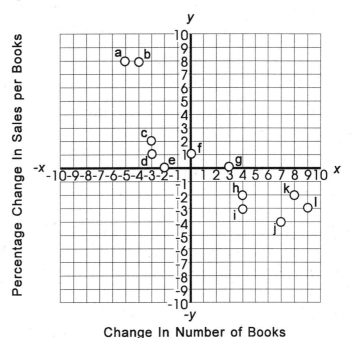

Change In Number of Books

b. After you match the graphed points with their corresponding months, the company president wants to know if there is a relationship. Your opinion is that there is a _____ (positive/negative/no) relationship. This means that as more "get rich" books are in print, sales per book (14) _____ (rise/fall/are unaffected).

Problem 3

Wall Street gurus constantly search for variables that predict stock market movements. A stockbroker develops a theory that percentage increases in sales of new yellow cars indicate consumer optimism and, hence, suggest that the Dow Jones stock market index (DJI) will rise by some percentage the next year.

a. Plot the data from the table below into the figure below for the broker, using a, b, c, and so on.

Point	Year	% Δ in Yellow Cars Sold	% Δ in next year's DJI
a	1976	1	10
b	1977	-5	10
c	1978	-8	-8
d	1979	6	-8
e	1980	4	4
f	1981	-5	-5
g	1982	9	-3
h	1983	5	-3
i	1984	0	5
j	1985	-7	-2

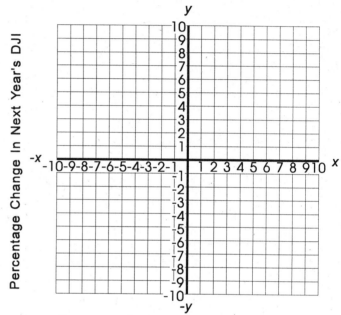

Percentage Change In Yellow Cars Sold

b. Looking at the data you just plotted, do you think the broker's theory is good or bad?_____ Why?_____

Problem 4

Graph the relationships between x and y (based on the formula $y = mx + b$) if the intercept b and the slope m have the following values. You need to set x equal to some arbitrarily selected values, and then calculate corresponding values for y. Label each line with the corresponding letter, from a through f. Identify negative relationships with an asterisk.

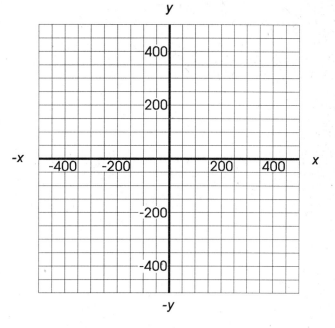

a. b = 100   m = 1
b. b = -100   m = 1
c. b = 100   m = -1
d. b = -100   m = -1
e. b = 200   m = -2
f. b = -200   m = 1/2

Descriptive Graphics

Problem 5

Age/earnings profiles show how people's incomes vary with their ages. Use the typical profile in the figure to answer the following questions.

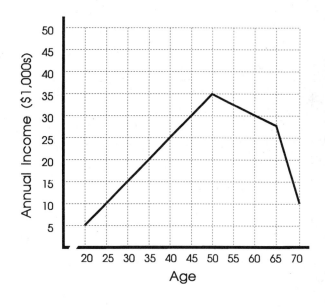

a. On average, the peak earning age is _____ ?

b. The slope of the line between age 20 and 50 is _____ ? How is that slope interpreted? _____ _____

c. The slope of the line between age 50 and 65 is_____? Between age 65 and 70, the slope is? _____

Graphical Analysis Of Areas

While in grade school you learned such formulas as: the area of a rectangle (A) equals the base (b) times the height (h), or A = bh. The following problems show how such calculations are useful in graphically analyzing individual expenditures or the costs of firms.

Problem 6

A world famous restaurant, Les Gourmandes, often features Quiche Lorraine as its luncheon special. Over the years, it has discovered how prices affect daily sales, as graphed in the figure below. If you draw lines from the points we have identified to the vertical and horizontal axes, you can calculate the areas of the resultant rectangles to fill in the table and find out how quiche revenues are influenced by the price charged. (Why? Because base times height (bh) is the same as price (P) times quantity (Q), and PQ equals total revenue.) Does the negative relationship between price and quantity seem reasonable? Why? (Answer this question for yourself at this point. We explore the reasons why such relationships are negative in Chapter 3.)

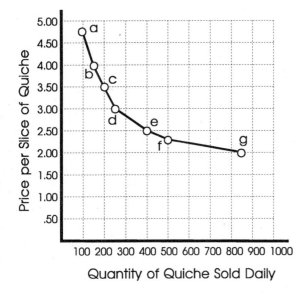

Point	Price (P)	Quantity (Q)	Total Revenue (P × Q)
a	_____	_____	_____
b	_____	_____	_____
c	_____	_____	_____
d	_____	_____	_____
e	_____	_____	_____
f	_____	_____	_____
g	_____	_____	_____

Problem 7

Suppose that a U.S. Department of Agriculture study suggests the relationship shown in the figure below between the price (P) of kumquats and the quantities (Q) that farmers are willing to produce. Fill in the table to indicate how the total dollar revenues of kumquat farmers vary with the changes in market conditions that cause prices to vary. (Hint: You must compute the areas of rectangles much as you did in the preceding problem.) Shade the area representing farmers' total income (P x Q) when kumquats are 50 cents a pound. Use a different shading technique to show how much extra revenue they receive if they sell as much as they want to when the price is 60 cents per pound. Does the positive relationship we have shown between price and farmers' willingness to produce seem reasonable? Why? (Answer this question for yourself at this point. We explore reasons for such positive relationships in Chapter 3.)

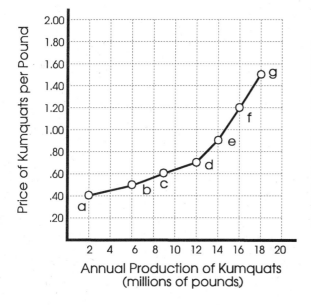

Point	Price (P)	Quantity (Q)	Total Revenue (P × Q)
a	_____	_____	_____
b	_____	_____	_____
c	_____	_____	_____
d	_____	_____	_____
e	_____	_____	_____
f	_____	_____	_____
g	_____	_____	_____

Problem 8

a. Plot the data from the table below into the figure, and connect all the data points with a smooth curve.

Y	X
6	1
8	2
10	3
8	4
6	5
4	6
3	7
4	8
6	9
7	10

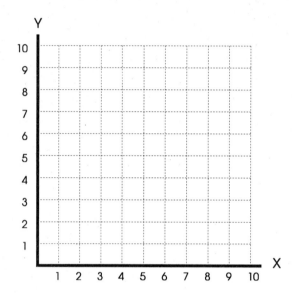

b. Based on your graph, this curve reaches a maximum when x takes on a value of _____ and the slope of the curve at this point is equal to _____.

c. This curve reaches a minimum when x takes on a value of _____ and the slope of the curve is equal to _____.

d. If one wished to find the slope of the curve at any particular point, it would be necessary to draw a _____ to the curve at that point.

ANSWERS

Problem 1

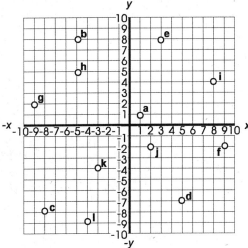

Problem 2

a. See table below
b. negative; fall

Letter	Month	Δ in # of Books	% Δ in Sales per Book
c	Jan.	-3	+2
a	Feb.	-5	+8
i	Mar.	+4	-3
f	Apr.	0	+1
e	May.	-2	0
h	Jun.	+4	-2
d	Jul.	-3	+1
j	Aug.	+7	-4
l	Sep.	+9	-3
k	Oct.	+8	-2
g	Nov.	+3	0
b	Dec.	-4	+8

Problem 3

a. See figure below.
b. This theory does not appear to work very well because the data points are randomly scattered without any apparent correlation.

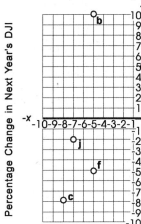

Percentage Change in Yellow Cars Sold

Problem 4

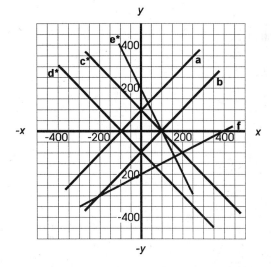

Problem 5

a. 50
b. 1000; for each extra year in age, the typical individual in this age range earns $1000 more annually.
c. -7500/15 = -500; -17,500/5 = -3,500.

Problem 6

POINT	PRICE (P)	QUANTITY (Q)	TOTAL REVENUES (P x Q)
a	4.75	100	475
b	4.00	150	600
c	3.50	200	700
d	3.00	250	750
e	2.50	400	1000
f	2.25	500	1125
g	2.00	850	1700

Problem 7

POINT	PRICE (P)	QUANTITY (Q)	TOTAL REVENUES (P x Q)
a	.40	2	.8 million
b	.50	6	3.0 million
c	.60	9	5.4 million
d	.70	12	8.4 million
e	.90	14	12.6 million
f	1.20	16	19.2 million
g	1.50	18	27.0 million

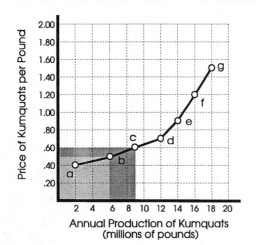

Problem 8

a. See the figure below
b. 3, 0
c. 7, 0
d. tangent

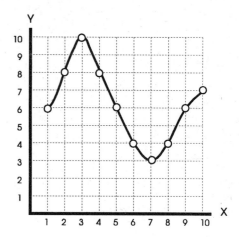

Chapter 2
Scarcity in a World in Transition

Chapter Objectives

After you have read and studied this chapter, you should be able to show how goods, resources, and incomes move among households through firms and government. You should be able to explain how comparative advantage, specialization, and trade can increase production and consumption. You should be able to use production possibilities curves to describe scarcity, increasing opportunity costs, and choice. You should be able to explain how alternative allocative mechanisms work, and understand some basic differences between capitalism and socialism.

Chapter Review: Key Points

1. *Households* ultimately own all wealth and provide all resources to business firms or government in exchange for income with which to buy goods. Interactions between households, firms, and government are shown in *circular flow* models.

2. *Comparative advantage* is a guide to efficient specialization: You gain by specializing in production where your opportunity costs are lowest and trading your output for things other people can produce at lower opportunity cost.

3. A *production-possibilities frontier (PPF)* shows the maximum combinations of goods a society can produce. *PPF* curves assume (**a**) fixed resources ; (**b**) constant technology; and (**c**) full and efficient employment of all scarce resources.

4. Opportunity costs are the values of outputs if resources were deployed in their next best alternatives. Opportunity costs are not constant because resources are not equally suited for all types of production. Increasing a particular form of production invariably leads to *diminishing returns* and *increasing opportunity costs*, so *PPF* curves are concave (bowed away) from the origin.

5. The idea that "a point of diminishing returns" has been reached is sometimes cited as a reason for ceasing an activity. This is usually a misuse of this phrase-- people intend to say that a point of negative returns has been reached. An activity is often worth doing even though diminishing returns are encountered.

6. *Economic growth* occurs when technology advances or the amounts of resources available for production increase. Economic growth is reflected in outward shifts of the production-possibilities curve; more of all goods can be produced.

7. The choices a society makes between consumption and investment goods affects its future production-possibilities curve. Lower saving and investment restricts economic growth and *PPF* expansion.

8. *PPF*'s shapes illustrate different countries' comparative advantages. Trade allows a nation's people to consume far more goods than they could produce in isolation.

9. Alternative *allocative mechanisms* include: (**a**) the *market system*, (**b**) *brute force*, (**c**) *queuing*, (**d**) *random selection*, (**e**) *tradition*, and (**f**) *government*.

10. Many different economic systems are used in attempts to resolve the problem of scarcity. They can be classified by who makes the decisions (*centralized* or *decentralized*) and who owns the resources (*public* versus *private*).

11. Property is privately owned under pure *capitalism* and government follows *laissez-faire* (hands-off) policies. Thus, decisions are decentralized and rely on individual choices in a market system. Under *socialism*, government acts as a trustee over the nonhuman resources jointly owned by all citizens, with many socialist economies also relying heavily on centralized production and distribution decisions.

Matching Key Terms And Concepts

SET I

___ 1. centralized decision making

___ 2. random selection

___ 3. laissez-faire

___ 4. tradition

___ 5. economic growth

___ 6. queuing

___ 7. technological advance

___ 8. brute force

___ 9. private property

___ 10. egalitarianism

a. Capitalism's answer to "who owns?".
b. When more goods can be produced with fewer resources.
c. "We do it this way because we always have."
d. Equal shares.
e. Might makes right, and right makes mine.
f. First-come/first-served.
g. A draft for military service is an example.
h. Minimal government.
i. One path to this is to increase investment.
j. System of economic planning that was used in the former Soviet Union.

SET II

_____ 1. socialism

_____ 2. increasing costs

_____ 3. mixed economy

_____ 4. law of diminishing returns

_____ 5. production possibilities frontier

_____ 6. markets

_____ 7. capitalism

_____ 8. command economy

_____ 9. "fee simple"

_____ 10. comparative advantage

a. The least restrictive form of property rights.

b. A society in which most major economic decisions are centralized.

c. Any activity eventually becomes more difficult the further it is extended.

d. When your opportunity cost of producing some good is lowest, so that you gain by trading for something else for which your opportunity cost is relatively high.

e. Government acts as "trustee" over most nonhuman resources.

f. Depicts limits to the amounts that given resources can produce.

g. Enables buyers and sellers to transact.

h. Emphasizes private property rights and laissez-faire policies.

i. A logical extension of the law of diminishing returns.

j. Some property and decisions are private, others are governmental.

True/False Questions

_____ 1. Queuing allocates on a first-come, first-served basis and may be used to discourage the consumption of particular goods.

_____ 2. In the United States most economic decisions are made in markets in which prices and productivity are major factors determining what is produced and who gets what.

_____ 3. Economic planners try to encourage high unemployment rates so that the economy will have the reserves needed for growth.

_____ 4. The means of production are individually owned by citizens in socialist economies.

_____ 5. High rates of investment tend to raise labor productivity and stimulate the creation of new products and technologies.

_____ 6. Most people view random selection as inequitable, but it is an extremely efficient mechanism for distribution choices.

_____ 7. Brute force inefficiently diverts productive resources into protecting what we have or taking from others.

___ 8. Laissez-faire policies mean that government play a minimal role.

___ 9. The broadest of property rights are called fee simple property rights.

___ 10. Tradition as a mechanism for resolving economic issues is used more today than at any previous time in history.

___ 11. Resolutions to intertribal and international disputes have historically often relied on brute force.

___ 12. Decreasing opportunity costs cause production possibilities frontiers to be concave from the origin.

___ 13. If an economy operates inside its production possibilities frontier, additional output can be produced without costs.

___ 14. Production possibilities curves can illustrate scarcity, opportunity costs, efficiency, and competitive choices.

___ 15. A society can move along its production possibility frontier without incurring any opportunity costs.

Standard Multiple Choice

There Is One Best Answer For Each Question.

___ 1. When you specialize in that which you can do at relatively low cost and buy from others that which they can produce at relatively low cost, all parties mutually gain by exploiting:
a. subdivisions of labor.
b. comparative advantage.
c. centralized coordination.
d. diversified investment.
e. diseconomies of scale.

___ 2. People have a comparative advantage in a good if their:
a. satisfaction from it exceeds that from other goods.
b. production costs are relatively low.
c. production of all goods is faster than their neighbors.
d. purchases of imports are cheaper than domestic goods.
e. psychic enjoyment exceeds the market price.

___ 3. Production possibilities curves can be used to illustrate:
a. scarcity.
b. full employment and efficiency.
c. opportunity costs, and choice.
d. diminishing returns and increasing costs.
e. All of the above.

___ 4. Production possibilities frontiers depend on the assumption that:
a. resources are variable in supply.
b. there are unlimited goods.
c. the economy is expanding.
d. all resources are efficiently employed.
e. technology advances quickly.

_____ 5. Operating inside society's PPF is a:
   a. way to stimulate economic growth.
   b. result whenever the capital stock depreciates rapidly.
   c. drawback of capitalism relative to socialism.
   d. sign that population is outstripping the food supply.
   e. symptom of inefficiency.

_____ 6. Production possibilities frontiers shift outward when the economy's:
   a. full employment level is reached.
   b. state of technology advances.
   c. demand for output increases.
   d. productive resources are efficiently utilized.
   e. capital stock depreciates rapidly.

_____ 7. If more goods can be produced from given resources than was previously possible, there has been a/an:
   a. technological advance.
   b. expansion of the resource base.
   c. change in the convexity of the PPF.
   d. increased investment and growth of the capital stock.
   e. enhanced financial investment.

_____ 8. If an economy is operating efficiently, economic growth will tend to be greater if:
   a. capital depreciates and becomes obsolete rapidly.
   b. threats of war divert resources to national defense.
   c. people's saving rises to allow greater investment.
   d. funds for research and development are reduced.
   e. the law of diminishing returns is fully operative.

_____ 9. One important reason why production possibilities frontiers are concave from the origin is that:
   a. production costs fall because of diminishing returns.
   b. capitalistic economies tend to operate inefficiently.
   c. technology advances faster than it can be utilized.
   d. prosperity reduces people's work incentives.
   e. resources vary in suitability among types of production.

_____10. A society in which your occupation is determined primarily by your parents' jobs bases many allocative decisions on:
   a. queuing.
   b. tradition.
   c. brute force.
   d. the market place.
   e. random selection.

_____11. Allocation by queuing entails waste because some people:
   a. are forced to work at the same profession their parents did.
   b. are randomly selected to perform jobs that do not maximize their potential productivity .
   c. must inefficiently protect themselves from other people's "bullying".
   d. are incapable of having their needs met in this fashion.
   e. spend long unproductive periods waiting in line.

___12. Rights to drill for oil on government property are often assigned by lottery. You submit your name and, if you are lucky, you win drilling rights. This is an example of:
a. brute force.
b. queuing.
c. random selection.
d. tradition.
e. egalitarianism.

___13. Trying to distribute goods according to needs is:
a. achieved in command economies.
b. an equitable answer to the basic "What" and "How" questions.
c. in practice, often a way for those who judge needs to be classed as needy.
d. an explanation of why many poor people prefer pure capitalism.

___14. Consumer tastes tend to be efficiently met when decisions are made:
a. individually.
b. by democratic voting.
c. in a command economy.
d. by queuing and random selection.

___15. John Locke thought that property rights derived from:
a. a person's inheritance.
b. the usefulness of goods.
c. saving and investing.
d. human labor.

___16. Most economists agree that property rights are determined primarily by:
a. laws and regulations.
b. the labor theory of value.
c. brute force.
d. supply and demand.

___17. The U.S. economy is most accurately characterized by relatively:
a. decentralized decisionmaking.
b. public ownership of productive resources.
c. egalitarian distributions of goods.
d. persistent full employment.
e. strict reliance on tradition to determine occupations.

___18. A government that follows laissez-faire policies:
a. specifies production plans in detail.
b. invariably aids the rich at the expense of the poor.
c. keeps "hands off" of most economic decisions.
d. stimulates investment through supply-side tax policies.
e. monitors trends to keep pace with what consumers want.

___19. A command economy:
a. uses laissez-faire government policies.
b. bases decisions on kolkhoz roundtables.
c. meets consumer wants most efficiently.
d. encourages a private property system.
e. requires detailed centralized decision making.

___20. Government acts as a trustee of nonhuman resources under:
a. laissez-faire capitalism.
b. traditional feudalism.
c. fee simple property rights systems.
d. socialism.
e. mercantilist monarchies.

Chapter Review (Fill-In Questions)

1. Interactions between households, business firms, and government are shown in _____ models.

2. Output and consumption rise when _____ advantage guides us into areas of _____ in which our opportunity costs of production are relatively low.

3. If the current output combination is inside the production possibilities frontier, some resources are _____; points outside the PPF are _____.

4. A typical production possibilities curve is concave (bowed away) from its origin because of _____ opportunity costs. The costs of producing any good eventually rise as output is expanded because _____ returns are encountered.

5. Diminishing returns are encountered along a PPF because resources are _____, and tend to be relatively _____ for different forms of production.

6. Several allocative mechanisms are available to any society to make choices between competing demands. They include _____, _____, _____, _____, _____, and _____.

7. The United States largely relies on a _____ form of decision making. The opposite of this form, used in China and elsewhere, is _____ decision making.

8. Government is minimal and follows _____ policies under pure capitalism. No society is either purely capitalistic or socialistic, so we all live in _____ economies.

Unlimited Multiple Choice

Warning: Each Question Has From Zero To Four Correct Answers.

___ 1. Production possibilities frontiers are concave from their origins because:
a. all forms of production use identical mixes of all resources.
b. costs fall consistently as resources are increased for any single output.
c. capital, land, and labor are used in different intensities to efficiently produce various goods.
d. resources are not equally suited to all forms of production.

___ 2. Economic growth can result from:
a. an increased resource base.
b. advances in production technology.
c. consumer saving that facilitates investment.
d. job-training programs for the unskilled.

___ 3. In a command economy,
  a. the central government makes major economic decisions.
  b. most nonhuman factors of production are held by government as "trustee" for the populace.
  c. matching production choices to people's wants is a very difficult task.
  d. there is relatively little private property.

___ 4. The foundations of pure capitalism include:
  a. private rights to property.
  b. inheritance as the major pathway to a high income.
  c. laissez-faire government policies.
  d. exploitation of labor, the real source of all wealth.

___ 5. A comparative advantage in some good requires that you:
  a. are able to produce it at relatively low opportunity cost.
  b. can make it better and faster than any other producers.
  c. encounter minimal marketing costs in finding buyers for it.
  d. be self-sufficient in all goods.

Problems

Problem 1

Some health care professionals use the slogan "the best care for the most people" to defend the American medical system against critics. Suppose current levels of medical resources (15% in 1994) yield this PPF curve going through points a and b.

a. Point _____ must be attained to make the above slogan true.

b. Attaining this point would require either more _____ or an advance in _____.

c. This PPF is concave from below because medical resources _____ in their _____ for different types of medical care.

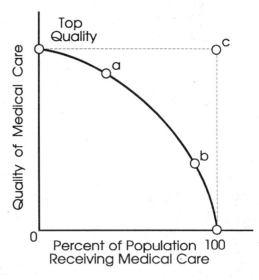

d. A PPF that conformed to the above slogan would look unusual because it would _____
_____.

Problem 4

Use this figure to answer the following True/False questions.

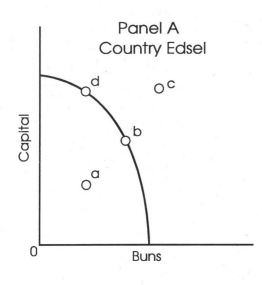

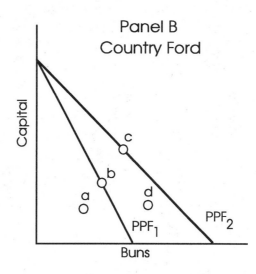

_____ a. The Edselian economy can move from point d to point b without incurring any opportunity costs.

_____ b. Fordic capital can be transformed into buns at constant opportunity costs along both production possibilities frontiers.

_____ c. Ever greater costs are incurred in producing buns as capital production is expanded in Edsel.

_____ d. Edselian capital is transformable into buns only at increasing opportunity costs.

_____ e. Increased demand could move Edsel from point b to point c.

_____ f. Edsel could move from point a to point b rather than point d costlessly.

_____ g. Edsel's production possibilities frontier suggests increasing opportunity costs.

_____ h. Land, labor, and capital probably are used in a fixed ratio in producing both capital and buns in Ford.

_____ i. Opportunity costs are incurred when Ford moves from point b to point d instead of point c.

_____ j. Point a is easily attained in both countries.

Problem 5

The countries of Vinlandia and Crude both produce wine and oil. More specifically, if all resources are used to produce a single good, Vinlandia could produce four times as much wine as Crude, which could produce four times as much oil as Vinlandia. Also, the maximum output of wine that Crude can produce is equal to the maximum output of oil that Vinlandia can produce; and the maximum output of oil that Crude can produce is equal to the maximum output of wine that Vinlandia can produce.

a. Vinlandia has a comparative advantage in the production of _____, while Crude has a comparative advantage in the production of _____.

b. Graph Vinlandia's and Crude's PPF in the figure and label both curves PPF_V and PPF_C respectively.

c. Graph the consumption possibilities frontier that Vinlandia and Crude can obtain if both countries specialize and trade, and label this curve as CPF.

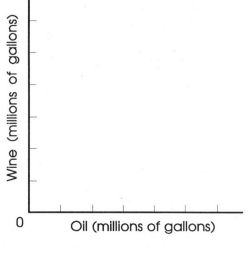

d. With the onset of specialization and trade, Vinlandia will trade _____ gallon(s) of _____ for _____ gallon(s) of _____ produced in Crude.

e. As a result of specialization and trade, Vinlandians will be able to consume more _____ and Crudeians will be able to consume more _____.

Problem 6

Use this figure to answer the following True/False questions.

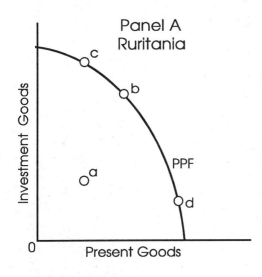

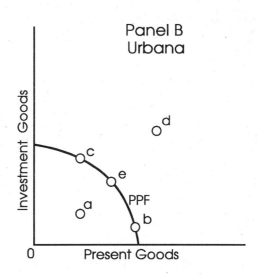

_____ a. If these countries have equal
resources, Urbana is more
technologically advanced than
Ruritania.

_____ b. Both countries confront diminishing
returns in producing both products.

_____ c. Ruritania invests more at point d than
at point c.

_____ d. If Ruritania were at point a, it could
move to point d.

_____ e. In both countries, point a implies
underemployment of resources and
inefficiency.

_____ f. Opportunity costs are constant along
Urbana's production possibilities
frontier.

_____ g. Ruritanian consumption exceeds
investment at point d.

_____ h. Each country can grow faster by
moving along its PPF frontier towards
the investment goods axis.

_____ i. Urbana can move from point e to point
c costlessly.

_____ j. If they share the same technologies,
Ruritania possesses more resources
than Urbana.

Problem 7

A map of Apabana, a Central American country divided into seven 1,000,000-acre sectors, is shown in the figure. The potential harvests of bushels of apples (A) or bananas (B) per acre are shown for each sector. Growing apples in a sector means that you lose bananas proportionally, and vice versa. For example, growing 60 million bushels of apples in sector X requires three-quarters of the land in X, leaving room for growth of only 25 million bushels of bananas.

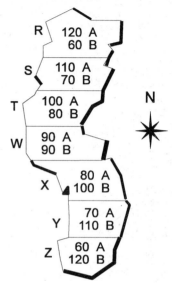

Sector	R	S	T	W	X	Y	Z
Costs: Apples in terms of Bananas							
Costs: Bananas in terms of Apples							

a. Fill in the table by computing the costs of apples in terms of bananas, and vice versa, for each sector.

b. Apple production costs the fewest bananas in sector _____.
c. Banana production costs the fewest apples in sector _____.

d. Suppose that only bananas were grown in all sectors except Z, which was reserved for apple production. Harvests, in millions of bushels, would be _____ bananas and _____ apples.

e. If only apples were grown in sector R, with all other sectors being used for bananas, output (in millions of bushels) would be _____ bananas and _____ apples.

f. Together, the results of answers d and e suggest that it would be _____ to grow _____ north of sector _____.

g. If you had to pay five apples for four bananas, where would only apples be produced? Only bananas? In which sector might both be produced?

h. Construct a production possibilities frontier for Apabana in the left-hand figure below.

i. Construct a curve in the right-hand figure below relating the cost of apples (in terms of bananas) to each possible output of apples. Put apple production on the horizontal axis, and the cost of extra apples on the vertical axis. (As you will soon learn, this is a supply curve.)

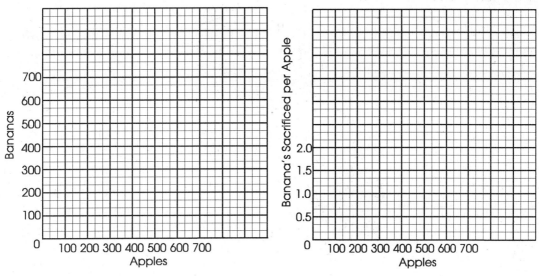

Problem 8

Two dimensional graphs limit the tradeoffs we normally illustrate with a PPF. However, with a little ingenuity we can accommodate a third output. We do this by drawing a family of PPF curves rather than a single curve, with each curve reflecting a different assumed level of production for the third good. Consider three commodities apples (a), bananas (b), and coconuts (c). The family of curves in this figure shows the tradeoff between apples and bananas, holding coconut production constant along each curve. We portray changes in coconut output possibilities by shifting among these curves.

a. How does the figure represent the law of increasing cost (diminishing returns) for apples?

   _____

   _____

   _____

   _____

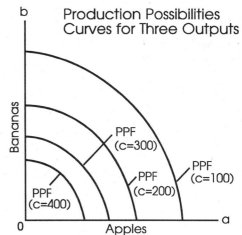

b. How does the figure represent the law of diminishing returns for coconuts?

   _____

   _____

   _____

   _____

Problem 9

When Alferd and Zachariah, two pioneers, operate independently, their average daily production and consumption over the course of a year are shown in the table.

	Daily Hours Worked	Average Daily Production and Consumption
Alferd	6	2 pounds of buffalo meat
	2	4 pounds of pinto beans
Zachariah	2	4 pounds of buffalo meat
	6	2 pounds of pinto beans

a. Who has the comparative advantage in hunting? _____

b. Who has the comparative advantage in farming? _____

c. Fill in the table below on the assumption that Alferd and Zachariah begin to specialize and trade, and that their tastes are sufficiently similar so that they end up eating identical diets.

	Daily Hours Worked	Average Daily Production	Average Daily Consumption
Hunter name: _____	8	___ pounds of _____	___ pounds of _____ ___ pounds of _____
Farmer name: _____	8	___ pounds of _____	___ pounds of _____ ___ pounds of _____

Problem 10

Suppose Bruno can brew 50 barrels of beer or bake 800 pizzas per year while Gino can brew 100 barrels of beer or bake 600 pizzas.

a. How much beer is sacrificed for each pizza Bruno bakes? _____

b. How much beer is sacrificed for each pizza Gino bakes? _____

c. In the absence of trade, both Bruno and Gino will devote half their time to producing both goods, and Bruno will consume _____ barrels of beer and _____ pizzas, while Gino will consume _____ barrels of beer and _____ pizzas.

d. If Bruno and Gino begin to specialize and trade, then overall pizza consumption will increase by _____ pizzas and overall beer consumption will increase by _____ barrels.

Problem 11[*]

We suggest that you tackle this challenging production-possibilities problem only after solving all previous questions. **Hint**: Efficiency requires that **scarce** resources be fully employed. In this problem, full employment for labor in some instances may require that other (nonscarce?) resources be unemployed.

Suppose an automobile may be produced by either (a) 5 workers and 1 robot, or (b) 3 workers and 2 robots; while a refrigerator requires either (c) 3 workers and 1 robot, or (d) 2 workers and 2 robots. Now suppose that an isolated factory has 60 workers and 15 robots employed. Filling in this table requires ingenuity and some trial-and-error experimentation. Good luck!

Autos	0	1	2	3	4	5	6	7	8	9	10	11	12
Refrigerators													
Idle Robots													
Unemployed Workers													

[*]Adapted with permission from Paul G. Coldagelli, author of "Production Possibilities Curves for Three Outputs", and "A Challenging Production Possibilities Problem" in *Great Ideas for Teaching Economics*, 4/e, edited by Ralph T. Byrns and Gerald W. Stone, Jr., Glenview, IL: Scott, Foresman and Company, 1989.

ANSWERS

	Matching		True/False			Multiple Choice		Unlimited Multiple Choice
Set I	Set II							
1. j	1. e	1. T	9. T	1. b	11. e	1. c, d
2. g	2. i	2. T	10. F	2. b	12. c	2. a, b, c, d
3. h	3. j	3. F	11. T	3. e	13. c	3. a, b, c, d
4. c	4. c	4. F	12. F	4. d	14. a	4. a, c
5. i	5. f	5. T	13. F	5. e	15. d	5. a
6. f	6. g	6. F	14. T	6. b	16. a	
7. b	7. h	7. T	15. F	7. a	17. a	
8. e	8. b	8. T		8. c	18. c	
9. a	9. a			9. e	19. e	
10. d	10. d			10. b	20. d	

Chapter Review (Fill-in Questions)

1. circular flow
2. comparative advantage; specialization
3. unemployed/underemployed; unattainable
4. increasing; diminishing
5. specialized; suited
6. brute force; random selection; queuing; tradition; government; the market system
7. decentralized; centralized
8. laissez-faire; mixed

Problem 1

a. c
b. resources; technology
c. vary; suitability
d. form a right angle

Problem 2

a-e. See figures a-e below.

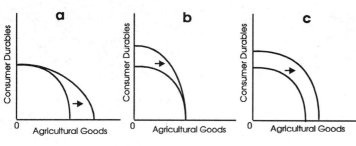

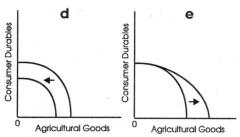

Problem 3

a. See figure at right.
b. concave from the origin
c. full employment and efficient use of all scarce inputs
d. 1/10, 1/9, 1/8, 1/7, 1/6, 1/5, 1/4
e. increasing

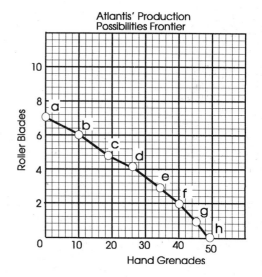

Problem 4	Problem 5	Problem 6	Problem 7
a. F	a. wine; oil	a. F	a. See table below.
b. T	b. See Figure 11.	b. T	b. R
c. F	c. See Figure 11.	c. F	c. Z
d. T	d. 1; wine; 1; oil	d. T	d. 510; 60
e. F	e. wine & oil;	e. T	e. 570; 120
f. F	wine & oil	f. F	f. inefficient; bananas; W
g. T		g. T	g. Sectors R and S would produce only apples T might produce both and W, X, Y, and Z would produce only bananas.
h. T		h. T	
i. T		i. F	h. See Figure 12.
j. T		j. T	i. See Figure 13.

Figure 11

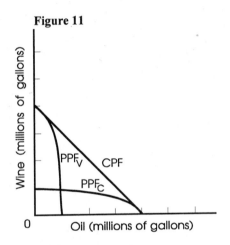

Sector	R	S	T	W	X	Y	Z
Costs: Apples in terms of Bananas	1/2	7/11	4/5	1.0	5/4	11/7	2.0
Costs: Bananas in terms of Apples	2.0	11/7	5/4	1.0	4/5	7/11	1/2

Figure 12

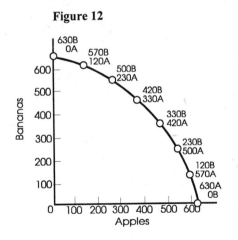

Figure 13

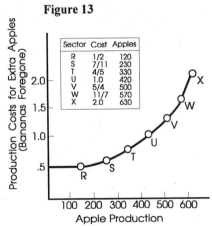

Problem 8

a. The concavity (from the origin) of all these PPFs yields increasing costs for apples: As the number of apples produced grows, the number of bananas sacrificed per extra apple rises.

b. Widening the gap between PPF curves as more coconuts are produced (shrinking the apple/banana PPF towards the origin) illustrates the increasing costs of coconuts in terms of either apples or bananas.

Problem 9

a. Zachariah
b. Alferd
c. See table.

	Daily Hours Worked	Average Daily Production	Average Daily Consumption
Hunter name: Zachariah	8	16 pounds of meat	8 pounds of meat 8 pounds of beans
Farmer name: Alferd	8	16 pounds of beans	8 pounds of meat 8 pounds of beans

Problem 10

a. 1/16 or .0625
b. 1/6 or .167
c. 25; 400; 50; 300
d. 100; 25

Problem 11

See table.

Autos	0	1	2	3	4	5	6	7	8	9	10	11	12
Refrigerators	15	14	13	12	11	10	9	8	6	5	3	2	0
Idle Robots	0	0	0	0	0	0	0	0	1	1	2	0	3
Unemployed Workers	15	13	11	9	7	5	3	1	2	0	1	1	0

Chapter 3
Demand and Supply

Chapter Objectives

After you have read and studied this chapter you should be able to explain the concept of marginalism in decisionmaking; explain the laws of demand and supply; describe the major determinants of demand and supply, and also show how they can respectively cause the demand and supply curves to shift; and show what is meant by a market equilibrium and explain how it is achieved.

Chapter Review: Key Points

1. Rational decision making is governed by evaluations of the relative benefits and costs of *incremental* or *marginal* changes.

2. The *law of demand.* People buy less of a good per period at high prices than at low prices. *Demand curves* slope downward and to the right, and show the quantities demanded at various prices for a good.

3. Changes in market prices cause changes in *quantity demanded*. There is a *change in demand* (the demand curve shifts) when there are changes in influences other than a good's own price. These determinants include:
   a. tastes and preferences;
   b. income and its distribution;
   c. prices of related goods;
   d. numbers and ages of buyers;
   e. expectations about prices, income, and availability;
   f. taxes, subsidies, and regulations.

4. Consumers buy more of a good per period only at lower prices because of:
   a. The *substitution effect*--the cheaper good will now be used more ways as it is substituted for higher priced goods;
   b. *Diminishing marginal utility*-- consuming the additional units ultimately does not yield as much satisfaction as consuming previous units, so demand prices fall as consumption rises;
   c. The *income effect*--a lower price for any good means that the purchasing power of a given monetary income rises.

5. *The law of supply*. Higher prices cause sellers to make more of a good available per period. The *supply curve* shows the positive relationship between the price of a good and the quantity supplied. Supply curves generally slope upward and to the right because:
   a. diminishing returns cause opportunity costs to increase;
   b. to expand output, firms must bid resources away from competing producers or use other methods (such as overtime) that increase cost;
   c. profit incentives are greater at higher prices.

6. In addition to the price paid to producers of a good, supply depends on:
   a. the number of sellers;
   b. technology;
   c. resource costs;
   d. prices of other producible goods;
   e. producer's expectations; and
   f. taxes, subsidies, and regulations.

7. Changes in prices cause *changes in quantities supplied*, while changes in other influences on production or sales of goods cause shifts in supply curves that are termed *changes in supply*.

8. When markets operate without government intervention, prices tend to move towards *market equilibrium* so that quantity supplied equals quantity demanded. At this point, the demand price equals the supply price.

9. When the market price of a good is below the intersection of the supply and demand curves, there will be *shortages* and pressures for increases in price. If price is above the intersection of the supply and demand curves, there will be *surpluses* and pressures for reduction in price.

10. Supply and demand are largely independent in the short run.

Matching Key Terms And Concepts

Set I

_____ 1.   market

_____ 2.   supply price

_____ 3.   *ceteris paribus*

_____ 4.   marginalism

_____ 5.   market price

_____ 6.   complementary goods

_____ 7.   substitute goods

_____ 8.   inferior goods

_____ 9.   demand price

_____ 10.   joint product

a. A consumer's subjective value from having a bit more of a good.

b. Right-hand gloves and left-hand gloves.

c. Goods for which demands increase as income decreases.

d. Coffee and tea.

e. The view that rational decision makers weigh the costs and benefits of the last extra bit of an activity.

f. Mechanism that enables buyers and sellers to transact.

g. Beef and leather.

h. The minimum payment that will induce a bit more production.

i. Must be in accord with consumers' subjective evaluations before they will purchase a good.

j. "All other influences are held constant".

Set II

_____ 1.   substitution effect

_____ 2.   law of demand

_____ 3.   change in quantity demanded

_____ 4.   income effect

_____ 5.   change in demand

_____ 6.   law of supply

_____ 7.   surpluses

_____ 8.   equilibrium

_____ 9.   shortages

_____ 10.   diminishing marginal utility

a. Relationships between quantities demanded and price are negative.

b. When neither shortages nor surpluses exist in a market.

c. Extra units of a good add declining amounts of satisfaction.

d. Adjustments people make solely because relative prices change.

e. Occurs when prices are below equilibrium.

f. Effect on a demand curve when the price of a substitute changes.

g. People's adjustments when price changes alter purchasing power.

h. Quantities supplied are positively related to price.

i. A movement along a demand curve.

j. Caused when prices are artificially held above equilibrium.

True/False Questions

____ 1. Most decisions (business and otherwise) are made at the margin.

____ 2. The term "demand" can mean that people desire a good, but are still unable to afford it.

____ 3. Supply must equal demand for equilibrium to occur.

____ 4. Other things constant, an increase in the wages of labor used in the production of a particular good will cause the supply curve of that good to shift to the right.

____ 5. For an entire demand curve to shift to the right, all determinants of demand except price must be stable.

____ 6. If a firm produces durable goods and expects the price of the good to fall in the future, it would not be unreasonable for the firm to deplete or sell down its inventory.

____ 7. Purchases by individuals can be considered "dollar votes" which signal and direct business decisions.

____ 8. Increases in income decrease supplies of inferior goods.

____ 9. The demand curve for a good shows the relationship between its price and the quantity demanded, assuming that all other determinants are constant.

____ 10. When a market is in equilibrium, a change in supply or demand always results in a shortage or surplus.

____ 11. Most markets maintain stable equilibria for long periods.

____ 12. Equilibrium supply prices exceed demand prices by the same ratio that quantity demanded exceeds quantity supplied.

____ 13. If quantity demanded exceeds quantity supplied, then a shortage exists.

____ 14. In equilibrium, a change in quantity demanded results if there is a change in supply.

____ 15. In equilibrium, a change in quantity supplied implies that demand has shifted.

Standard Multiple Choice

There Is One Best Answer For Each Question.

___ 1. If Jill's demand price for a mountain bike exceeds the $500 price tag, then:
   a. Jill will purchase the bike.
   b. mountain bikes are an inferior good.
   c. Jill will not purchase the bike.
   d. mountain bikes are a normal good.
   e. surpluses of mountain bikes are likely.

___ 2. Which term implies that people are able and willing to pay for something?
   a. Need.
   b. Demand.
   c. Requirement.
   d. Necessity.
   e. Desire.

___ 3. The market demand for a good is least affected by the:
   a. incomes of consumers.
   b. prices of related goods.
   c. costs of resources.
   d. number of buyers.
   e. expectations about price changes.

___ 4. When demand decreases, the demand curve shifts:
   a. down and to the left.
   b. in a clockwise rotation.
   c. up and to the right.
   d. counter-clockwise.
   e. away from the origin.

___ 5. A demand curve would not shift if there were changes in the:
   a. tastes and preferences of consumers.
   b. size or distribution of national income.
   c. price of the good.
   d. number or age composition of buyers.
   e. expectations of consumers about availability.

___ 6. Demand is positively related to income for:
   a. inferior goods.
   b. normal goods.
   c. complementary goods.
   d. joint products.
   e. substitute goods.

___ 7. People's adjustments to relative price changes are termed:
   a. demonstration effects.
   b. substitution effects.
   c. wealth effects.
   d. adaptive effects.
   e. income effects.

___ 8. If price cuts in video recorders cause expanded cable TV hookups, these are:
   a. luxury goods.
   b. substitute goods.
   c. normal goods.
   d. inferior goods.
   e. complementary goods.

___ 9. In the short run, an increase in the relative price of a good increases the:
   a. state of technology.
   b. supply of the good.
   c. quantity of the good demanded.
   d. quantity of the good supplied.
   e. profits of capital owners.

___10. Improvements in technology shift:
   a. demand up and to the right.
   b. production possibilities towards the origin.
   c. demand down and to the right.
   d. supply to the right, away from the vertical axis.
   e. supply up and to the left.

___11. When quantity supplied exceeds quantity demanded:
   a. a surplus will occur.
   b. equilibrium is achieved.
   c. a shortage will occur.
   d. consumers will bid up prices.
   e. suppliers' inventories will be depleted.

___12. Decreases in the desire and willingness to pay for additional units of some good are best explained by the:
   a. substitution effect.
   b. principle of diminishing marginal utility.
   c. income effect.
   d. law of diminishing supply.
   e. law of demand.

___13. Examples of joint goods (by-products in production) would include:
   a. shirts, ties, and socks.
   b. cameras and film.
   c. college tuitions and textbooks.
   d. vitamin pills and surgery.
   e. water skiing and electricity from a hydroelectric dam.

___14. Expectations of price hikes for a durable good tend to:
   a. increase production, but only for later sale.
   b. cause firms to increase their inventories.
   c. decrease supply in the very short run.
   d. increase consumers' demands.
   e. All of the above.

___15. Which of the following will NOT result in a change in the supply of camcorders?
   a. New firms enter the industry.
   b. Capital costs increase.
   c. Prices of photographic equipment increase dramatically.
   d. Production technology advances rapidly.
   e. Consumers increasingly prefer camcorders over cameras.

___16. The market for a good is in equilibrium if the:
   a. supply and demand are equal.
   b. price equals costs plus a fair profit.
   c. rate of technological change is steady.
   d. quantity supplied equals the quantity demanded.
   e. government properly regulates demands and supplies.

___17. An increase in the quantity demanded of a good can be caused by an increase in:
  a. supply.
  b. inflationary expectations.
  c. consumer incomes.
  d. the price of a substitute good.
  e. federal income tax rates.

___18. Other things constant, an improvement in overall technology that allows more output to be produced with the same level of inputs causes:
  a. a movement up and along the supply curve, resulting in both a higher equilibrium price and quantity.
  b. a leftward shift of the supply curve so that less is offered for sale at every price.
  c. no movement of the supply curve but a fall in price and an increase in the quantity supplied.
  d. a rightward shift of the supply curve so that more is offered for sale at every price.
  e. None of the above are correct.

___19. Market prices that are below equilibrium tend to create:
  a. surpluses of the good.
  b. declines in resource costs.
  c. pressures for research and development.
  d. shortages of the good.
  e. buyers' markets.

___20. Given the list below, all of the following will cause the demand curve to shift to the left except:
  a. an increase in the price of a substitute good.
  b. a reduction in consumer income if the good is normal.
  c. an increase in the price of a complementary good.
  d. an increase in income if the good is inferior.
  e. consumer tastes change so that they no longer want the good.

Chapter Review (Fill-In Questions)

1. The _____ unit of a thing is the last bit of that thing; _____ is the idea that rational decisions are based on the assessments of the costs and benefits of the final increments of an activity.

2. The law of demand states that consumers will purchase _____ of a good the lower its opportunity cost (relative price), and vice versa. The basic reason for this is the _____ effect, which reflects the adjustments people make solely because of changes in relative prices. A secondary reason for most goods is the _____ effect, which measures the adjustments people make because price changes alter consumers' _____ .

3. Another way to explain the negative relationship between relative prices and quantities demanded is the principle of _____ , which suggests that a point is eventually reached where added consumption of any good yields ever _____ gains of satisfaction.

4. Factors other than the price of a good that can affect purchases include _____ , _____ , _____ , _____ , and _____ .

5. The law of supply states that higher prices induce sellers to offer consumers _____ of their product, and vice versa. The supply curve depicts the _____ amounts of a good that firms are willing to place on the market at various prices.

6. Markets permit buyers and sellers to communicate their desires and complete transactions. In so doing, markets reach _____ . When quantity demanded exceeds quantity supplied, the current price is too low and a _____ exists. This is known as a _____ market. If the current price is above the equilibrium price, there is a _____ of the good, which is known as a _____ market.

Unlimited Multiple Choice

Warning: Each Question Has From Zero To Four Correct Answers.

___ 1. According to the law of demand, consumers will purchase more of a good when:
   a. the relative price of the good falls.
   b. incomes increase.
   c. the market price of the good rises.
   d. the supply price increases.

___ 2. In the short run, the market demand for ice cream should:
   a. shift to the right upon the arrival of a heat wave.
   b. slope upwards to depict the inverse relationship between its price and the quantity of ice cream demanded.
   c. remain stationary when the price of ice cream falls.
   d. grow to accommodate any increase in the supply of ice cream.

___ 3. In the market for gasoline, one would expect the:
   a. supply curve to be stable in spite of OPEC's uneven history of trying to establish inordinately high oil prices.
   b. demand curve to continually shift to the right, if more and more gas-guzzling automobiles are purchased.
   c. demand for gasoline to decrease when acceptable and economical substitutes are developed and marketed.
   d. supply curve to shift to the right if the government began taxing oil companies more heavily.

___ 4. The quantity demanded of a good adjusts to changes in:
   a. the price of a substitute good.
   b. the price of a complementary good.
   c. consumers' income.
   d. tastes and preferences.

___ 5. Marginalism is a term that is generally used to describe:
   a. the idea that most decisions entail weighing the relative costs and small changes in behavior.
   b. the price of purchasing more of a normal good.
   c. the manner in which the supply curve shifts in response to an increase in the price of a good.
   d. changes in consumer tastes and preferences that occur only in the long run.

Problems

Problem 1

Use the data in this table to answer the following questions.

a. Draw demand curves for consumers X, Y, and Z, respectively, in Panels A, B, and C of the figure below, and label them as D_0.

Consumer X's Demand Schedule		Consumer Y's Demand Schedule		Consumer Z's Demand Schedule	
Price	Quantity Demanded	Price	Quantity Demanded	Price	Quantity Demanded
$10	0	$10	0	$10	0
9	0	9	3	9	1
8	0	8	5	8	5
7	1	7	7	7	8
6	2	6	9	6	11
5	4	5	12	5	12
4	6	4	15	4	15
3	10	3	18	3	18
2	15	2	21	2	20
1	21	1	24	1	23
0	25	0	25	0	25

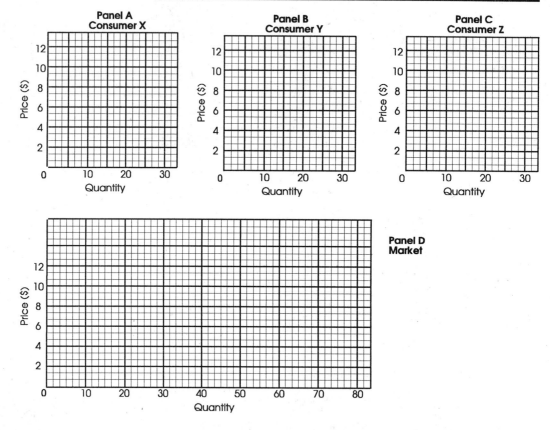

b. Draw the resulting market demand curve in Panel D and label it as D_M. Explain how you derived the demand curve for the entire market. _____

c. Assume that demands for this good by individuals X and Y double, but fall by half for individual Z. Revise their demand curves (labeling them as D_1 in the figure above), and then redraw the market demand curve and label it as D_{M1}.

Problem 2

Use the market demand curves D_0, D_1, and D_2, in this figure to answer the following questions.

a. A movement from point a to point b represents what?_____
Why? _____
What might account for this movement? _____
_____

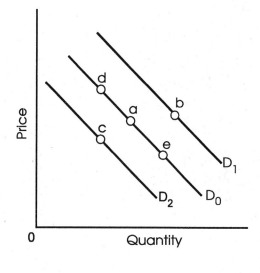

b. A movement from point a to point c represents what?_____
Why? _____
What might account for this movement? _____
_____

c. A movement from point a to point d represents what?_____
Why? _____
What might account for this movement? _____

d. A movement from point a to point e represents what?_____
Why? _____ What might account for this movement? _____
_____

Problem 3

Use the market supply curves S_0, S_1, and S_2 in this figure to answer the following questions .

a.   A movement from point a to point b represents
     what?_____
     Why? _____
     What might account for this movement? _____

     _____

b.   A movement from point a to point c represents
     what?_____
     Why? _____
     What might account for this movement? _____

     _____

c.   A movement from point c to point d represents
     what?_____
     Why? _____
     What might account for this movement? _____

d.   A movement from point b to point e represents what?_____
     Why? _____ What might account for this movement? _____

     _____

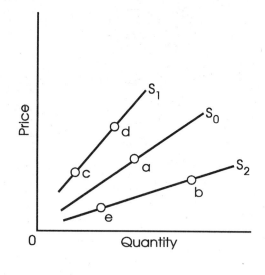

Problem 4

Use these market supply and demand schedules for electric drills to answer the following
questions.

Price	Quantity Demande d (1,000s)	Quantity Supplied (1,000s)
$10	32	4
$20	28	7
$30	24	10
$40	20	13
$50	16	16
$60	12	19
$70	8	22

a.   Draw the market supply and demand
     curves for electric drills in the figure.

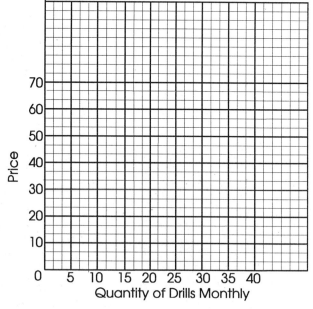

b. The equilibrium price in this market is _____.

c. The equilibrium quantity of drills is _____ thousand monthly.

d. If the price were $30, there would be a _____ of _____ thousand drills monthly.

e. If the price were $60, there would be a _____ of _____ thousand drills monthly.

Problem 5

The demand curve for Xebs is represented by D_X. The demand curves for Yoozs , (a substitute good for Xebs) and Zorks (a complement to Xebs) are given by D_Y and D_Z respectively.

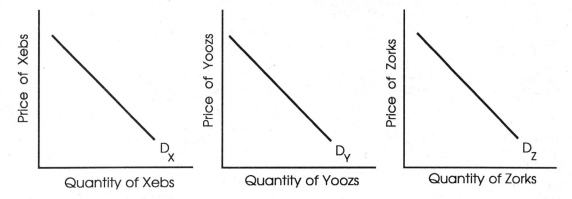

Suppose the price of Xebs increases. Indicate the effect(s) of this price change on the graphs in the figure.

Problem 6

The concepts of average and marginal occur in many areas other than economics.

a. What happens to your average for this class if your score on the next (marginal) test is above your current average? _____ Suppose that you do not do quite as well on the final exam as on your next test. How is it possible for your average to rise even though the marginal test (final exam) score is falling? _____

b. Shaquille O'Neal, a 7' center for the Orlando Magic basketball team, walks into your class. What happens to the average height of people in your classroom? _____ To the average income? _____

c. How could an increase in the rate of inflation this year reduce the average rate of inflation over a decade? _____

d. How are marginal and average values related? _____
_____

Problem 7

Identify the following pairs of goods as substitutes (S), complements (C) or joint products (JP).

a. VCRs and rental video cassettes. _____

b. Salt and pepper. _____

c. Yogurt and ice cream. _____

d. Ball-point pens and paper. _____

e. Beer and wine. _____

f. Wool and cotton. _____

g. Tea and honey. _____

h. Lumber and paper. _____

i. Eggs and hash browns. _____

j. Footballs and ham. _____

Problem 8

If oil prices suddenly fell after rising rapidly for years, what would you expect to happen to the:

a. demand for small cars? _____

b. demand for luxury sedans? _____

c. demand for air travel? _____

d. supply of synthetic fabrics? (Most are made from petroleum products) _____

e. demand for wool and cotton? _____

Problem 9

Around the middle of January, the annual crop of mink furs is put on the auction block. How will the supplies and demands for mink pelts be affected when:

a. wearing fur in public increasingly elicits jeers and harassment from strangers? _____
    _____

b. other fur-bearing animals become increasingly classified as endangered species. _____
    _____

c. the price of mink food rises. _____

d. a sharp, worldwide (1929-type) depression occurs. _____

e. higher income tax rates and a new wealth tax are imposed while the revenues are used to raise welfare payments. _____

ANSWERS

Matching		True/False		Multiple Choice		Unlimited Multiple Choice
Set I	**Set II**					
1. f	1. d	1. T	9. T	1. a	11. a	1. a
2. h	2. a	2. F	10. F	2. b	12. b	2. a, c
3. j	3. i	3. F	11. F	3. c	13. e	3. b, c
4. e	4. g	4. F	12. F	4. a	14. e	4. None
5. i	5. f	5. F	13. T	5. c	15. e	5. a
6. b	6. h	6. T	14. T	6. b	16. d	
7. d	7. j	7. T	15. T	7. b	17. a	
8. c	8. b	8. F		8. e	18. d	
9. a	9. e			9. d	19. d	
10. g	10. c			10. d	20. a	

Chapter Review (Fill-in Questions)

1. marginal; marginalism
2. more; substitution; income; purchasing power
3. diminishing marginal utility; smaller
4. tastes and preferences; income; number of buyers; price of related goods; and expectations
5. more; maximum
6. equilibrium; shortage; sellers; surplus; buyers

Problem 1

a. See panels A-D on next page.
b. Horizontal summation of individual demand curves.
c. See panels A-D on next page.

Problem 2

a. increase in demand; curve shifted rightwards; increase in income, more favorable consumer preferences, or some other parallel change in a determinant besides the good's own price.
b. decrease in demand; curve shifted leftward; decrease in income, increase in the price of a complement, or some other parallel change in a determinant besides the good's own price.
c. decrease in quantity demanded; movement along the curve; increase in the price of the good.
d. increase in quantity demanded; movement along the curve; decrease in the price of the good.

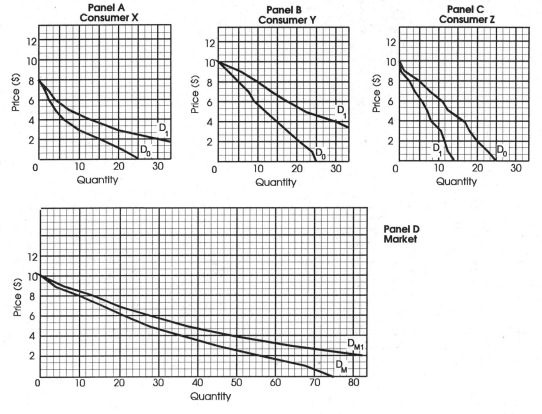

Problem 3

a. increase in supply; curve shifted to the right; decrease in resource price, technological advances, or some other change in determinant besides the good's price.
b. decrease in supply; curve shifted to the left; increasing resource prices, reduction in the number of sellers, or some other change in a determinant besides the good's price.
c. increase in quantity supplied; movement along a curve; increase in price.
d. decrease in quantity supplied; movement along a supply curve; decrease in price.

Problem 4

a. See figure at right.
b. $50
c. 16
d. shortage, 14
e. surplus, 7

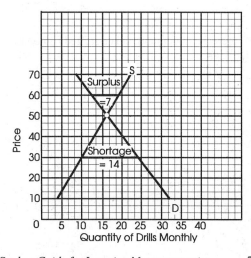

Problem 5

Demand for substitute good (Yoozs) increases, demand for complement (Zorks) decreases.

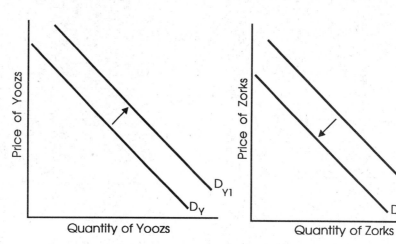

Problem 6

a. Your average increases; as long as your marginal grade is above your average grade, it will pull up your average grade.
b. Average height increase; average income increases.
c. As long as this year's (marginal) increase is less than the decade's average, the average rate of inflation for the decade will decline.
d. Whenever a marginal value is greater than the average value, the average will be pulled up; whenever a marginal value is below the average, the average will be pulled down.

Problem 7

a. C
b. C
c. S
d. C
e. S
f. S
g. C
h. JP
i. C
j. JP

Problem 8

a. Demand will decrease.
b. Demand will increase.
c. Demand will most likely increase.
d. Supply will increase.
e. Demand will decrease (price of synthetics will fall).

Problem 9

a. Demand will decrease.
b. Demand will rise as substitutes become scarce.
c. Supply will decrease.
d. Demand will decrease because mink pelts are a luxury.
e. Demand will decrease, and higher taxes might reduce supply.

Chapter 4
Markets and Equilibrium

Chapter Objectives

After you have read and studied this chapter you should be able to explain how prices and quantities change to reflect movements in supplies and demands; describe the effects of government price controls (price ceilings and price floors) on the market's ability to efficiently allocate society's scarce resources and also show how price controls prohibit a market from achieving an equilibrium price and quantity; list some of the activities performed by speculators, arbitrageurs, and intermediaries in the market place; offer suggestions about how supply and demand interact to shape the activities in markets that you might encounter in the future; state how the market system answers the "**what**", "**how**", and "**for whom**" questions; and list the five economic goals for government in a market economy.

Chapter Review: Key Points

1. Increases in supplies or decreases in demands tend to reduce prices. Decreases in supplies or increases in demands tend to raise prices. Increases in either supplies or demands tend to increase quantities. Decreases in either supplies or demands tend to shrink quantities. If both supply and demand shift, the effects on price and quantity may be either reinforcing or at least partially offsetting. (You need to review this important material if these points make little sense to you.)

2. *Transaction costs* arise because information and mobility are costly. This allows the price of a good to vary between markets, and to approach its equilibrium erratically.

3. *Intermediaries* prosper by reducing transaction costs incurred in getting goods from ultimate producers to ultimate consumers. *Speculators* facilitate movements towards equilibrium because they increase demand by trying to buy when prices are below equilibrium, and increase supply by selling when prices exceed equilibrium. This dampens price swings and cuts the costs and risks to others of doing business.

4. *Arbitrage* involves buying where prices are low and selling where prices are higher. If price spreads exceed transaction costs, arbitrage is risklessly profitable. Competition for opportunities to arbitrage dampens profit opportunities and facilitates efficiency by ensuring that price spreads between markets are minimal.

5. Government can set monetary prices at values other than equilibrium price, but *price ceilings* or *price floors* do not "freeze" opportunity costs; instead, these *price controls* create economic inefficiency and either shortages or surpluses, respectively.

6. The market system tailors production according with consumers' demands in answering the basic economic question of "*What?*" will be produced. Competition tends to compel efficient forms of production in answering "*How?*" production will occur. Markets answer the "*Who?*" question by producing for those who own valuable resources .

7. Where the price system is incapable of providing certain goods or fails to supply the socially optimal levels, government steps in to supplement the private sector in five major ways. It attempts to:
   a. provide a legal, social and business environment for stable growth;
   b. promote and maintain competitive markets;
   c. redistribute income and wealth equitably;
   d. alter resource allocations in an efficient manner where public goods or externalities are present; and
   e. stabilize income, employment, and prices.

8. If *negative externalities* (costs) exist, the private market will provide too much of the product and the market price will be too low because full production costs are not being charged to consumers. If *positive externalities* (benefits) exist, too little of the product will be produced by the private market and market price will be too high, requiring government subsidy or government production or provision of the commodity.

9. Once *public goods* are produced, it is costly to exclude people from their use (the *nonexclusion* problem), and everybody can consume the goods simultaneously with everyone else (the *nonrivalry* problem). The free market fails to provide public goods efficiently because of the "free-rider" problem.

10. Total spending on goods and services by all three levels of government exceeds 20 percent of U.S. GDP. State and local governments spend the bulk of their revenues on services that primarily benefit people in their community and rely heavily on the property and sales taxes as a source of revenue. Federal spending is generally aimed at activities that are national in scope. Over 90 percent of federal revenue comes from individual and corporate income taxes plus Social Security and other employment taxes. Transfer payments through government account for an additional 10% of U.S. national income.

Matching Key Terms And Concepts

Set I

___ 1. arbitrage

___ 2. price controls

___ 3. externalities

___ 4. speculator

___ 5. public goods

___ 6. price floor

___ 7. price ceiling

___ 8. intermediaries

___ 9. invisible hand

___10. minimum wage laws

___11. transaction costs

a. Government imposed price ceilings or price floors that hinder the market's ability to ration goods efficiently.

b. Adam Smith's name for automatic market adjustments.

c. Their incomes depend on cutting transaction costs for others.

d. Emerge because information and mobility are costly.

e. Risklessly buying at a low price in one market and then selling at a higher price in another market.

f. Can be enjoyed by many people simultaneously, but restricting access is prohibitively expensive.

g. Floors that may cause the unskilled to be unemployed.

h. A legal limitation that causes a surplus.

i. A legal limitation that causes a shortage.

j. Examples include ticket scalpers.

k. Benefits or costs of an activity spill over to third parties.

Set II: An answer may be used more than once.

What happens to equilibrium price and quantity when:

___ 1. both supply and demand increase?

___ 2. both supply and demand decrease?

___ 3. supply increases and demand decreases?

___ 4. supply decreases and demand increases?

___ 5. supply grows and demand is constant?

___ 6. demand grows; supply remains the same?

___ 7. supply falls and demand is constant?

___ 8. demand declines and supply is constant?

___ 9. corn prices rise--what happens to wheat?

___10. How will an oil discovery affect the price of gasoline?

a. Price and quantity will increase.

b. Price and quantity will fall.

c. Equilibrium price will fall and quantity will rise.

d. Equilibrium price will rise and quantity will fall.

e. Equilibrium price rises, but quantity changes are indeterminate.

f. Equilibrium price falls, but quantity changes are indeterminate.

g. Equilibrium quantity rises, but price changes are indeterminate.

h. Equilibrium quantity falls but price changes are indeterminate.

True/False Questions

___ 1. Prices depend on demand alone, while quantities depend primarily on supply.

___ 2. Long-term shortages or surpluses are, with very few exceptions, the results of government price controls.

___ 3. Federal minimum wage laws are examples of price ceilings, and most utility rates are examples of price floors.

___ 4. Increases in supplies put upward pressure on market prices and tend to increase the quantities of a good sold.

___ 5. Price controls are legal restrictions that often prevent monetary prices from reaching equilibrium levels.

___ 6. Speculation tends to hinder movements of prices and quantities towards market equilibrium.

___ 7. Allocative efficiency is aided if decision makers consider all costs of their actions.

___ 8. According to Adam Smith, the behavior of both business firms and individual consumers is governed by altruism.

___ 9. If the equilibrium price is below a price ceiling, a market tends to generate surpluses.

___ 10. The opportunity costs of consumption tend to increase if price ceilings below equilibrium price are imposed.

___ 11. Transaction costs arise because consumers do not have complete information about the price and availability of goods in all markets.

___ 12. Arbitrage generates riskless profits from buying low in one market and then selling at a higher price in another.

___ 13. Intermediaries will not be successful unless they reduce the transaction costs of getting goods   from ultimate producers to consumers.

___ 14. Price supports for agricultural products generate surpluses that consumers value less than their   costs to society.

___ 15. Black markets and consumer queues are signs that price ceilings restrict monetary prices below equilibrium.

___ 16. A tax is progressive if higher incomes are taxed proportionately less than lower incomes.

___ 17. Externalities occur when parties other than those directly making decisions are affected by an activity.

___ 18. At present, well over half of all goods produced in our economy are directly controlled or allocated by government.

___ 19. Efficiency requires government to produce public goods.

___ 20. National defense is the classic example of a negative externality.

Standard Multiple Choice

There Is One Best Answer For Each Question.

___ 1. The first comprehensive work on economics was written by Adam Smith in 1776 and entitled An Inquiry into the Nature and Causes of the:
  a. Laws of Supply and Demand.
  b. Wealth of Nations.
  c. Sovereignty of the Marketplace.
  d. Distribution of Income Among the Social Classes.
  e. Efficiency Gained from Competition.

___ 2. When the price of a good is below the intersection of its supply and demand curves, there will be:
  a. surpluses.
  b. shortages.
  c. "frozen" opportunity costs.
  d. excessive unemployment.
  e. None of the above.

___ 3. If the supply and demand for a product both increase, the:
  a. price will rise.
  b. quantity will increase.
  c. price will remain stable.
  d. profits of competitors will increase.
  e. welfare of society rises.

___ 4. The market price of video recorders will rise if:
  a. reading becomes more popular.
  b. supply increases.
  c. technology advances.
  d. imports are prohibited.
  e. consumers substitute towards cable TV.

___ 5. Buying at a low price in one market and selling at a higher price elsewhere is not:
  a. a risk-free way to make profits.
  b. called arbitrage.
  c. a cause of price spreads between markets.
  d. a mechanism that increases demand in the low-price market.
  e. a mechanism that increases supply in the high-price market.

___ 6. The transaction costs of conveying goods from producers to consumers are reduced by agents known as:
  a. arbitrageurs.
  b. efficiency consultants.
  c. commission houses.
  d. intermediaries.
  e. consortiums.

___ 7. Speculators tend to:
  a. increase the risks to other firms.
  b. reduce the volatility of prices.
  c. cause economic booms and busts.
  d. eliminate transaction costs.
  e. always make profits.

___ 8. Providing a stable business environment, promoting growth, and maintaining competitive markets are examples of the:
  a. social allocation of resources.
  b. economic functions of government.
  c. externalities of government.
  d. economic incidence on consumers.
  e. duties of trade unions.

9. All transaction costs would be zero if:
    a. a law was passed that required prices to be cut in half.
    b. information and transportation were costless.
    c. prices could not legally exceed production costs.
    d. rapidly rising input and output prices were eliminated.
    e. the operation by intermediaries was efficient.

10. Government price controls may reduce the supply of a good to the extent that they:
    a. artificially stimulate demand.
    b. prevent pollution and industrial blight.
    c. raise the costs of production.
    d. are based on laissez faire government policies.
    e. generate cyclical shortages and then surpluses.

11. Laws used to keep market prices from rising are called:
    a. wage and/or price ceilings.
    b. rationing and subsidies.
    c. allocations and redemptions.
    d. arbitrage and arbitration.
    e. None of the above.

12. Long term price ceilings are likely to cause:
    a. shortages.
    b. queues.
    c. black markets and corruption.
    d. economic inefficiency.
    e. All of the above.

13. Minimum wage laws are examples of:
    a. government assistance that aid people on welfare.
    b. direct benefits from union membership.
    c. price floors, and create surplus labor and unemployment.
    d. arbitrage exercised by government bureaucrats.
    e. price ceilings that create labor shortages.

14. Ignoring economic factors when designing social policies is:
    a. appropriate because morality does not depend on money.
    b. likely to cause results that are incompatible with intentions.
    c. recommended by advocates of laissez faire policies.
    d. a major reason why income is equitably distributed.
    e. mandated by the 27th amendment to the U.S. Constitution.

15. Harsher punishments for drug pushers than addicts cannot be blamed for higher:
    a. prices for illegal drugs than free market prices.
    b. rates of street crime by addicts.
    c. profits reaped by successful pushers who are uncaught.
    d. rates of addiction than would exist in a free market.
    e. police corruption because pushers can offer big bribes.

___16. Government's macroeconomic role is most closely related to the goal of providing or promoting:
   a. a common defense.
   b. a stable legal system and business environment.
   c. purchasing power, employment, and economic growth.
   d. equity in the distribution of income.
   e. positive externalities in public goods.

___17. Negative (cost) spillovers:
   a. result in too much of a product at too low a price.
   b. are exemplified by air pollution and education.
   c. are exemplified by transportation an immunization.
   d. result in too little of a product at too high a price.
   e. are caused by wastes of taxpayers' dollars.

___18. Government provision of a public good does not require the good to be:
   a. scarce so that opportunity costs exist.
   b. nonrival.
   c. nonexclusive.
   d. produced by government.
   e. exclusive.

___19. Which of the following activities is least likely to generate negative externalities?
   a. Driving while intoxicated.
   b. Smoking a cigar in a restaurant.
   c. Parking on your front lawn for months while repairing your car.
   d. Failing to bathe during the hot summer months.
   e. Getting an inoculation against a contagious disease.

___20. If a good is nonexclusive, people will:
   a. all vote for maximum possible government provision
   b. buy the good according to their tastes and preferences.
   c. not care if the good generates negative externalities.
   d. try to be "free riders".
   e. have a high benefit/cost ratio from its purchase.

Chapter Review (Fill-In Questions)

1. Market _____ occurs at the price where quantity demanded equals quantity _____ .

2. A shortage occurs when the market price is _____ the equilibrium price because a greater quantity of the good is _____ than supplied. If the market price exceeds the equilibrium price, there is a _____ because greater quantities of the good are _____ than are demanded by consumers.

3. If demands increase while supplies decline, prices _____ but quantity changes are _____ . When there are increases in both demands and supplies, _____ will increase but the change in _____ is indeterminate.

4. When a maximum legal price is set, it is called a price _____ , whereas if the government sets a minimum legal price, it is called a price _____ .
Price ceilings do not hold economic prices down; opportunity costs rise because of increases in _____ costs, and price ceilings typically cause _____ .
Price floors on the other hand often cause _____ ; and the production costs of these surpluses are _____ their values to consumers.

5. Successful speculators tend to reduce the volatility of _____ and absorb the _____ to others of doing business. Intermediaries are successful only to the extent that they are able to reduce the _____ incurred in transmitting goods from producers to consumers. The process of _____ entails buying at a low price in one market and selling at a higher price elsewhere.

6. When a consumer enters the market for a particular good, he might "shop" in order to gather information. This "shopping", however, generates _____ as the consumer accumulates information about product prices and availability.
_____ costs are also associated with the mobility of goods, resources, and people between markets.

7. If market (price) signals from consumers to business are incorrect, too little or too much of a good will be provided. These problems usually exist when _____ are involved or when the commodity or service in question is a _____ good.

8. A tax is said to be progressive if the percentage tax rate _____ as income rises. Regressive taxes are those where the tax rate _____ as income rises.

Unlimited Multiple Choice

The following questions have from zero to four correct answers.

___ 1. Market equilibrium is said to occur when the:
  a. government strictly controls price-gouging businesses.
  b. market experiences neither surpluses nor shortages.
  c. market price equates the quantities demanded and supplied.
  d. quantity demanded equals a governmentally imposed quota.

___ 2. The economic functions of government include:
  a. providing a reasonably certain legal, social, and business environment for stable growth.
  b. promoting and maintaining competitive markets.
  c. providing public goods and adjusting for externalities.
  d. stabilizing income, employment, and the price level.

___ 3. Price ceilings that are below market-clearing prices keep:
  a. monetary prices from rising except in black markets.
  b. a lid on opportunity costs.
  c. consumers from being "ripped off."
  d. incentives strong for the Invisible Hand to work its magic.

___ 4. Examples of "intermediary" operations include:
  a. speculators.
  b. retail outlets.
  c. arbitrating.
  d. ticket scalpers.

___ 5. Competitive markets:
  a. translate consumer wants into production by firms.
  b. are stationary by nature.
  c. aid buyers and sellers in communicating their wants, and facilitate beneficial exchanges of goods and resources.
  d. are all very similar.

Problems

Problem 1

Use the information in this table to answer the following questions about the market for battery-powered thermal socks. (Quantities are in millions of pairs of socks annually.)

Quantity Demanded	Price ($)	Quantity Supplied
0	10.00	20
2	9.50	18
4	9.00	16
6	8.50	14
8	8.00	12
10	7.50	10
12	7.00	8
14	6.50	6
16	6.00	4
18	5.50	2
20	5.00	0

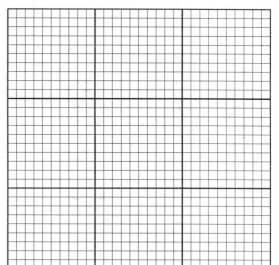

a.   Plot the supply and demand curves in the figure, being sure to label both axes; label the curves S_0 and D_0 respectively.

b.   What is the equilibrium price? _____ Quantity? _____

c.   Does the demand schedule illustrate the law of demand? _____ Why?
   _____

d.   Does the supply schedule illustrate the law of supply? _____ Why? _____

e.   Draw in a price ceiling of $6.00. What would occur? _____

f.   Draw a price floor of $9.50. What would occur? _____

g.   Assume that the quantities demanded and supplied double at each price. Plot the new supply and demand curves and label them S_1 and D_1 respectively.

h.   What is the new equilibrium price? _____ Quantity? _____

i.   List factors that could have increased demand: _____

j.   List factors that could have increased supply _____

Problem 2

Consider the (hypothetical) market for rental apartments in Paris as illustrated in this figure. Assume that the model represents a typical two-bedroom, single bath apartment.

a. Suppose that the rental market for single family apartments in Paris is initially competitive. The equilibrium rent for a typical apartment is _____, and at this rate, _____ apartments will be rented.

b. Now let the government impose rent controls or a _____ of $400 per apartment. This controlled price is _____ (above/below) the market equilibrium price by an amount equal to _____ per apartment. The government's motive for imposing the rent control is most likely to be that of making the typical apartment more _____ for the average family.

c. As a result of the controls, there is a _____ (surplus/shortage) of apartments in Paris equal to _____ rental units. At the controlled rent, _____ apartments could be rented; however, landlords will be willing and able to supply only _____ units.

d. At the controlled rent, apartment hunters would be willing and able to pay _____ per unit when only _____ apartment units are available rather than go without housing.

e. Even though rent controls ideally would help maintain affordable housing, they introduce several distortions in the rental housing market. One likely distortion is that it will take the average family _____ (more/less) time to find an apartment in Paris. Another likely distortion is that landlords will be _____ (more/less) willing to pay for maintenance, and so the quality of apartments will most likely _____. A third problem that rent controls may cause in Paris is that the return on the landlord's investment in apartments will likely _____ (increase/decrease), and as a result, the stock of available rental apartments will _____ (rise/decline) over time.

Problem 3

Supply and demand curves S_0 and D_0 represent the original situation in the market for top quality Brahma bulls. Use information from the figure to answer these questions about this market.

a. What is the original equilibrium price? _____
   Quantity? _____

b. If demand moves to D_1 because dietitians recommend that all people over 40 become vegetarians, what is the new equilibrium price? _____ Quantity? _____

c. Beginning with the original curves, if supply shifts to S_1 with the introduction of beef-up antibiotics, what is the new market-clearing price? _____ Quantity? _____

d. Assuming simultaneous shifts to D_1 and S_1, what is the new equilibrium price? _____ Quantity? _____

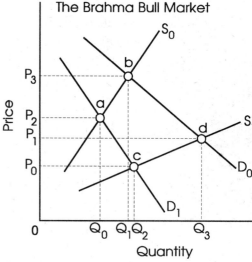

The Brahma Bull Market

e. The movement from point a to point c represents what on the demand side? _____
   What on the supply side? _____

f. The movement from point a to point b represents what on the demand side? _____
   What on the supply side? _____

g. The movement from point b to point d represents what on the demand side? _____
   What on the supply side? _____

h. The movement from point c to point d represents what on the demand side? _____
   What on the supply side? _____

i. Looking only at the original set of demand and supply curves (D_0, S_0), what would occur if the price were set at P_2? _____ Why? _____

j. Looking only at the new set of demand and supply curves (D_1, S_1) what would occur if the price were set at P_1? _____ Why? _____

Problem 4

Demand curve D_L in this figure represents the demand for unskilled labor services by business firms, and S_L represents the supply of unskilled labor services offered by households. Money wage rate W_e is the market-clearing wage rate, but W_m denotes the minimum money wage rate imposed on this labor market by federal law. Use this information to answer the following true/false questions.

____a. The minimum money wage rate is an example of a price floor.

____b. At wage rate W_e, the quantity of labor demanded equals the quantity supplied.

____c. Employment is greater at W_m than at W_e.

____d. The federal government has created a buyers' market in the labor market.

____e. At wage rate W_m, unemployment equals L_2 minus L_1.

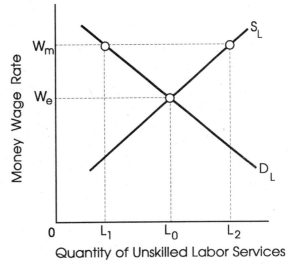

____f. Unemployment would fall if the government discontinued its legal minimum for the money wage rate.

____g. The minimum wage reduces employers' costs of discriminating.

Problem 5

Draw supply and demand diagrams on scratch paper to help you answer the following questions.

a. There is a major technological breakthrough in producing natural gas from coal. What happens in the market for natural gas? _____
   The market for coal? _____

b. Gasoline prices soar. What happens in the markets for big cars? _____
   Bicycles? _____ Tune-up shops? _____
   Rapid -transit systems? _____

c. What happens to quantity, if a price ceiling of $10 a pair is imposed on denim jeans?
   _____ To quality? _____
   Is the government doing jeans wearers a favor? _____

d. In 1994, the government announces a major renewal of space exploration. In 2001, this program is discontinued. What will happen in the market for aeronautical engineers in 1994-1995? _____ Between 1995 and 2001? _____
   Between 2001 and 2002? _____ After 2002? _____

e. There is a radical overhaul and simplification of the income tax system. What happens in the market for accountants? _____ Lawyers?
   _____ Erasers? _____

Problem 6

Use the tax and income information listed in this table to answer the following questions.

a. Fill in the average tax rate column in the table.

b. What is the marginal rate of taxation (ΔTax /ΔIncome) when income increases from $10,000 to $15,000?

   _____

c. What kind of tax is depicted in the table? _____

Income($)	Total Taxes ($)	Average Tax Rate
10,000	5,000	_____
15,000	6,750	_____
20,000	8,000	_____
25,000	8,750	_____
35,000	9,000	_____
50,000	10,000	_____

d. Can you think of any taxes that fit this pattern?_____

ANSWERS

Matching		True/False		Multiple Choice		Unlimited Multiple Choice
Set I	Set II					
1. e	1. g	1. F	11. T	1. b	11. a	1. bc
2. a	2. h	2. T	12. T	2. b	12. e	2. abcd
3. k	3. f	3. F	13. T	3. b	13. c	3. a
4. j	4. e	4. F	14. T	4. d	14. b	4. abcd
5. f	5. c	5. T	15. T	5. c	15. d	5. ac
6. h	6. a	6. F	16. F	6. d	16. c	
7. i	7. d	7. T	17. T	7. b	17. a	
8. c	8. b	8. F	18. F	8. b	18. d	
9. b	9. d	9. F	19. F	9. b	19. e	
10. g	10. c	10. T	20. F	10. c	20. d	
11. d						

Chapter Review (Fill-in Questions)

1. equilibrium; supplied
2. lower than; demanded; surplus; supplied
3. rise; indeterminate; quantity; price
4. ceiling; floor; transaction; shortages; surpluses; above
5. prices; risks; transaction costs; arbitrage
6. costs; transaction
7. externalities; public
8. rises; falls

Problem 1

a. See figure.
b. $7.50; 10 million.
c. Yes; The relationship between price and quantity demanded is inverse (negative).
d. Yes; The relationship between price and quantity supplied is direct (positive).
e. See figure; a shortage, since 16 units would be demanded but only 4 units would be supplied.
f. See figure; a surplus, since 18 units would be supplied but only 2 units would be demanded.
g. See figure.
h. $7.50; 20 million pairs.
i. favorable change in tastes and preferences; rise in income or the number of buyers; drop in price of a complementary good or rise in the price of a substitute good; increase in price expectations.
j. decline in resource costs; increase in technology; decreases in the prices of substitutes in production; an increase in the numbers of suppliers, expectations that durables' prices will fall.

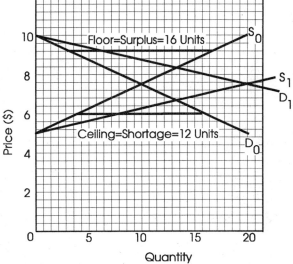

Problem 2

a. $800; 20 thousand
b. price ceiling; below; $400; affordable
c. shortage; 20 thousand; 30 thousand; 10 thousand
d. $1,200; 10 thousand
e. more; less; decline; decrease; decline

Problem 3

a. P_3, Q_1
b. P_2, Q_0
c. P_1, Q_3
d. P_0, Q_2
e. increase in quantity demanded; increase in supply
f. increase in demand; increase in quantity supplied
g. increase in quantity demanded; increase in supply
h. increase in demand; increase in quantity supplied
i. shortage; quantity demanded at P_2 exceeds quantity supplied
j. surplus; quantity supplied at P_1 exceeds quantity demanded

Problem 4

a. T
b. T
c. F
d. T
e. T
f. T
g. T

Problem 5

a. supply increases; demand increases
b. demand decreases; demand increases; demand increases; demand increases
c. quantity supplied decreases while quantity demanded increases; quality decreases; no
d. demand increases; supply increases; demand decreases; supply decreases
e. demand decreases; demand decreases; demand decreases

Problem 6

a. See table.
b. 35% (($6,750 - $5,000)/($15,000 - $10,000))
c. regressive
d. some sales taxes, tobacco and alcohol taxes

Income($)	Total Taxes ($)	Average Tax Rate
10,000	5,000	50%
15,000	6,750	45%
20,000	8,000	40%
25,000	8,750	35%
35,000	9,000	25.7%
50,000	10,000	20%

Chapter 5
Foundations of Macroeconomics

Chapter Objectives

After you have read and studied this chapter you should be able to describe different phases of business cycles and explain early business cycle theories; identify the major determinants of Aggregate Supply and Aggregate Demand; use Aggregate Demand and Aggregate Supply curves to (crudely) illustrate movements of economy wide levels of prices, output, and employment; and describe the historical record of American business fluctuations.

Chapter Review: Key Points

1. *Business cycles* are alternating periods of expansion and contraction, which break down into four phases: (a) *peak* (boom), (b) *contraction* (recession or downturn), (c) *trough* (depression), and (d) *expansion* (recovery or upturn). As measured from peak to peak by the National Bureau of Economic Research, cycles average about 4 years, with some as short as 18 months, while others have lasted a decade. Reference dates are established after detailed scrutiny of data from past cycles.

2. Marriages and divorces alike tend to be positively related to the business cycle. Mental disorders, some physical diseases, suicides, crimes, and illegitimate births are inversely related to business conditions. That is, they all rise when the economy turns down. Declines in income and the negative social effects of slumps have prompted policy-makers to look for ways to keep the economy on a steady path.

3. Many early business cycle theories were *external shock* theories, focusing on sources of instability outside the economic system such as war or weather conditions.

4. *Joseph Schumpeter* developed a business cycle theory around major innovations that may partially explain major long-term business fluctuations. He cited the developments of railroads, automobiles, and similar innovations as generating significant investment leading to tremendous spurts of economic growth.

5. *Psychological theories* of business cycles use people's herd instincts to explain extended optimism or pessimism. These theories may partially account for the cumulative nature of business cycle downturns or recoveries, but provide little insight into the reasons for turning points.

6. *Classical macroeconomics* focuses on the supply side. It relies on market forces to automatically ensure full employment, and views recessions as self-extinguishing without a role for government.

7. The prolonged Great Depression seemed to refute classical theory. The demand-oriented theories of John Maynard Keynes dominated economic thought from 1936 through the 1960s. *Keynesian macroeconomics* concludes that government can adjust Aggregate Demand through its tax and spending policies.

8. *Aggregate Demand* is based on spending by (**a**) consumers, (**b**) investors, (**c**) government, and (**d**) foreigners (i.e., net exports). The *Aggregate Demand curve* is negatively sloped because a higher price level causes reduced spending on our domestic output because of (**a**) the *wealth effect*, (**b**) the *foreign sector substitution effect*, and (**c**) the *interest rate effect*.

9. The single most important determinant of *consumer spending* is disposable income. Other major determinants of consumption and saving include: (**a**) wealth and expectations of future income, (**b**) the average size and age composition of typical households, (**c**) household balance sheets and stocks of consumer goods, and (**d**) consumer expectations regarding prices and availability of products.

10. *Investment* in capital refers to purchases of new output that can be used in the future to produce other goods and services. There are three major components of investment: (**a**) new business and residential structures, (**b**) machinery and equipment, and (**c**) inventory accumulation.

11. The quantity of investment is determined primarily by expected returns from investment which, in turn, depend on (**a**) expectations about the business environment, (**b**) rates of technological change and innovation, (**c**) existing stocks of capital relative to total production, and (**d**) investment costs, which depend most on the interest rate.

12. *Exports* (X) add to Aggregate Demand, but reduce Aggregate Supply. (Goods sold to foreigners are not available to Americans.) *Imports* (M) boost Aggregate Supply but may reduce Aggregate Demand. (Buyers of imports spend less on American goods.) Exports and imports are reasonably balanced, so *net exports* ($X - M$) affect Aggregate Demand relatively little. The foreign sector is, however, vital, because it provides (**a**) markets for our production and (**b**) imported goods that would be more costly if produced only domestically.

13. The *Aggregate Supply curve* is positively sloped because, when business conditions change, firm can adjust prices more rapidly than production costs. Prosperity increases profit per unit, so firms hire more resources and produce more output.

14. Aggregate Supply curves shift in response to changes in (**a**) supplies of resources, (**b**) technology, (**c**) government policies that affect costs, or (**d**) net imports.

15. Increases in Aggregate Demand raise national income and output, the price level, and employment. Expansion of Aggregate Supply pushes prices downwards and facilitates growth of employment and national income and output.

Matching Key Terms And Concepts

Set I

___ 1. Aggregate Demand curve

___ 2. business cycles

___ 3. wealth effect

___ 4. Joseph Schumpeter

___ 5. external shock theories

___ 6. classical economics

___ 7. Aggregate Supply curve

___ 8. Keynesian economics

___ 9. stagflation

___10. increase in Aggregate Supply

a. Cycles are caused by outside disturbances.

b. Can be caused by technological advances.

c. Believes government can counter business cycles by adjusting Aggregate Demand.

d. One reason why the Aggregate Demand curve is negatively sloped.

e. Declines in output precipitate rising prices.

f. Major innovations partly explain long cycles.

g. A positive relationship between goods available economy-wide and the price level.

h. Alternating expansion and contraction.

i. A negative relationship between economy-wide domestic production and the price level.

j. Market forces ensure long-run full employment.

Set II

___ 1. Aggregate Supply shifts leftward

___ 2. Aggregate Supply shifts rightward

___ 3. Aggregate Demand shifts leftward

___ 4. Aggregate Demand shifts rightward

___ 5. contraction

___ 6. foreign sector substitution effect

___ 7. recovery

___ 8. trough

___ 9. "capitalistic crisis"

___10. the Great Depression

a. May be caused by interest rate hikes.

b. Increased preference for leisure by labor.

c. Reductions in monopoly power.

d. May be caused by an increase in planned government purchases.

e. Marxian view that business cycles would become more severe.

f. The low point of a cyclical downturn.

g. Typically follows a peak.

h. Typically follows a trough.

i. Lasted from 1929 until World War II.

j. A reason why Aggregate Demand is negatively sloped.

True/False Questions

___ 1. During the Great Depression, the U.S. unemployment rate approached 25 percent.

___ 2. In the U.S. the unemployment rate plummeted from 25 percent in 1929 to only 3.2 percent in 1933.

___ 3. The long wave theory of business cycles gained wide acceptance after several studies proved their existence.

___ 4. Between 1830 and 1894, Karl Marx expounded a long-wave theory of business cycles by suggesting that economic growth and development in capitalistic systems are fueled by innovations.

___ 5. During the Great Depression, the burden of economic assistance fell largely on private charities.

___ 6. The decade of the 1950s in the US was a period of rapidly accelerating economic growth, with double-digit inflation becoming slightly more serious as the years progressed.

___ 7. In the U.S., the middle 1970s witnessed our first serious brush with supply induced double-digit inflation.

___ 8. Classical economics relies heavily on the self-correcting power of automatic market adjustments to cure macroeconomic instability.

___ 9. The Great Depression was responsible for many of the governmental institutions that exist today.

___10. Other things constant, if the labor force became better trained and educated, the Aggregate Supply curve would shift to the left.

___11. All else equal, if the government were to increase its spending on national defense, the Aggregate Demand curve would shift to the right.

___12. Major discoveries of new deposits of raw materials would immediately expand the Aggregate Demand curve.

___13. Aggregate Demand curves shift when planned spending changes for consumption, investment, government, or net exports to foreigners.

___14. The Aggregate Supply curve reflects a positive relationship between the price level and real national output.

___15. Growth of Aggregate Supply is the major cause of unemployment.

Standard Multiple Choice

There Is One Best Answer For Each Question

___ 1. Which of the following is **not** one of the four phases of a business cycle?
   a. peak
   b. inflation
   c. recession
   d. trough
   e. recovery

___ 2. "Sunspot" theories of business cycles:
   a. say that booms commence when business becomes optimistic.
   b. correlate sunspot activity with innovations that spark growth.
   c. are intrinsically psychological.
   d. may be resurrected if solar energy becomes relatively inexpensive.
   e. conform to modern astrology.

___ 3. Joseph Schumpeter's theory of business cycles was:
   a. sunspot theory: that sunspots affect agricultural production.
   b. psychological: herd instincts propel waves of optimism and pessimism.
   c. long-wave innovation theory: the economy expands with significant innovation, reaches saturation, and then moves into a recession until another great innovation.
   d. "long-waves" theory: economic sine waves last 50 to 60 years.
   e. that population adjusts to the resources available, creating swings in supplies and demands.

___ 4. Psychological theories of business cycles can be used to help explain:
   a. the timing of cyclic turning points.
   b. the cumulative nature of economic recoveries or downturns.
   c. why people do not behave as if they possess a "herd instinct."
   d. why pessimism or optimism won't affect economic cycles in any way.
   e. psychoeconomic problems.

___ 5. Prosperous periods tend to engender:
   a. fewer suicides.
   b. more marriages and divorces.
   c. less crime.
   d. fewer illegitimate births.
   e. All of the above.

___ 6. Keynesian theory developed as a response to:
   a. the stagflation of the 1970s.
   b. external business cycle theories.
   c. Say's Law.
   d. extensive and prolonged unemployment in the 1930s.
   e. inflation after World War I.

___ 7. Humans are destined to live at a subsistence level according to:
   a. new classical macroeconomics.
   b. Thomas Malthus.
   c. Keynesian theory.
   d. Marxism.
   e. innovation theory.

___ 8. Which of the following could shift the Aggregate Demand curve rightward?
   a. New resources are discovered.
   b. The supply of labor increases.
   c. Tax rates are reduced.
   d. Household wealth is reduced.
   e. Investors become more pessimistic.

___ 9. Stagflation occurs when Aggregate:
   a. Technology shifts vertically.
   b. Demand shifts right.
   c. Demand shifts left.
   d. Supply shifts right.
   e. Supply shifts left.

___10. The Aggregate Demand curve is negatively sloped because of the:
   a. wealth effect.
   b. interest rate effect.
   c. foreign sector substitution effect.
   d. all of the above.
   e. none of the above.

___11. The foreign sector substitution effect suggests that a drop in the U.S. price level relative tends to increase U.S.:
   a. exports and decrease U.S. imports.
   b. imports and decrease U.S. exports.
   c. Aggregate Supply.
   d. production possibilities.
   e. None of the above.

___12. Increased Aggregate Demand tends to increase all of the following EXCEPT:
   a. national income.
   b. the price level.
   c. unemployment.
   d. national output.
   e. employment.

___13. Which of the following statements about the Great Depression is FALSE:
   a. The unemployment rate rose to a high of nearly 25 percent.
   b. Real disposable income fell sharply.
   c. Average prices fell--the economy actually experienced deflation.
   d. Most economic relief came from public welfare programs.
   e. The depression was global.

___14. Which of the following could increase both real output and the price level?
   a. An external shock that drives up resource costs.
   b. An increase in government purchases of goods and services.
   c. An increase in taxes.
   d. An external shock that reduces resource costs.
   e. Consumer expectations of price deflation.

___15. Pressure for stagflation would be most likely to emerge from increases in:
   a. average income tax refunds.
   b. the money supply.
   c. labor force education and training.
   d. the length of annual vacation leave.
   e. consumer indebtedness.

Chapter Review (Fill-In Questions)

1. Most early theories of business cycles focused on forces that were _____ to the economic system. Sunspot theories and other early theory stressed wars and shocks to _____. Psychological theories of the cycle concentrate on the herd instinct coupled with prolonged periods (or waves) of _____ and _____.

2. According to _____, variations in the magnitudes and timing of _____ and then the process of adjusting to them were the driving forces behind long cycles.

3. _____ predicted the decline and eventual overthrow of capitalism as it moved through extended business expansions and contractions because of ever greater _____ of wealth in the hands of capitalists.

4. The business cycle exhibits a strong relationship with many _____ institutions and maladies. Suicides, crime, and illegitimate births tend to be _____ related to economic activity.

5. Classical economics relies heavily on market forces to _____ move the economy to _____.

Chapter (
Employment and Unemployment

Chapter Objectives

After you have studied this chapter you should be able to explain how unemployment is measured, identify and give reasons for the differing types of unemployment, and enumerate the costs and benefits of unemployment.

Chapter Review: Key Points

1. *Voluntary unemployment* occurs when people could find work quickly, but choose to look for what they view as better jobs in terms of pay or working conditions. *Involuntary unemployment* occurs when people lack jobs, but are willing and able to work at wages commensurate with their skills.

2. *Wage stickiness* describes needed downward adjustments of wages that occur only slowly, and tends to prolong periods of unemployment. Wages tend to be "sticky" because of minimum wage laws, union contracts, and the personnel policies firms use in attempts to reduce turnover in jobs regarded as career positions by employers.

3. The *labor force* consists of all employed or unemployed civilians plus military personnel. A *labor force participation rate* is the proportion in the labor force from a specific group.

4. Part-time workers who would like to work full time are officially categorized as employed, but they also experience *part-time unemployment*. Unemployed people who are so discouraged about job prospects that they do not look for work are not counted in unemployment statistics. Some people who are not truly out of work indicate that they are to collect unemployment compensation. Thus, data for unemployment may either understate the true unemployment rate because of *discouraged workers* or overstate it because of *dishonest nonworkers*.

5. *Frictional unemployment* arises because of transaction costs associated with normal entry and exit from labor markets, layoffs or firings, or voluntary job changes. Both workers and firms "invest in information" by *searching* for jobs or screening applicants until their expected marginal benefits no longer exceed their expected marginal costs.

6. *Seasonal unemployment* arises from the annually recurring influences of weather, vacations, and the like on labor markets.

7. *Structural unemployment* results from mismatches between workers and jobs because of changes in the skill requirements of job openings or individuals lack marketable skills.

8. *Cyclical unemployment* results from recessions.

9. Government policies that reduce work incentives or that prevent workers from securing employment (e.g., minimum wage laws) cause *induced unemployment*.

10. Unemployment causes both *economic* and *social costs.* Society as a whole suffers because of lost income and output that unemployed individuals could have produced. Individuals and their families suffer socially and psychologically when they are unemployed for long periods. Personal losses are, however, partially cushioned by such programs as unemployment compensation.

11 Unemployment is not distributed equally across all groups. Workers in manufacturing and construction are hit harder by cyclical unemployment during recessions than employees in most other lines of work, but this tendency seems to be weakening, with cyclically rising rates of unemployment among service workers and professional and technical personnel and mid level managers.

Matching Key Terms And Concepts

___ 1. cyclical unemployment

___ 2. contingency work force

___ 3. structural unemployment

___ 4. lost income costs of unemployment

___ 5. seasonal unemployment

___ 6. discouraged workers

___ 7. wage stickiness

___ 8. involuntary unemployment

___ 9. frictional unemployment

___10. induced unemployment

a. Caused by transaction costs in labor markets.

b. Typesetter replaced by computer programs.

c. Persons who want to work but have given up.

d. Annual experience of many life guards and golf pros.

e. Caused by slumps in the economy.

f. Wages are slow to adjust downward.

g. Include the opportunity costs of the output and income unemployed individuals could have produced.

h. Mostly brought about by government policies.

i. Consists of part-timers, temps, and the self-employed.

j. Persons willing to work at wages commensurate with their skills, but unable to find jobs.

True/False

___ 1. Seasonal unemployment is that unemployment associated with the business cycle.

___ 2. Globalization, the decline of manufacturing, and government policies have all contributed to the dramatic change in the demand for labor over the past few decades

___ 3. Reducing frictional unemployment is a major goal of government policymakers.

___ 4. Discouraged workers tend to overstate the unemployment rate.

___ 5. Unemployment is costly, individually and socially, and yields no benefits.

___ 6. Structural unemployment can occur if individuals have very little education.

___ 7. Cyclical unemployment tends to result in longer periods of unemployment.

___ 8 Government retraining programs are primarily targeted at people whose job losses have been induced.

___ 9. Reduced transactions costs in the labor market would also reduce frictional unemployment.

___10. Total labor force participation rates have grown over time primarily because women increasingly choose to pursue careers.

Standard Multiple Choice

There Is One Best Answer For Each Question.

_____ 1. Unemployment statistics will be understated because of:
   a. welfare cheaters.
   b. unemployed college dropouts.
   c. discouraged workers.
   d. housewives.
   e. cyclical layoffs.

_____ 2. Official unemployment data are based on surveys of:
   a. all firms in the country.
   b. all households in the country.
   c. all workers in the country.
   d. a sample of all U.S. households.

_____ 3. People who do not work for pay because of physical disability are defined by the BLS as:
   a. in the labor force.
   b. unemployed.
   c. discouraged.
   d. not in the labor force.

_____ 4. Macroeconomic policy makers are most concerned with reducing:
   a. frictional unemployment.
   b. cyclical unemployment.
   c. structural unemployment.
   d. voluntary unemployment.
   e. union strikes in key industries,

_____ 5. Allocative benefits of unemployment do NOT include improvements in:
   a. the economy's overall efficiency.
   b. matches between workers and jobs.
   c. total returns from investment in labor market information.
   d. job satisfaction among workers who don't look for better jobs.

_____ 6. The social and psychic costs of unemployment include the:
   a. declines in the self esteem of unemployed breadwinners.
   b. value of loot from more frequent bank robberies.
   c. transaction costs incurred by job seekers.
   d. output not produced because of inefficiency.
   e. menu and distortion costs.

_____ 7. Periods of high U.S. unemployment since the 1930s have been usually been characterized by substantial:
   a. voluntary poverty for virtually all seasonally unemployed workers.
   b. induced unemployment--welfare now pays them more income than most jobless workers could earn.
   c. cyclical unemployment.
   d. structural unemployment caused by wartime dislocations
   e. seasonal unemployment.

_____ 8. Defining full employment as occurring when the numbers of job vacancies and the numbers of unemployed are equal implies that, at full employment, people who want work but who lack jobs would be experiencing:
   a. cyclical unemployment.
   b. structural and frictional unemployment.
   c. involuntary unemployment.
   d. motivational underemployment.
   e. induced unemployment.

9. Induced unemployment as a concept is least relevant for a:
   a. machinist laid off by automation.
   b. person drawing unemployment compensation to help pay the costs of looking for a perfect job.
   c. teenager who could provide work worth $3.00 per hour, but not enough to cover the minimum wage of $3.35 per hour.
   d. welfare recipient who would lose all benefits by accepting a minimum wage job.

10. Discouraged workers are those who are:
    a. disenchanted with their jobs.
    b. employed in jobs that underutilize their skills.
    c. unhappy because search hasn't generated an acceptable job.
    d. so pessimistic about job prospects that they quit looking for work.

11. An ex-convict who landed a job as a college president by fraudulently claiming a Ph.D. in Marketing is officially classified by the BLS as:
    a. employed.
    b. unemployed.
    c. unreliable.
    d. overemployed.

12. Structural unemployment would apply LEAST to an individual who was a:
    a. convicted murderer with a life sentence and no chance of parole.
    b. thin department store Santa Claus in February.
    c. deposed dictator willing to retake his old job at his old income.
    d. former all-Pro guard banned from the NFL because of drug addiction.

13. Unemployed slide rule mechanics, typesetters displaced by automation, or ex-convicts whose only legal skills are making license plates, exemplify:
    a. structural unemployment.
    b. seasonal unemployment.
    c. cyclical unemployment.
    d. frictional unemployment.
    e. institutional unemployment.

14. On average, the duration of unemployment tends to be longer:
    a. during cyclical downturns.
    b. for white collar workers than in earlier eras, especially since the advent of corporate down-sizing.
    c. for people deemed over-qualified.
    d. as more generous unemployment compensation is offered.
    e. All of the above.

15. The best example of induced unemployment is given by:
    a. migrant workers in the winter time.
    b. workers who lose their jobs during a recession.
    c. laws that prohibit teenagers under 16 from working full time.
    d. workers who quit their jobs.
    e. companies that demand workers have a college education.

16. Jennifer is looking for full time work, but ignores the help wanted sign in a fast food restaurant, because she will not do this type of work. Jennifer would be considered as:
    a. involuntarily unemployed.
    b. cyclically unemployed.
    c. structurally unemployed.
    d. voluntarily unemployed.
    e. seasonally unemployed.

___17. Employees may quickly adjust to wage hikes, but are loath to take pay cuts, leading to a concept known as:
   a. voluntary unemployment.
   b. wage stickiness.
   c. cyclical unemployment.
   d. involuntary unemployment.
   e. induced unemployment.

___18. Allocative benefits from unemployment occur primarily because:
   a. slackers are easily shed.
   b. wages fall relative to capital costs.
   c. of worker retraining programs.
   d. of unemployment insurance.
   e. transaction costs are reduced for workers and firms.

___19. A split minimum wage, in which teenage trainees could be paid less than the prevailing minimum wage, would most likely:
   a. reduce induced unemployment.
   b. fuel cyclical unemployment.
   c. decrease structural unemployment.
   d. increase seasonal unemployment.
   e. reduce frictional unemployment.

___20. As long as transaction costs are positive:
   a. cyclical employment will persist.
   b. structural employment will rise.
   c. seasonal unemployment declines.
   d. frictional unemployment will exist.
   e. induced employment will be zero.

Chapter Review (Fill-In Questions)

1. The _____ consists of all employed and unemployed civilians over age 16 plus member of the military. The _____ is the percentage of the population that is in the labor force.

2. People who could find work quickly, but who choose to search for better jobs, are considered _____ unemployed. However, people are considered _____ unemployed if they are unable to find work at wages commensurate with their skills.

3. _____ unemployment occurs because matching workers with jobs absorbs time and is costly. _____ unemployment results from downturns in the business cycle.

4. Unemployment statistics as reported may understate true unemployment due to the failure to include _____, and may overstate the true level because of _____.

5. When skill requirements for a given occupation change or people have no marketable skills, _____ unemployment results. _____ unemployment occurs because some types of work are dependent upon weather or the time of the year.

6. Unemployment results in _____ as well as _____ costs such as foregone education, increased family debt, and higher crime and suicide rates.

Unlimited Multiple Choice

There Are From Zero To Four Correct Answers For Each Question.

___ 1. Frictional unemployment:
   a. could be eliminated by appropriate government programs.
   b. is a result of normal economic activity.
   c. usually results from serious structural change in the economy.
   d. arises due to transaction costs in labor markets.

___ 2. Cyclical unemployment:
   a. tends to increase the duration of unemployment.
   b. moves in tandem with business cycle.
   c. could be reduced if minimum wage legislation was repealed.
   d. historically affected construction workers more than professionals.

___ 3. Persons are classified as:
   a. unemployed if they are not employed but are available for work and made recent attempts to find jobs.
   b. unemployed if during the survey week they were waiting to report to a new job in three months.
   c. unemployed if during the survey week they were waiting to be recalled to a job from which they were laid off.
   d. part of the labor force if they were employed during the survey week.

___ 4. Structural unemployment:
   a. is of little concern to government policymakers.
   b. affects persons with antiquated skills.
   c. can be combated with job training programs.
   d. affects primarily overeducated people.

___ 5. Federal laws to punish firms that hire illegal immigrants might help reduce:
   a. induced unemployment.
   b. cyclical unemployment.
   c. seasonal unemployment.
   d. frictional unemployment.

Problems

Problem 1

In 1993, the U.S. population was 256,394,000, of whom 192,690,000 were age 16 or over. The labor force including the Armed Forces was 132,724,000, the civilian labor force was 131,387,000, and civilian employment was 123,414,000.

a. The employment/population ratio is? _____

b. The labor force participation rate for ages 16 and over is? _____

c. The total unemployment rate (including the military) is? _____

d. The civilian unemployment rate is? _____

e. Why is the total unemployment rate lower than that for civilians? _____

Problem 2

In the following scenarios, determine if the individual would be considered employed, unemployed, or not part of the labor force by the Bureau of Labor Statistics.

a. A Ph.D. in anthropology who works full-time as a cab driver while devoting three hours daily to searching for a job as a researcher or an assistant professor. _____

b. After quitting work as a cab driver, the anthropologist remodels her home six days a week, devoting only Monday mornings to looking for work as an anthropologist. _____

c. An eighth-grader who temporarily loses her job delivering papers when the printer's union at the local newspaper goes on strike.

d. A chef who chops off two fingers the day before his restaurant closes forever, draws disability pay while vacationing before looking for another job.

e. A novelist who has not written a page in months because he is unable to think of a good plot.

f. A construction worker who has free time for three weeks until the next big job starts.

Problem 3

This table illustrates population and employment data for the hypothetical country of Paradisio.

	July 1994	December 1994
Non-institutional Population	2,000,000	2,100,000
Labor Force	1,000,000	
Employed	920,000	900,000
Unemployed		50,000
Employment Rate		
Unemployment Rate		
Labor Force Participation Rate		

a. For simplicity, assume that Paradisio has no military personnel. Complete the table.

b. What are likely causes of the population increase? _____

c. What has happened to the number employed? _____; and the employment rate?_____ Does this result seem perverse? _____ Why or why not?

_____

d. Why do you think the labor force declined over this period? _____ This type of "unemployment" is usually called _____

e. Are discouraged workers counted in any of these statistics? _____ Which one(s)?

_____

Answers

Matching	True/False	Multiple Choice		Unlimited	Chapter Review (Fill-in Questions)
1. e	1. F	1. c	11. a	1. bd	1. labor force;
2. i	2. T	2. d	12. a	2. abd	labor force participation rate
3. b	3. F	3. d	13. a	3. abcd	2. voluntary; involuntary
4. g	4. F	4. b	14. e	4. bc	3. Frictional; Cyclical
5. d	5. F	5. d	15. c	5. none	4. discouraged workers;
6. c	6. T	6. a	16. d		dishonest nonworkers
7. f	7. T	7. c	17. b		5. structural; seasonal
8. j	8. F	8. b	18. e		6. lost income; social
9. a	9. T	9. a	19. a		
10. h	10. T	10. d	20. d		

Problem 1

a. Total employment civilian plus armed forces (=124,751) divided by population (256,394,000) = 48.7%.
b. 68.9% (132,924,000/192,690)
c. Employment rate equals 94.0% (124,751,000/132,724,00), so the unemployment rate equals 6.0% (100% - 94.0%)
d. 6.1% (100% - 123,414,000/131,387,000)
e. 100% of military personnel are considered employed, so their inclusion must decrease the total unemployment rate.

Problem 2

a. employed
b. unemployed
c. not in labor force
d. not in labor force
e. employed
f. unemployed

Problem 3

a. See table.
b. Immigration, and the birth rate exceeds the mortality rate.
c. Employment has fallen. The employment rate has risen. No, because the labor force has declined substantially over this period.

	JULY 1994	DECEMBER 1994
Non-institutional Population	2,000,000	2,100,000
Labor Force	1,000,000	950,000
Employed	920,000	900,000
Unemployed	80,000	50,000
Employment Rate	92%	94.7%
Unemployment Rate	8%	5.3%
Labor Force Participation Rate	.50	.45

d. The July figures include high school students no longer in the labor force in December. The term seasonal unemployment is usually used to describe such situations.
e. Discouraged workers are included in population and, therefore, the labor force participation rate.

Chapter 7
Inflation

Chapter Objectives

After you have studied this chapter you should be able to explain how inflation is measured and how index numbers are constructed and used; be able to distinguish between different types of inflation as well as their causes, and enumerate the benefits and costs associated with inflation.

Chapter Review: Key Points

1. *Index numbers* are used to compare particular variables over time. The *Consumer Price Index (CPI)* measures average price changes for a given bundle of consumer goods over time. The *CPI* is based on typical consumer patterns for most of the urban population.

2. The *CPI* is used to convert nominal values to real values. It is also used extensively as an escalator clause (cost-of-living adjustment) in many contracts.

3. *Deflating* nominal variables means dividing their monetary values by (1 percent of) a price index.

4. Major difficulties in computing the *CPI* include problems inherent in adjusting the index for: (*a*) new products; (*b*) changes in the qualities of existing products; (*c*) changes in the composition of consumer expenditures; and, (*d*) already owned consumer durables such as housing.

5. The *Producer Price Index (PPI)* measures changes in the prices of goods in other than retail markets. The *GDP Deflator* adjusts GDP for changes in prices. It is composed of relevant portions of the *CPI* and the *PPI,* plus some additional prices covered by neither.

6. *Creeping inflation* occurs relatively slowly; *galloping inflation* occurs when average prices move at double-digit rates. *Hyperinflation* entails average price hikes exceeding 50 percent monthly. Inflation is generally less harmful if it is anticipated than if it is a surprise to people.

7. Inflation increases *transaction costs* by making price information obsolete faster, and it causes resources that could be used productively elsewhere to be used for repricing. These are the *menu costs* of inflation.

8. Inflation also distorts relative prices and economic decision making, and depresses incentives to save. Capital accumulation may or may not be hampered by inflation, depending on business expectations and the availability of funds for investment. These are the *distortion costs* of inflation.

9. The *discomfort (misery) index* is the sum of the inflation rate and the unemployment rate. It averaged 6-7 percent during the 1950s and 1960s. During the late 1970s and early 1980s, the index ranged from 13 to more than 20 percent. By 1990, economic growth had pushed the index below 10 percent.

10. There are *social costs of inflation* because people feel greater uncertainty during inflationary periods. People living on fixed incomes are hurt by inflation, but many transfer payments and wage contracts now have escalator clauses that adjust payments for price level changes. Borrowers tend to gain from unexpected inflation, while the ultimate lenders (e.g., savers with bank deposits) lose. When inflation boosts income, meeting a fixed mortgage payment becomes easier, so heavily mortgaged homeowners tend to gain.

Matching Key Terms And Concepts

Set I

____ 1. "deflating" nominal values

____ 2. demand-pull inflation

____ 3. discomfort (misery) index

____ 4. inflation

____ 5. real values

____ 6. cost-push inflation.

____ 7. hyperinflation

____ 8. menu costs of inflation.

____ 9. composition-shift inflation

____ 10. creeping inflation

a. Cost of upward revisions of price schedules.
b. Rising demand in one sector causes price hikes; falling demand in another causes layoffs.
c. An upward movement in general prices.
d. Adjusting for price level changes by dividing monetary variables by (1% of) a price index.
e. Occurs, e.g., if costly resources are increasingly wasted and misused by incompetent managers.
f. Low levels of persistent price hikes.
g. The sum of the rates of inflation and unemployment.
h. Variables measured by money but adjusted for price level changes.
i. Arises, e.g., if the money supply grows too rapidly.
j. Experienced in Germany after World War I.

Set II

_____ 1. deflation

_____ 2. supply side inflation

_____ 3. administered price inflation

_____ 4. expectational inflation

_____ 5. galloping inflation

_____ 6. anticipated inflation

_____ 7. Consumer Price Index (CPI)

_____ 8. distortion costs of inflation

_____ 9. Producers Price Index (PPI)

_____ 10. nominal values

a. Measures changes in wholesale prices.

b. Wage hikes are used as an excuse to raise prices by huge firms.

c. It is common for people to hedge when guarding against this type of inflation.

d. Double-digit annual rates of inflation.

e. A decline in the general price level.

f. Measures average prices by comparing the costs of consumer market baskets over time.

g. Speeded by peoples' concerns and beliefs about future inflation.

h. Current dollar values of economic variables.

i. Caused by a leftward shift of the Aggregate Supply curve.

j. Arise, in part, because inflated prices rise at different rates.

True/False

_____ 1. The value of an index for the base period is normally 100.

_____ 2. Consumer buying patterns seldom if ever change.

_____ 3. Incomes or other money payments received by over 80 percent of our population are directly tied to the CPI.

_____ 4. Direct measurement of the value that consumers ascribe to quality changes in consumer goods is relatively easy.

_____ 5. The CPI undoubtedly understates hikes in the level of industrial prices.

_____ 6. Inflation roughly represents a zero sum game in terms of distribution.

_____ 7. The income redistribution effects of inflation invariably reduce the real level of national production.

_____ 8. In the short run, the Consumer Price Index (CPI) assumes fixed consumption patterns.

_____ 9. When prices are rising consistently, but at relatively low rates, we must be suffering "demand-pull" inflation.

_____ 10. Uncontrolled growth of Aggregate Supply is a major cause of stagflation.

_____ 11. The only country to suffer any significant hyperinflation in the twentieth century was Germany during World War II.

___12. Powerful unions that are able to increase the wages of their members are undoubtedly the principal reason for the inflation we face today.

___13. Widespread expectations of inflation generate inflationary pressures.

___14. When items on the shelf must be repriced due to inflation, the economy actually gains since workers are needed to accomplish these changes.

___15. Aggregate Supply and Demand curves operate quite differently from market demand and supply for individual goods.

Standard Multiple Choice

There Is One Best Answer For Each Question.

___ 1. In the short run, rapid growth of Aggregate Demand relative to Aggregate Supply is LEAST likely to yield:
   a. deflationary growth.
   b. growth of aggregate output.
   c. inflation of the price level.
   d. declines in unemployment rates.
   e. widespread shortages if there are economy-wide price ceilings.

___ 2. If Aggregate Supply shrinks relative to Aggregate Demand, a likely result is:
   a. stagflation, with simultaneous inflation and rising unemployment.
   b. a deep depression, like that suffered during the 1930s.
   c. deflationary growth, with income rising and the price level falling.
   d. accelerating inflation of the sort suffered in post-WWI Germany.
   e. creeping inflation accompanied by moderate real growth, like the U.S. experience of the 1950s and 1960s.

___ 3. Real income:
   a. always increases along with inflation.
   b. is the same as nominal income.
   c. is current monetary income divided by CPI/100.
   d. remains the same regardless of inflation.
   e. always rises when deflation occurs.

___ 4. The real costs of inflation do NOT include:
   a. lost income when a recession raises unemployment.
   b. the values of resources used in repricing goods.
   c. declines in capital accumulation caused by inflation.
   d. distortions due to uneven price increases.
   e. lost production because of mistakes emerging from inflation-caused confusion about what prices mean.

_____ 5. The producer price index (PPI):
    a. currently includes over 50,000 retail products.
    b. is a general purpose index, measuring changes in prices in markets other than retail.
    c. does not distinguish list from transaction prices.
    d. will be less than 100 because markups are ignored.
    e. is synonymous with the GDP deflator.

_____ 6. Business firms may mark up their prices to compensate for increased risks they perceive from inflation. This is primarily an example of:
    a. menu costs.
    b. escalator costs.
    c. frictional costs.
    d. distortions costs.
    e. capitalist exploitation of misfortune.

_____ 7. When the supply of money expands too rapidly relative to the growth of the supplies of goods, or when we are close to full employment and the government spends far more than its tax revenues, the likely result is:
    a. cost-push inflation.
    b. administered-price inflation.
    c. composition-shift inflation.
    d. expectational inflation.
    e. demand pull inflation.

_____ 8. Which country experienced the most rapid hyperinflation?
    a. China (1940-1950).
    b. Brazil (1950-1970).
    c. Germany (1919-1923).
    d. United States (1929-1933).
    e. Hungary (1945-1946).

_____ 9. The Consumer Price Index (CPI) is used:
    a. to convert real values to long-term nominal values.
    b. as an escalator in many contracts calling for future payments.
    c. to indicate the strength of policies to dampen seasonal unemployment.
    d. to directly measure of real growth.
    e. to ascertain consumer savings from using coupons at discount stores.

_____ 10. The most persistent period of rapid inflation in the United States occurred:
    a. in the Great Depression (1929-39).
    b. after the Civil War (1865-1895).
    c. during World War II (1940-1946).
    d. during the Korean and Vietnam War eras (1950-1968).
    e. from the late 1960s into the early 1980s.

_____ 11. The Consumer Price Index (CPI) is most likely to overstate the inflation most consumers experience if the:
    a. quality of goods changes little.
    b. real values are used instead of nominal values.
    c. market basket used to determine the CPI is seldom updated.
    d. economy is at full employment.
    e. money supply grows at a fixed rate.

_____ 12. The major reason why comparing nominal incomes at different time periods can be meaningless is:
    a. varying unemployment rates.
    b. price level changes.
    c. population growth.
    d. technological stagnation.
    e. hyperactivity.

Chapter Review (Fill-In Questions)

1. Inflation is defined as an increase in the _____ level of money prices. The average level of prices is measured using a(n) _____.

2. The _____ (CPI) measures the changes in purchasing power by comparing the cost of a sample _____ today with its cost at an earlier date.

3. If inflation is at a relatively low rate, the economy is said to be suffering from _____ inflation. However, when inflation exceeds roughly 50 percent monthly, inflation is defined as _____.

4. The discomfort index is a combination of the rates of _____ and _____.

5. When Aggregate Demand grows relatively faster than Aggregate Supply, the economy experiences _____ inflation, while if Aggregate Supply shrinks, the economy experiences _____ inflation.

6. Powerful unions that ask for excessive wage hikes are the culprit of inflation according to the _____ theory of inflation. Diametrically opposed to this theory is the notion that huge firms are the true instigators of what is known as _____ inflation.

Unlimited Multiple Choice

There Are From Zero To Four Correct Answers For Each Question.

___ 1. The major conceptual and statistical problems with the CPI occur because:
a. the CPI is constructed primarily to adjust Social Security payments and fails to measure changes in the cost of living for other groups.
b. such things as alcohol consumption and rock concerts are routinely excluded from all price indexes.
c. the value and prices for personal services cannot be estimated.
d. criminal activity is missing from the market basket of goods and services.

___ 2. Society may gain from inflation if:
a. firms invest more today, viewing rising prices as a signal that more profits can be made and that future capital acquisitions will cost more.
b. needed changes in relative prices occur more easily during inflation.
c. needed expansion of government is easier because tax revenues rise at a faster rate because the personal income tax are progressive.
d. the discomfort index for the economy grows as the inflation rate increases.

_____ 3. Moderate rates of inflation:
   a. impose no real costs on society.
   b. are irrelevant to policymakers.
   c. can distort relative prices.
   d. imply that average prices rise.

_____ 4. Aggregate Demand and Aggregate
   Supply are both major influences on:
   a. cost-push inflation.
   b. compositional-shift inflation.
   c. expectational inflation.
   d. administered-price inflation.

_____ 5. When an economy is experiencing
   hyperinflation:
   a. people have an incentive to spend
      their money as quickly as possible.
   b. uncertainty stymies investment.
   c. barter for goods and services
      becomes more common.
   d. people have more incentive to save

Problems

Problem 1

Use the numbers in this table for nominal GDP and the GDP implicit price deflator to answer the following questions.

a. Compute real GDP in 1982 prices and complete the table above.

b. What was the percentage increase in real GDP from 1929 to 1989? __478.7__.

c. What has been the percentage increase in nominal GDP from 1929 to 1989? __4905.6__

d. What accounts for the difference between (b) and (c)? __inflation__

e. Compute the percentage increase in real GDP for the following decades:

Year	Nominal GDP (Billions)	GDP Implicit Price Deflator (1982=100)	Real GDP
1929	103.9	14.6	711.6
1933	56.0	11.2	500.0
1939	91.3	12.7	718.9
1949	260.4	23.5	1108.1
1959	495.8	30.4	1630.9
1969	963.9	39.8	2421.9
1979	2,508.2	78.6	3191.1
1989	5,200.8	126.3	4117.8

1940s __54.1__   1950s __47.2__   1960s __48.5__

1970s __31.8__   1980s __29.0%__

Problem 2

These current-dollar data cover the same bundle of consumer goods over a ten year period.

a. Compute the price index for each year, assuming that year 6 represents the base year.

b. Assume that during year 8 the industry producing one of the commodities in the market basket experienced a technological revolution, greatly enhancing product quality. If the price index was adjusted for this change in quality, what would happen to the values in the table? _they would be less after that_

Year	Dollar Value Of Bundle	Price Index
1	20	40
2	22	44
3	25	50
4	30	60
5	40	80
6	50	100
7	70	140
8	80	160
9	90	180
10	110	220

Problem 3

Complete this table of hypothetical data for a specific wage earner over the period 1967-1990.

Year	CPI (1983=100)	Nominal Income (current dollars)	Real Income (1983 dollars)
1967	30	20,000	66667
1974	50	28000	56,000
1980	66	40,000	60,606
1983	100	42,000	42000
1990	130	45,000	34615

$$\frac{x}{50} = \frac{56000}{100}$$

$$\frac{40000}{x} = 606$$

Problem 4 Use these shifts of AD and AS curves to answer the following true/false questions.

___ a. A shift from AD_1 to AD_0 would cause recession and deflationary pressure on prices.

___ b. "Supply-siders" would recommend policies that shift Aggregate Supply from AS_1 to AS_0.

___ c. Unemployment is likely to increase if Aggregate Demand moves from AD_0 to AD_1.

___ d. Stagflation is consistent with a movement from AS_1 to AS_0.

___ e. Deflationary growth is likely if the economy's equilibrium moves from w to z.

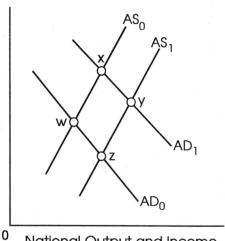

___ f. Employment and inflation will both increase if the economy moves from point z to x.

___ g. Real output is likely to be comparatively unaffected, but prices will soar if Aggregate Supply moves from AS_0 to AS_1 while Aggregate Demand goes from AD_0 to AD_1.

___ h. Substantial economic growth will occur with little inflation or deflation if Aggregate Demand moves from AD_0 to AD_1 while Aggregate Supply moves from AS_0 to AS_1.

___ i. A growing production possibilities frontier is paralleled by an upward movement of Aggregate Supply from AS_1 to AS_0.

___ j. The Great Depression followed a path like $y \rightarrow x \rightarrow w$.

Problem 5

Draw an Aggregate Demand curve and an Aggregate Supply curve, and label them, respectively, AD_0 and AS_0. Now show how demand pull inflation can occur by labeling a new Aggregate Demand curve AD_1. Label the new intersection I. Finally, using the new Aggregate Demand curve AD_1, illustrate stagflation. Label the new Aggregate Supply curve AS_1, and the new intersection S.

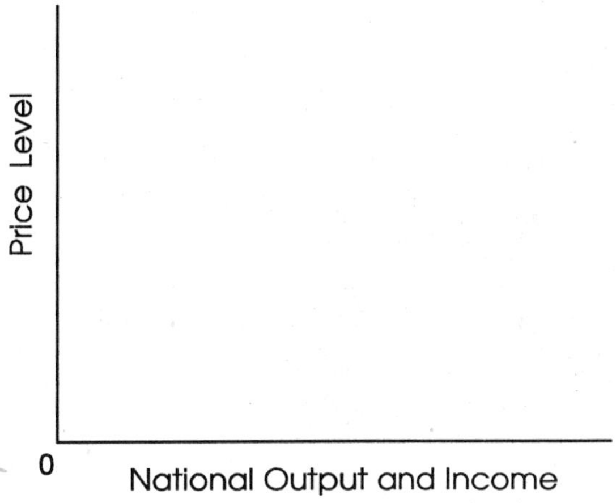

(Graph: vertical axis labeled "Price Level", horizontal axis labeled "National Output and Income", origin labeled 0)

Problem 6

This table lists aggregate personal income in billions of current (nominal) dollars for selected years since 1929 and the CPI for the same years.

a. Convert the CPI to a base year of 1990 = 100 and fill in the table.

b. By what percentage did prices fall between 1929 and 1933? _____

c. If between 1990 and 1991, nominal personal income grew 6 percent and the inflation rate was 4 percent, what was the percentage growth of real personal income? _____ By how much did real personal income grow? _____

Year	Personal Income $B (Current Dollars)	CPI 1982-84 = 100	CPI 1990 = 100
1929	84.3	15.5	_____
1933	46.3	11.6	_____
1960	409.4	29.6	_____
1970	831.8	38.8	_____
1980	2258.5	82.4	_____
1983	3290.0	100.0	_____
1990	4645.6	130.7	_____

Problem 7

Spending patterns for Jennifer and Melissa are shown in this table.

	Price Year 1	Price Year 2	Price Year 3	Units Purchased Jennifer	Melissa	Average
candy bars	$0.50	$0.75	$1.00	10	30	xxx
gasoline	$1.00	$1.50	$1.80	10	8	xxx
computer disks	$1.50	$1.00	$0.80	10	2	xxx
Price Index Year 1	xxx	xxx	xxx	____	____	____
Price Index Year 2	xxx	xxx	xxx	____	____	____
Price Index Year 3	xxx	xxx	xxx	____	____	____

a. The CPI uses spending on particular goods in the base year as a proportion of total spending that year to "weight" price changes of particular goods over time. Using year 1 as the base year, compute personal price indices and fill in the price index blanks for Jennifer and Melissa. The easy way to do this is to compute how much each would have to spend in years 2 and 3 to buy their "market basket" from year 1. Then divide this amount by what each spent in year 1.)

b. Determine the average price index for Jennifer and Melissa for each year, then fill in the average column in the table.

c. Who is harmed relatively more by these changes in average prices? _____ Why?
    _____

ANSWERS

	Matching Multiple Choice		True/False		Multiple Choice		Unlimited
	Set I	Set II					
1.	d	1. e	1. T	9. F	1. a	9. b	1. none
2.	i	2. i	2. F	10. F	2. a	10. e	2. abc
3.	g	3. b	3. F	11. F	3. c	11. c	3. cd
4.	c	4. g	4. F	12. F	4. a	12. b	4. bc
5.	h	5. d	5. F	13. T	5. b		5. abc
6.	e	6. c	6. T	14. F	6. d		
7.	j	7. f	7. F	15. F	7. e		
8.	a	8. j	8. T		8. e		
9.	b	9. a					
10.	f	10. h					

Chapter Review (Fill-In Questions)

1. average, index
2. Consumer Price Index; market basket
3. creeping; galloping or hyperinflation
4. unemployment; inflation
5. demand-side; supply-side
6. cost-push; administered price

Problem 1

a. See table.
b. (4,117.8 - 711.6)/711.6 = 478.7%
c. (5,200.8 - 103.9)/103.9 = 4,905.6%
d. inflation
e. 1940s = (1,108.1 - 718.9)/718.9 = 54.1%
   1950s = (1,630.9 - 1,108.1)/1,108.1 = 47.2%
   1960s = (2,421.9 - 1,630.9)/1,630.9 = 48.5%
   1970s = (3,191.1 - 2,421.9)/2,421.9 = 31.8%
   1980s = (4,117.8 - 3,191.1)/3,191.1 = 29.0%

Year	Nominal GDP (Billions)	GDP Implicit Price Deflator (1982=100)	Real GDP
1929	103.9	14.6	711.6
1933	56.0	11.2	500.0
1939	91.3	12.7	718.9
1949	260.4	23.5	1,108.1
1959	495.8	30.4	1,630.9
1969	963.9	39.8	2,421.9
1979	2,508.2	78.6	3,191.1
1989	5,200.8	126.3	4,117.8

Problem 2

a. See table at right.
b. The price index numbers should be lower after year 8.

Year	Current Dollar Value Of Bundle	Price Index
1	20	40
2	22	44
3	25	50
4	30	60
5	40	80
6	50	100
7	70	140
8	80	160
9	90	180
10	110	220

Problem 3

Year	CPI (1983=100)	Nominal Income (current dollars)	Real Income (1983 dollars)
1967	30	20,000	66,667
1974	50	28,000	56,000
1980	66	40,000	60,606
1983	100	42,000	42,000
1990	130	45,000	34,615

Problem 4

a. T
b. F
c. F
d. T
e. T
f. F
g. F
h. T
i. F
j. F

Problem 5

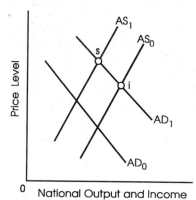

Problem 6

a. See table.
b. $(11.9 - 8.9)/11.9 = 25.2\%$.
c. $(6\% - 4\%) = 2\%$; $(\$4,645.6 \times .02) = \$92.91$ billion

Year	Personal Income $B (Current Dollars)	CPI 1982-84 = 100	CPI 1990 = 100
1929	84.3	15.5	11.9
1933	46.3	11.6	8.9
1960	409.4	29.6	22.6
1970	831.8	38.8	29.7
1980	2258.5	82.4	63.0
1983	3290.0	100.0	76.5
1990	4645.6	130.7	100.0

Problem 7

a. See table.
b. See table.
c. Melissa is harmed relatively more because she purchases larger quantities of the item (candy bars) whose price has increased by the largest percent.

	Price Year 1	Price Year 2	Price Year 3	Units Purchased in Year 1		
				Jennifer	Melissa	Average
candy bars	$0.50	$0.75	$1.00	10	30	xxx
gasoline	$1.00	$1.50	$1.80	10	8	xxx
computer disks	$1.50	$1.00	$0.80	10	2	xxx
Price Index Year 1	xxx	xxx	xxx	100.0	100.0	100.0
Price Index Year 2	xxx	xxx	xxx	108.3	140.4	124.4
Price Index Year 3	xxx	xxx	xxx	120.0	176.9	148.5

Chapter 8
Measuring Economic Performance and Growth

Chapter Objectives

After you have studied this chapter you should be able to: explain the concept and uses of Gross Domestic Product (GDP); explain how income and expenditure approaches estimate GDP; explain the concept of value-added; explain how disposable personal income, personal income, national income and net national product are derived from GDP accounts; explain some limitations of GDP accounting, and evaluate GDP as a measure of social well-being.

Chapter Review: Key Points

1. *GDP* is the total market value of a nation's annual production. GDP measures estimate the economic performance of an economy and are important for government policy and business decisions.

2. The *expenditures* approach to GDP sums *consumption* spending (*C*), business *investment* spending (*I*), *government purchases* (*G*), and *net exports* (*X-M*): **GDP = C + I + G + (X - M).**

3. *Gross Private Domestic Investment (GPDI)* is the economic term for business spending. To arrive at net investment, we need to subtract depreciation from GPDI.

4. Government purchases (**G**) do not include *transfer* (welfare) *payments*, which are treated as flows of income from some households to others.

5. The *income* approach to GDP sums wages, interest, rent, and profits. We use the figures available, which are (**a**) wages and salaries, (**b**) proprietors' income, (**c**) corporate profits, (**d**) rental income, and (**e**) interest. The sum of these figures is *National Income (NI)*. Addition of *indirect business taxes*, which is not anyone's income, yields *Net National Product (NNP)*. The *capital consumption allowance* (*depreciation*) is the difference between GDP and NNP.

6. The *value-added* approach to GDP sums the sales of all firms and subtracts their purchases of intermediate products, which are goods bought by one firm from another for further processing. Failure to exclude purchases of intermediate goods from GDP figures would result in substantial *double counting* of production.

7. GDP figures should be used cautiously. One problem is that they may be systematically biased and are often presented in an artificially precise fashion. Another is that most nonmarket production is ignored (e.g., homemakers' services, do-it-yourself projects, and the like). GDP accounts include as production many disproducts (for instance, pollution abatement equipment is added to GDP, but environmental decay is not subtracted).

8. Currencies from different countries are traded in international financial markets at *exchange rates* (relative prices) set primarily by market forces, although governments affect exchange rates directly (by buying and selling currencies), and indirectly (by imposing quotas and tariffs on goods traded internationally).

9. *Purchasing power parity* reflects cost-of-living differentials between countries.

10. According to the *law of one price*, if transactions costs are zero, relative prices for given goods or resources will be identical everywhere in the world.

11. International comparisons of GDP are especially problematic because countries differ in relative importance of do-it-yourself production, and the extent of barter and the underground economy. Ideally, per capita incomes should be adjusted for the relative purchasing power parity of currencies in different countries, but most comparisons are based on exchange rates between currencies because such data are much more readily available.

Matching Key Terms And Concepts

Set I

___ 1. exports

___ 2. Gross Domestic Product

___ 3. Measure of Economic Welfare (MEW)

___ 4. imports

___ 5. indirect business taxes

___ 6. Net National Product

___ 7. Purchasing power parity approach

___ 8. Law of one price

___ 9. transfer payments

___ 10. Exchange rate approach

a. GDP adjusted to better estimate economic welfare.

b. A way to account for cost-of-living differences between countries when comparing their GDPs.

c. National Income + Indirect business taxes + depreciation.

d. GDP minus depreciation of capital stock.

e. Uses relative nominal values of countries' currencies to make international comparisons of GDP.

f. Homogenous goods should have same price everywhere if transactions costs are zero.

g. Domestic production that is sold to foreigners.

h. Income taxed from one set of households and given to another set.

i. Sales, excise, and property taxes.

j. Goods produced abroad and purchased by consumers in this country.

Set II

____ 1. net private domestic investment
____ 2. value-added
____ 3. personal income
____ 4. capital consumption allowance
____ 5. retained earnings
____ 6. government purchases
____ 7. net exports
____ 8. personal taxes
____ 9. income approach
____ 10. expenditure approach

a. NI + transfer payments - corporate taxes - retained earnings.
b. C + I + G + (X - M)
c. Corporate income after taxes and dividends.
d. A way to avoid the double-counting problem.
e. X - M
f. Capital accumulation after adjusting for depreciation.
g. w + i + r + Π
h. Plus transfer payments equals government outlays.
i. Subtracted from Personal Income to calculate Disposable PI.
j. Known by accountants as depreciation.

True/False Questions

____ 1. For national income accounting purposes, sales of stocks and bonds are considered real investments.

____ 2. Final economic goods are those goods used in the production of other economic goods.

____ 3. Included in farm income is an estimate of the value of home-consumed food grown on farms but not marketed.

____ 4. Indirect business taxes are treated as a part of NI because they are payments to the factors of production.

____ 5. One way to avoid overstatement of GDP is to total the sales of firms after subtracting the values of intermediate goods purchased by each firm.

____ 6. National Income accounts consider only productive activity is transacted through the marketplace.

____ 7. For GDP accounting, the costs of the inputs government uses are treated as the value of government services.

____ 8. GDP includes adjustments for the changing value of leisure time.

____ 9. Individual income and spending are related positively to the level of economic activity.

____ 10. Changes in inventories are considered consumption.

____ 11. The expenditure approach adds up all income received by U.S. citizens to arrive at GDP.

___12. International GDP comparisons are most accurate when exchange rates are used to convert currencies to a common denominator.

___13. The purchasing power parity approach yields results which suggest that many countries are not as poor as the exchange rate approach indicates.

___14. Consumption expenditures equal income derived from wages and salaries since the expenditure approach and income approach yield identical GDP figures.

___15. The law of one price will not be valid for homogenous goods and services if transactions costs are positive.

Standard Multiple Choice

There Is One Best Answer For Each Question.

___1. Gross Domestic Product is the total market value of all:
a. commodities sold in a year.
b. services produced in a year.
c. production during a year.
d. consumer goods sold during a year.
e. None of the above.

___2. National Income is the sum of ALL of the following EXCEPT:
a. wages.
b. savings.
c. interest.
d. rent.
e. profits.

___3. GDP computations include only rough adjustments for changes in:
a. the amounts of leisure time.
b. such disproducts' as pollution or crowding.
c. the quality of the goods we buy.
d. how equitably wealth is distributed.
e. values of homemakers' services.

___4. Purchases of foreign-made goods should NOT be:
a. included with other expenditures to compute our GDP.
b. included in the GDP of the exporting country.
c. included in the personal expenditures category of GDP, which is then adjusted by subtracting imports.
d. value-added for the exporting country.

___5. The problem of "double counting" is partially cured by:
a. summations of sales by all firms.
b. the expenditures approach.
c. the income approach.
d. summations of only the values added by each firm.
e. capital consumption allowances.

___6. The "father of GDP accounting" was:
a. Oskar Morgenstern.
b. Franscois Quesnay.
c. John Stuart Mill.
d. James Buchanan.
e. Simon Kuznets.

___ 7. Transfer payments include:
   a. consumption expenditures.
   b. Social Security taxes.
   c. corporate managers' incomes.
   d. funds paid to foreign investors.
   e. Social Security benefits.

___ 8. Legalization of marijuana would cause
      the growth of GDP to:
   a. more accurately reflect well-being.
   b. be overstated in the very short run.
   c. be understated in the long run.
   d. decline precipitously.
   e. become stagnant.

___ 9. GDP measures do not include the:
   a. market prices of harmful goods.
   b. costs incurred to reduce pollution.
   c. government's military spending.
   d. increases in inventories during
      business downturns.
   e. values of "do-it-yourself" projects.

___10. Net National Product (NNP) equals:
   a. C + GPDI + G + X - M.
   b. C + S + T + M.
   c. GDP - indirect business taxes.
   d. GDP - depreciation.
   e. DPI + S.

___11. The value-added approach estimates
      GDP as the sum of all:
   a. sales of all firms.
   b. intermediate goods all firms use.
   c. sales of all firms minus purchases
      of all intermediate products.
   d. final goods minus production costs.
   e. sales minus labor costs.

___12. Corporations use their profits to pay
   a. salaries to employees.
   b. salaries and taxes or invest in
      capital goods.
   c. taxes to the government, dividends
      to stockholders, and to finance the
      firm's operations or expansion.
   d. buy insurance.
   e. graft to politicians, contribute to
      charities, and distribute foreign aid.

___13. The most accurate international
      measures of GDP per capita use the:
   a. expenditure approach.
   b. income approach.
   c. exchange rate approach.
   d. purchasing power parity approach.
   e. law of one price.

___14. Limitations to GDP accounting would
      not include problems associated with
   a. ambiguity.
   b. conceptualization.
   c. incompleteness.
   d. inaccuracy.
   e. misclassification.

___15. GDP accounting overstates a country's
      economic welfare if:
   a. it includes homemade production.
   b. based on purchasing power parity.
   c. negative aspects of production are
      not taken into account.
   d. real prices and figures are used.
   e. estimates of underground activities
      are included in GDP accounts.

Chapter Review (Fill-In Questions)

1. Gross Domestic Product (GDP) is the total _____ of all production during one year. One of the major reasons for measuring GDP is to provide policymakers a regular, continuing and comparable _____ of total economic activity.

2. The two main conceptual approaches to measuring GDP are the _____ approach and the _____ approach.

3. The expenditure approach looks at the expenditures of the _____ users of goods and services, which include _____, _____, _____, and _____. By adding these four expenditure categories _____ is obtained.

4. Alternatively, national income can be obtained by adding together all payments to the _____. The biggest component of national income is _____. To reconcile national income and GDP, _____ and _____ must be added to NI to obtain GDP.

5. While GDP does a pretty fair job of measuring economic performance, some notable limitations exist. Some national economic data is provided to the exact _____ where rounding would make more sense. Many forms of _____ production, such as the value of homemaker's services, are excluded.

6. Since many _____ services are not sold, valuing the output is difficult, so GDP statisticians use the next best estimate, the value of the _____.

7. One way to make international comparisons of per capita GDP is to use _____ to convert currencies to a common denominator. This approach, however, is not as accurate as the _____ approach which attempts to take into account cost of living differences between countries.

8. As a measure of well-being, GDP has many limitations. The value of _____ activities is ignored while expenditures for removing litter and pollution are included. To overcome these problems, two economists developed a(n) _____.

Unlimited Multiple Choice

There Are From Zero To Four Correct Answers For Each Question.

___ 1. Economic investment includes all:
   a. purchases of new capital equipment.
   b. changes in inventories.
   c. construction.
   d. purchases of stocks and bonds.

___ 2. Profits are used by corporations to:
   a. pay corporate profit taxes.
   b. finance investment projects.
   c. pay dividends to households.
   d. reward managers who own stock.

___ 3. Interest income:
   a. includes payments made for the use of borrowed capital (usually financial capital).
   b. has been the most rapidly growing proportion of National Income since 1990.
   c. is usually associated with the renting of real property.
   d. represents profits received by entrepreneurs

___ 4. National income:
   a. is the sum of incomes paid to owners of the various factors of production, plus retained earnings and corporate profit taxes.
   b. is normally broken down into wages, interest, rent, corporate income, and proprietor's income.
   c. equals Consumption + GPDI + Government purchases.
   d. equals GDP - (depreciation + indirect business taxes).

___ 5. Gross Domestic Product (GDP) is:
   a. an important measure of total economic activity.
   b. a crude yardstick with which to measure national well-being.
   c. based on various accounting methods, depending on the specific output or income being measured.
   d. a valuable guide when policy-makers try to determine the needs of the economy.

Problems

Problem 1

Listed below are various categories of expenditures and income used in GDP accounting. Using the numbers for these categories, specify formulas (e.g., 5 + 10 + 15) that answer questions a-f.

1. Wages and salaries
2. Rental income
3. Interest
4. Indirect business taxes
5. Capital consumption allowance
6. Personal consumption expenditures
7. Gross Private Domestic Investment
8. Corporate profits
9. Proprietors' income
10. Government expenditures on goods
11. Personal income tax
12. Government transfer payments
13. Social security taxes
14. Corporate profits tax
15. Exports
16. Imports
17. Retained earnings
18. Personal savings
19. Consumer interest payments plus personal transfers to foreigners

a. Compute GDP using the expenditure approach. _____

b. Compute GDP using the income approach. _____

c. Compute National Income. _____

d. Compute Personal Income. _____

e. Compute Disposable Income. _____

f. Compute NNP in two different ways. _____

Problem 7

Use these U.S. data for 1990 to answer questions a through h. (Dollar values are in billions).

Personal Consumption Expenditures	3,728.1
Compensation of Employees	3,286.9
Personal Taxes	718.1
Consumer Interest Payments and Personal Transfer Payments to Foreigners	109.3
Capital Consumption Allowance:	585.2
Net Interest Income	470.2
Federal Purchases of Goods and Services	438.5
Rental Income of Persons	8.5
Gross Private Domestic Investment	714.0
Corporate Profits with Inventory Adjustment	306.6
State and Local Purchases of Goods and Services	694.2
Exports	687.7
Proprietors' Income	406.1
Imports	743.7
personal income	4,719.0
Gross Domestic Product in 1982 dollars	4,147.6
U.S. population size	252.5 million

a.   GDP equals? _____

b.   Net National Product equals? _____

c.   National Income equals? _____

d.   Indirect Business Taxes equal? _____

e.   Personal Saving equals? _____

f.   The GDP deflator (1982=100) equals? _____

g.   GDP per capita equals? _____

h.   Disposable Personal Income per capita equals? _____

Problem 8

Fill in the blanks in this table which shows the various steps in making a wooden table (the sum of all the values added is $80).

Stage	Cost of Input	Sales Receipts	Value Added
Mill	___	___	___
Lumber distributor	15	___	___
Table maker	30	___	___
Delivered table	___	___	25

Problem 9

Assume a simple economy with two people, Robinson and Friday. Robinson is the boss because Friday possesses a meek personality. Robbie pays Friday $400 a year in wages to gather food and to make clothing, and $100 a year to build new housing. Friday takes the $500 total wages and gives $100 to Robinson for rent and $400 to Robinson for clothes and food that Robbie has stored for Friday. Robbie reinvests the rental income into housing and assumes that $300 of Friday's money is for wages and $100 is entrepreneurial profit.

a. What does GDP equal? _____

b. What does NNP equal? _____

c   What does NI equal? _____

ANSWERS

Matching

Set I		Set II	
1.	g	1.	f
2.	c	2.	d
3.	a	3.	a
4.	j	4.	j
5.	i	5.	c
6.	d	6.	h
7.	b	7.	e
8.	f	8.	i
9.	h	9.	g
10.	e	10.	b

True/False

1.	F	9.	T
2.	F	10.	F
3.	T	11.	F
4.	F	12.	F
5.	T	13.	T
6.	F	14.	F
7.	T	15.	T
8.	F		

Multiple Choice

1.	c	9.	e
2.	b	10.	d
3.	c	11.	c
4.	a	12.	c
5.	d	13.	d
6.	e	14.	b
7.	a	15.	c
8.	b		

Unlimited Multiple Choice

1.	abc
2.	abc
3.	a
4.	abd
5.	abcd

Chapter Review (Fill-In Questions)

1. market value; estimate
2. income; expenditure
3. final or ultimate; consumers; business investors; government; foreigners; Gross Domestic Product
4. resource owners; wages; capital consumption allowance; indirect business taxes
5. dollar; nonmarket
6 government; inputs
7. exchange rates; purchasing power parity
8. leisure; Measure of Economic Welfare (MEW)

Problem 1

a. $(6) + (7) + (10) + ((15) - (16))$.
b. $(1) + (2) + (3) + (8) + (9) + (4) + (5)$.
c. $(1) + (2) + (3) + (8) + (9)$
d. $(18) + (6) + (19) + (11)$.
e. $(18) + (6) + (19.$
f. $(6) + (7) + (10) + ((15) - (16)) - (5)$ or $(1) + (2) + (3) + (8) + (9) + (4)$

Problem 2

a. See table.
b. $2,500
c. $2,500

	Dollar Value of Inputs	Dollar Value of Good in Market	Value Added
Stage 1	0	100	100
Stage 2	100	300	200
Stage 3	300	900	600
Stage 4	900	1,500	600
Stage 5	1,500	2,500	1,000

Problem 3

a. $4,016.9 (2,606.1 + 666.1 + 832.5 + 363.2 - 451.0)
b. $3,575.5 (4,016.9 - 441.4)
c. $194.2 (3,298.5 - 2,606.1 -498.2)

Problem 4

a. $9,000 (to car maker); $1,400 (dealer value added); $600 (repairs); -$1,500 (trade in minus repairs and resale value)
b. $9,500

Problem 5

a. $1,300 (900 + 150 + 200 + 100 - 50)
b. $1,150 (800 + 100 + 100+ 75 + 75)
c. $75 (1,300 - 1,150 - 75)
d. $1,225 (1,150 + 75)
e. $1,075 (1,150 + 50 - 50 - 75)
f. $975 (1,075 - 100)

Problem 6

a. F
b. F
c. T
d. T
e. T
f. T
g. F
h. T
i. F
j. T

Problem 7

a. 5,518.9 (C + I + G + X - M)
b. 4,933.7 (GDP - CCA)
c. 4,478.3 (w + r + i +Π)
d. 455.4 (NNP - NI)
e. 163.5 (PI - PT - C - $109.3)
f. 133.1 (($5,518.8/$4,147.6) x 100))
g. 21,857 ($5,518.8 billion/252.5 million)
h. 15,845 (PI - PT/252.5 million)

Problem 8

Stage	Cost of Input	Sales Receipts	Value Added
Mill	0	15	15
Lumber distributor	15	30	15
Table maker	30	55	25
Delivered table	55	80	25

Problem 9

a. $1,000 (GDP = C + I + G + (X-M) = 900 + 100 + 0 + 0)
b. $1,000 (GDP = NNP since there is no depreciation.)
c. $1,000 (NNP = NI since there is no government to collect indirect business taxes.)

Chapter 9
Classical Macroeconomics and
Keynesian Aggregate Expenditures

Chapter Objectives

After you have read and studied this chapter you should be able to explain why classical economists believed the economy would tend to operate at full-employment; describe the major conceptual differences between Classical and Keynesian theory; enumerate the components of Keynesian Aggregate Demand; discuss average and marginal propensities to consume and save; describe the major determinants of consumption and saving; explain the major determinants of investment; and describe how the major components add together to form Keynesian Aggregate Demand.

Chapter Review: Key Points

1. *Classical theory* is a conglomeration of the thoughts of many economic thinkers dating back to Adam Smith.

2. Classical economists based their theory on *Say's Law: Supply creates its own demand.* Coupled with assumptions that wages, prices, and interest rates are all perfectly flexible, Say's Law quickly drives a market economy towards full employment. All unemployment is considered voluntary--simply a refusal to work at the equilibrium wage. The protracted unemployment of the early 1930s diluted acceptance of classical theory and led to the development of the radically different Keynesian theory.

3. Keynesian analysis focuses on Aggregate Demand. Much of economic capacity was idle during the Great Depression. During a slow recovery from 1933 to 1940, real output expanded by over 60 percent with only slight increases in the price level. Keynesian economics treats Aggregate Supply as flat during a depression so that the price level can be ignored; it focuses primarily on how to maintain Aggregate Demand consistent with full employment.

4. *Aggregate Expenditures (AE)* encompass total spending on domestic output during a year. Aggregate Expenditures include four components: (*a*) personal consumption expenditures, (*b*) gross private domestic investment, (*c*) government purchases, and (*d*) net exports of goods and services:
$$AE = C + I + G + (X - M)$$

5. The single most important determinant of consumer spending is disposable income through its influence on *induced consumption*. Consumer spending is related directly to disposable income and is a stable component of Aggregate Expenditures. Other important determinants of consumption and saving include (*a*) wealth and expectations of future income, (*b*) customary living standards, (*c*) the sizes and age composition of typical households, (*d*) consumer goods on hand and household balance sheets, and (*e*) consumer expectations about prices and product availability. These determine the level of *autonomous consumption* (C_a).

6. The *marginal propensity to consume* (**mpc**) is the change in planned consumption arising from a given small change in disposable income; it tells us how much of an additional dollar of income will be consumed. Similarly, the *marginal propensity to save* (**mps**) is how much of an additional dollar in income will be saved, so *mpc + mps = 1*.

7. Capital investment refers to purchases of new output that can be used in the future to produce other goods and services. The three major components of investment are (*a*) new business and residential structures, (*b*) machinery and equipment, and (*c*) inventory accumulation.

8. Investment is the least stable component of Aggregate Expenditures, fluctuating widely over the course of a business cycle. The most volatile component of investment is inventory accumulation.

9. The primary factors determining the quantity of investment are (*a*) expected returns from investment, (*b*) market interest rates, (*c*) expectations about the business environment, (*d*) rates of technological change and innovation, (*e*) the level of existing stocks of business capital relative to total production, and (*f*) the costs of capital goods. All else equal, changes in items (*c*) through (*f*) shift rate of return curves, while changes in interest rates cause movements along an expected rate of return curve. In simple Keynesian models, investment is treated as *autonomous* (I_a).

10. While government spending is probably influenced by changes in income, it is even more strongly affected by the state of international relations and domestic politics. Thus government spending as a component of Aggregate Expenditures is also treated as autonomous.

11. Exports and imports are reasonably balanced, so *net exports* (*X - M*) make a comparatively small contribution to Aggregate Expenditures. Simple Keynesian models treat net exports as autonomous.

Matching Key Terms And Concepts

____ 1. Classical economics

____ 2. Say's Law

____ 3. autonomous expenditures

____ 4. induced expenditures

____ 5. marginal propensity to save

____ 6. Keynesian Aggregate Expenditures

____ 7. 45-degree Keynesian reference line

____ 8. rate of return

____ 9. marginal propensity to consume

____10. break-even level of income

____11. dissaving

a. Annual percentage by which profits will grow if reinvested.

b. Economy will automatically adjust to full-employment.

c. Borrowing or drawing down savings.

d. $C + I + G + (X-M)$.

e. Supply creates its own demand.

f. The change in consumption divided by the change in income.

g. Related to income.

h. Not a function of income.

i. 1-MPC.

j. $Y = C + S$.

k. The point where S is zero.

True/False Questions

____ 1. Classical economists strongly reject the idea that a capitalistic, laissez-faire economy automatically produces a full employment level of output.

____ 2. Whenever Aggregate Demand exceeds Aggregate Supply, the level of economic activity will tend to rise, and there will be pressures for output or prices, or both, to increase.

____ 3. John Maynard Keynes was the first major economist to put forth the revolutionary notion of a positive relationship between consumption and the income level.

____ 4. It is impossible for households to have negative savings.

____ 5. The marginal propensity to consume tells us how much of an additional dollar of income will be consumed.

____ 6. When the interest rate increases, the investor's opportunity cost of investment falls.

____ 7. The marginal propensity to save indirectly indicates how much of an additional dollar of income will be consumed.

____ 8. Consumption as a percentage of income increases as income increases.

____ 9. Investment spending is unaffected by changes in business expectations about the economy.

___10. Some economists attribute much of the volatility of investment to changes in the interest rate.

___11. Keynesian Aggregate Expenditure is a vertical summation of consumption, investment, government spending, and net exports.

___12. The marginal propensity to save refers to the proportion of total income saved.

___13. The marginal propensity to save is equal to the slope of the consumption function.

___14. The purchase of 100 shares of General Motors stock is not considered an investment for aggregate economic analysis.

___15. The marginal propensity to consume and marginal propensity to save added together equal one in a simple Keynesian model.

Standard Multiple Choice

There Is One Best Answer For Each Question.

___ 1. Say's Law refers to:
   a. the concept that demand creates its own supply.
   b. an insignificant part of classical macroeconomic theory.
   c. the idea that the act of production creates an equivalent level of demand.
   d. an old law that held that workers could not sue business for on-the-job injuries because they (the workers) had assumed the risks of employment by accepting the job in the first place.
   e. a tendency towards unionization of the labor force.

___ 2. Classical economists thought that:
   a. flexible wages and prices were the principal causes of recessions.
   b. government policies and spending were needed to keep the economy at full employment.
   c. the Great Depression confirmed their view of the business cycle.
   d. price, wage, and interest rate flexibility can quickly cure any tendencies for a recession.
   e. communist revolutions would overthrow capitalism.

___ 3. Classical macroeconomics assumes:
   a. Say's law.
   b. flexible prices.
   c. flexible wages.
   d. flexible interest rates.
   e. All of the above.

___ 4. The marginal propensity to consume (MPC) is between zero and one according to:
   a. Keynesian consumption functions.
   b. the Law of Diminishing Returns.
   c. the Law of Demand.
   d. Say's Law.
   e. the Law of Entropy.

___ 5. Keynesian Aggregate Demand does not include:
   a. consumption (C).
   b. government purchases (G).
   c. investment (I).
   d. saving (S).
   e. net exports (X-M).

___ 6. I spent $8,000 of my $10,000 income last year. My salary has increased to $12,000 and my MPC is .8. What will be the growth in my consumption?
   a. $2,000.
   b. $9,600.
   c. $1,600.
   d. $11,000.
   e. $400.

___ 7. Investment is $100 billion at 6 percent interest. If the interest rate increases to 8 percent, investment will:
   a. climb to over $100 billion.
   b. remain at $100 billion.
   c. cause the rate of return from investment to fall.
   d. drop below $100 billion.
   e. decline until interest falls substantially below 6 percent, to compensate for the short term interest rate penalty.

___ 8. The largest component of Aggregate Demand is:
   a. government spending.
   b. consumer spending.
   c. new office construction.
   d. inventory accumulation.
   e. investment.

___ 9. Which one of the following is NOT an example of economic investment?
   a. Inventory growth.
   b. Manufacturers replacing worn out equipment.
   c. Purchases of government bonds.
   d. Newly constructed residential housing.
   e. Newly installed telephone lines.

___ 10. If a wave of inflationary expectations newly arose and you were a new car dealer, you might expect your sales to:
   a. drop drastically.
   b. increase rapidly.
   c. remain constant.
   d. fluctuate up and down until the rumors subside.
   e. fall initially, but ultimately rise, stabilizing at a new high.

___ 11. Keynesian theory suggests that when Aggregate Supply exceeds Aggregate Demand, economic activity will:
   a. decline, with pressure on prices to fall.
   b. decline, with pressure on prices to rise.
   c. rise, with pressure on prices to fall.
   d. remain the same.
   e. rise, with pressure on prices to rise.

___12. Which of the following is NOT an important determinant of consumption and saving?
   a. Average size and age of the household.
   b. Consumer expectation about prices and availability of products.
   c. Stocks of consumer goods on hand.
   d. Wealth.
   e. Wages relative to rates of return on capital.

___13. If income increases from $7,000 to $12,000 and saving increases by $500, the Marginal Propensity to Save is:
   a. .2.
   b. .3.
   c. .1.
   d. .05.
   e. .5.

___14. Investors will pursue investment opportunities as long as:
   a. the expected rate of return is greater than zero.
   b. saving is available for investment.
   c. they are more optimistic than pessimistic.
   d. the expected total profits over time exceeds current monetary outlays.
   e. the expected rate of return is at least as great as the interest rate.

___15. Increases in which of the following will reduce Aggregate Demand?
   a. imports (M).
   b. investment (I).
   c. government spending (G).
   d. consumption (C).
   e. marginal propensity to consume (MPC).

Chapter Review (Fill-In Questions)

1. Classical economic theory was the result of numerous studies of how markets operate. Classical theory suggested that several automatic mechanisms operate to ensure _____. The first mechanism is Say's Law, which asserts that the very act of production creates an equivalent level of _____.

2. Classical economists suggested that full employment is assured by flexible _____ and _____ in labor and product markets.

3. The high and prolonged unemployment of the Great Depression caused many to doubt classical theory. Many economists turned away from classical theory which emphasized long-run changes in _____ toward Keynesian theory which emphasized short-run changes in _____.

4. The largest component of Keynesian Aggregate Demand is consumption and the most volatile is _____. The most important determinant of consumer spending is _____.

5. Keynes's fundamental psychological law asserted that people will _____ their consumption as income increases, but by _____ than the increase in income.

6. When consumption exceeds income, _____ occurs. Autonomous consumption is _____ income.

7. The level of investment is affected by business expectations about the business climate, new technologies and the stocks of _____ relative to total output. Production from capital, as with other factors of production, is subject to _____.

8. One crucial cost of investment is the _____, which represents the opportunity cost of using funds. _____ investment refers to investment that is unrelated to income.

9. Many _____ purchases are like investment in that the benefits are received over a long period. Government _____ are not considered a part of Keynesian Aggregate Expenditures because they do not directly affect demand until the recipient actually spends the money.

10. Graphically, Keynesian Aggregate Expenditures are the _____ sum of all types of spending; consumption, investment, and government spending. Since exports and imports are reasonably balanced, _____ are sometimes ignored because they represent such a small part of Aggregate Expenditures.

Unlimited Multiple Choice

There Are From Zero To Four Correct Answers For Each Question.

___ 1. Classical economic theory:
   a. easily explained the persistence of the Great Depression.
   b. viewed full employment in the economy as unattainable.
   c. was not a theory of the business cycle per se, but rather a systematic study of the functioning of the economy.
   d. relies heavily on unhindered supply and demand to work.

___ 2. The marginal propensity to save:
   a. is the change in income caused by a small change in saving.
   b. is the proportion of income saved.
   c. is computed as $\Delta S/\Delta Y$.
   d. plus the marginal propensity to consume balances to zero.

___ 3. Major determinants of consumption and saving include:
   a. wealth and the average size and age of the household.
   b. stocks of consumer goods on hand.
   c. household balance sheets.
   d. consumer expectations about product prices and availability.

4. Changes in inventories:
   a. are the most volatile component of investment spending.
   b. are signals to business firms of changing economic conditions.
   c. are controlled only by the actions of business firms.
   d. are uncontrollable by most business firms on a day-to-day basis.

5. The marginal propensity to consume (MPC) is:
   a. the proportion of total income consumed.
   b. the proportion of additional income consumed.
   c. inconsistent with the fundamental psychological law of consumption as expressed by Keynes.
   d. is equal to (1-MPS).

Problems

Problem 1

Use this illustration of a classical capital market to answer the following True/False questions.

____a. The economy is in equilibrium at point b after saving increases from S_0 to S_1.

____b. Say's Law holds at point b.

____c. Say's Law does not hold at point a.

____d. The new saving curve (S_1) indicates that people have decided to save less, and, therefore, to consume more, at each income level.

____e. The movement from point a to point b represents an increase in investment demand.

____f. The movement from point a to point b reflects an increase in the willingness to save.

____g. In moving from point a to point b, the interest rate must fall to eliminate the excess supply of commodities created by the decrease in consumption.

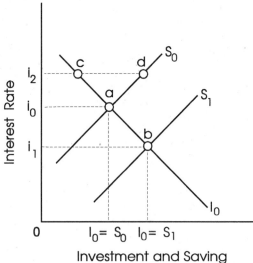

____h. Interest rate i_2 is an equilibrium rate of interest.

____i. Say's Law holds true at point c.

____j. The horizontal segment dc represents excess demand in the investment and savings market.

Problem 2

Use this figure, which illustrates the classical labor market, to answer the following questions. The original supply and demand curves are denoted S_0 and D_0 respectively. The Ps in parentheses indicate the price level.

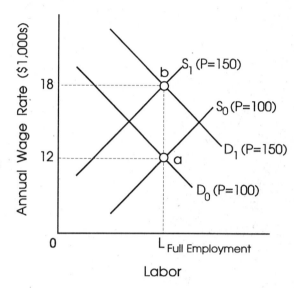

_____a. Labor decisions are based on the real wage rate.

_____b. The quantity of labor services demanded varies inversely with the money wage rate, assuming a constant price level.

_____c. When the demand for labor shifts from D_0 to D_1, this is an indication that the general price level has declined.

_____d. A 50 percent general increase in prices could cause the labor supply curve to shift from S_0 to S_1.

_____e. A movement from point a to point b indicates an increase in the wage rate.

_____f. A movement from point a to point b necessarily represents an increase in real wages.

_____g. At point b, voluntary unemployment is zero.

_____h. At point a, involuntary unemployment exists.

_____i. The movement from a to b shows that, as a result of an increase in the real wage rate, business firms decide to hire fewer workers and to produce less output.

_____j. A movement from point a to point b would occur if the wage rate and the general price level experience the same 50 percent increase.

_____k. The average level of prices has increased 50 percent as we move from point a to point b.

Problem 3

Use responses a through g (representing line segments) to answer the following questions based on this figure:

a. -0G

b. 0G

c. df/cf

d. -ab

e. 0Y1

f. ed

g. dY2

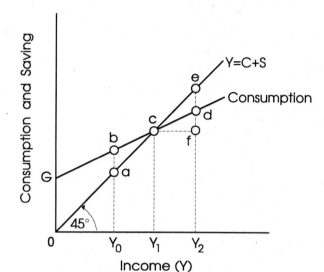

1. The break-even level of income is ____?

2. Saving at income Y_0 is equal to ____?

3. The MPC is equal to ____?

4. Autonomous consumption is equal to ____?

5. Autonomous saving is equal to ____?

6. Consumption at income Y_2 is equal to ____?

7. Saving when income is Y_2 is equal to ____?

Problem 6

Use this saving -income diagram to answer the following questions.

a. In this situation the level of autonomous saving equals _____; and the level of autonomous consumption equals

    _____.

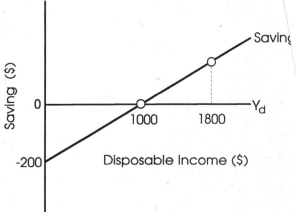

b. The mpc equals _____; and the mps equals _____.

c. If the level of income is $1,800, then the level of induced consumption is _____, and the total level of consumption equals _____.

d. If the level of income were to rise to $2,200, then the amount of induced savings would equal _____; and the total level of savings would be _____; which naturally means that autonomous saving is still _____.

Problem 7

Refer to this Aggregate Expenditures diagram to answer the following questions.

a. The equilibrium level of $800 is based on a marginal propensity to consume of _____.

b. In equilibrium, the level of autonomous consumption equals_____ and induced consumption is _____; therefore, total consumption equals _____.

c. The corresponding savings function that would go with this diagram would have autonomous saving equal to _____; a mps equal to _____; and induced savings of _____ at equilibrium.

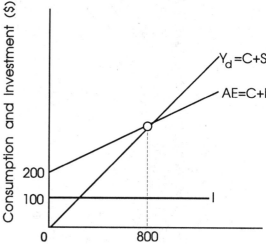

d. If the level of autonomous consumption fell to $50, then the new level of equilibrium income would equal _____, and induced consumption would equal _____. At equilibrium, total consumption equals _____; and total saving equals _____.

ANSWERS

Matching	True/False		Multiple Choice		Unlimited Multiple Choice
1. b	1. F	9. F	1. c	9. c	1. cd
2. e	2. T	10. T	2. d	10. b	2. c
3. h	3. T	11. T	3. e	11. a	3. abcd
4. g	4. F	12. F	4. a	12. e	4. abd
5. i	5. T	13. F	5. d	13. c	5. bd
6. d	6. F	14. T	6. c	14. e	
7. j	7. T	15. T	7. d	15. a	
8. a	8. F		8. b		
9. f					
10. k					
11. c					

Chapter Review (Fill-In Questions)

1. full employment; demand
2. wages; prices
3. Aggregate Supply; Aggregate Demand
4. investment; disposable income
5. increase; less
6. dissaving; unrelated to
7. capital; diminishing returns
8. interest rate; Autonomous
9. government; transfer payments
10. vertical; net exports

Problem 1		Problem 2		Problem 3	
a.	T	a.	T	1.	e
b.	T	b.	T	2.	d
c.	F	c.	F	3.	c
d.	F	d.	T	4.	b
e.	F	e.	T	5.	a
f.	T	f.	F	6.	g
g.	T	g.	F	7.	f
h.	F	h.	F		
i.	F	i.	F		
j.	F	j.	T		
		k.	T		

Problem 4

Y (Billions)	C	S	MPC	MPS
$0	$100	$-100	---	---
100	175	-75	.75	.25
200	250	-50	.75	.25
300	325	-25	.75	.25
400	400	0	.75	.25
500	475	25	.75	.25
600	550	50	.75	.25
700	625	75	.75	.25
800	700	100	.75	.25
900	775	125	.75	.25
1,000	850	150	.75	.25

a. See table at left.
b. $100
c. See figure below.
d. one

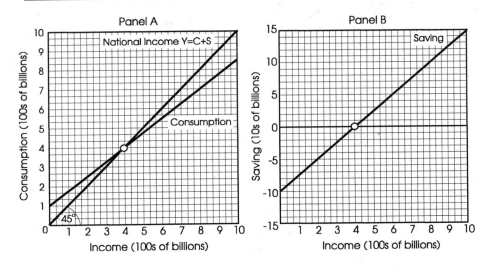

Problem 5

a. F
b. F
c. F
d. F
e. F
f. T
g. T
h. F
i. T
j. F

Problem 6

a. -$200; $200; (Autonomous saving and income are based on zero income.)
b. .8; .2; (As income rises from $0 to $1,000, savings increases by $200 (0-(-200)). Thus MPS = 200/1,000 = .2 and MPC = 1 - MPS = 1 - .2 = .8.)
c. $1,440; $1,640; (Induced consumption is equal to MPC x Y = .8 x $1,800 = $1,440. The total level of consumption is induced plus autonomous ($1,440 + 200 = $1,640).)
d. $440; $240; -$200; (Induced saving is equal to MPS x Y = .2 x $2,200 = $440. The total level of savings is induced plus autonomous ($440 + (-200) = $240).)

Problem 7

a. .75; (Since autonomous spending is $200 for an equilibrium income of $800, the multiplier must equal 4 and therefore the MPC is .75.)
b. $100; $600; $700; (Since autonomous spending is $200 and autonomous investment is $100, autonomous consumption must equal $100. Induced consumption is MPC x Yd = .75 x $800 = $600. Total consumption is equal to autonomous plus induced or $100 + $600 = 700.)
c. -$100; .25; $200; (Autonomous saving is the negative of autonomous consumption or -$100. The marginal propensity to save, MPS = 1 - MPC = 1 - .75 = 25. At equilibrium induced saving is equal to MPS x Y = .25 x $800 = $200.)
d. $600; $450; $500; $100 (Equilibrium income is equal to autonomous spending ($150) times the multiplier (4) or $600. At equilibrium induced consumption is MPC x Y = .75 x $600 = $450 and total consumption is autonomous plus induced ($50 + $450 = $500). Therefore, since S = Y - C, savings is $100 ($600 - $500 = $100).)

Chapter 10
Macroeconomic Equilibrium

Chapter Objectives

After you have read and studied this chapter you should be able to explain equilibrium income and employment using the Aggregate Expenditures - National Income approach, and why Keynesians differ from classical economists by emphasizing demand over supply forces; explain macroequilibrium with the savings-investment approach; explain the differences between potential and actual GDP and the concepts of recessionary and inflationary gaps; and explain the relationships between Keynesian Aggregate Supply and Demand and the average level of prices in the economy.

Chapter Review: Key Points

1. Keynesian theory suggests that erratic changes in *business investment spending* (especially inventories) play a major role in causing fluctuations in aggregate income and employment.

2. Equilibrium income and employment occur at the output level at which *Aggregate Spending equals National Output*; firms desire to produce and sell exactly the amounts consumers and investors want to purchase. Any deviation from equilibrium income sets forces in motion to drive the economy towards a new equilibrium.

3. When *planned saving equals planned investment (S = I)*, the economy will be in *equilibrium*. Actual saving and investment are equal at all times because inventory adjustments and similar mechanisms ensure this balance.

4. When *autonomous spending* in the economy increases by $1, income rises by an amount equal to the *autonomous spending multiplier* times the original $1. The multiplier exists because the original $1 in new spending becomes $1 in new income, parts of which are then spent by successive consumers and businesses. The simple autonomous spending multiplier equals: $\Delta Y/\Delta A = 1/mps = 1/(1 - mpc)$, where A represents some form of autonomous spending.

5. Investment spending fell precipitously during the 1929-33 period. The effect of this decline was to reduce equilibrium income sharply. This may have been a principal cause of the Great Depression.

6. The *paradox of thrift* appears to be an important challenge to our conventional wisdom. If more consumers decide to increase their saving, the result might be declining income, consumption, and saving.

7. *Potential GDP* is an estimate of the output the economy could produce at full employment. The *GDP gap* is the difference between potential and actual GDP.

8. The *recessionary gap* is the amount by which autonomous spending falls short of that necessary to achieve a full employment level of income; it is measured on the vertical axis. An *inflationary gap* is the amount that autonomous spending exceeds what is necessary for a full employment equilibrium and is a measure of upward pressure on the price level.

9. Aggregate Expenditure curves are constructed for a given (fixed) price level. If the price level rises, Aggregate Expenditures fall, and vice versa. This leads to a unique relationship that allows us to derive an Aggregate Demand curve from specific levels of Aggregate Spending at various price levels.

10. If the price level is constant, higher autonomous spending increases Aggregate Demand by shifting the Aggregate Demand curve to the right, and vice versa.

11. Keynes thought that raising Aggregate Demand will boost output during a depression without raising the price level. Simple Keynesian theory suggests that the Aggregate Supply curve is horizontal up to the point of full employment. Once full-employment GDP is reached, classical reasoning reigns: The Aggregate Supply curve is vertical, and increases in Aggregate Demand cannot generate extra output. In a fully-employed economy, additions to Aggregate Demand simply bid up prices and result in inflation.

Matching Key Terms And Concepts

_____ 1. Keynesian equilibrium

_____ 2. withdrawals

_____ 3. GDP gap

_____ 4. recessionary gap

_____ 5. inflationary gap

_____ 6. paradox of thrift

_____ 7. potential GDP

_____ 8. actual investment

_____ 9. planned investment equals planned savings

_____ 10. autonomous spending multiplier

a. The reciprocal of the marginal propensity to save.

b. Difference between what GDP currently is and what it would be at full employment.

c. Planned investment adjusted for unintended inventory changes.

d. Aggregate Output and Income equal planned Aggregate Expenditures.

e. Condition for a private economy macroequilibrium.

f. Deficiency in autonomous expenditures needed to reach full employment.

g. Attempts to save more actually yields less saving.

h. Occur when income is not spent on domestic output.

i. Amount that autonomous spending exceeds that needed to achieve full-employment equilibrium with price level stability.

j. National output when resources are fully employed.

True/False Questions

_____ 1. Increasing government spending could eliminate an inflationary gap.

_____ 2. Keynes viewed savers and investors as different groups who saved and invested for different reasons.

_____ 3. In Keynesian theory, planned saving always equals planned investment.

_____ 4. According to Keynesian theory, consumption expenditure is a function of the level of income.

_____ 5. By definition, the recessionary gap is the amount by which Keynesian Aggregate Expenditures exceeds National Income at the full employment level of income.

_____ 6. Keynes supported Say's Law in his _General Theory_.

_____ 7. Firms increase employment and production in response to rising sales and unplanned declines in inventories.

_____ 8. An economy will stay in equilibrium whenever actual investment equals actual saving.

_____ 9. An inflationary gap occurs when Aggregate Expenditures exceed National Income at full employment.

_____ 10. The Keynesian model suggests that autonomous injections into the economy are translated into much larger changes in incomes.

Standard Multiple Choice

There Is One Best Answer For Each Question.

___ 1. The Keynesian autonomous spending multiplier equals:
   a. government spending.
   b. 1 - MPC.
   c. 1/(1-MPS).
   d. 1/(1-MPC).
   e. unity.

___ 2. As autonomous investment rises, Keynesians expect increases in:
   a. income.
   b. employment.
   c. consumption.
   d. Aggregate Demand.
   e. All of these.

___ 3. If the MPC equals .67, then the autonomous spending multiplier equals:
   a. 3.
   b. 4.
   c. 5.
   d. 6.
   e. 7.

___ 4. The Aggregate Supply curve during a Keynesian depression:
   a. is horizontal.
   b. is vertical.
   c. tilts downward to the right.
   d. tilts upward to the right.
   e. is the negative relation between unemployment and inflation.

___ 5. A recessionary gap measures the:
   a. amount by which autonomous spending is below that needed to achieve a full employment equilibrium.
   b. amount Aggregate Spending exceeds that needed to achieve full employment.
   c. difference in real output between the classical model and the Keynesian depression model.
   d. paradox of thrift.
   e. None of the above.

___ 6. The paradox of thrift suggests that:
   a. "a penny saved is a penny earned."
   b. as consumption increases, saving decreases.
   c. as saving increases, investment declines.
   d. attempts to save more may actually reduce total saving.
   e. the less you pay, the lower your satisfaction.

___ 7. Macroequilibrium is achieved in a private economy when desired:
   a. consumption equals Aggregate Expenditures.
   b. consumption equals desired savings.
   c. investment equals desired saving.
   d. inventories equal desired saving.
   e. income equals net wealth.

8. Inventories play an important role in the economic equilibrium because:
   a. unintended inventory changes act as signals to producers to change their production plans.
   b. they are a major component of the multiplier effect.
   c. Aggregate Expenditures would be too hard to accurately measure without inventory changes.
   d. savings could not be converted to investment without inventories as the means of doing so.
   e. inventories are an extremely stable component of investment.

9. The Keynesian point of view suggests that:
   a. supply creates its own demand.
   b. demand creates its own supply.
   c. the market is always at equilibrium.
   d. full employment is achieved as the result of natural market forces.
   e. None of the above.

10. Keynesians believe the depression of the 1930s was most attributable to:
   a. excessive government spending.
   b. reduced foreign exports.
   c. reductions in investment.
   d. declines in the money supply.
   e. None of the above.

11. If the marginal propensity to consume is .8, how much will total income rise in response to new investment of $25?
   a. $5.
   b. $20.
   c. $25.
   d. $125.
   e. $200.

12. An excess in autonomous spending relative to that needed for full employment is referred to as a(n):
   a. inflationary surplus.
   b. inflationary gap.
   c. recessionary gap.
   d. deflationary shortfall.
   e. demand shortage.

Chapter Review (Fill-In Questions)

1. Keynesian analysis focused on _____ problems and illustrated that the economy might be stuck in a short run equilibrium in which substantial excess _____ existed.

2. In the simple Keynesian Aggregate Expenditures - National Income model, the National output schedule could be thought of as a Keynesian _____ schedule. All points along the National Income schedule represent potential equilibrium because aggregate output and income just equal aggregate spending. Whenever aggregate spending differs from aggregate income there is _____ .

3. Equilibrium occurs when Keynesian Aggregate Expenditures are just equal to _____. At this point, firms do not experience pressures to expand or contract output and they are able to maintain _____ at a level consistent with their desires.

4. Keynesian analysis assumes that only _____ adjustments will occur in situations of excess capacity. Whenever Keynesian Aggregate Expenditures exceed national output, firms typically find their _____ shrinking. To correct for this problem, business will _____ output and as a result, _____ will increase. Consequently, national income and output expands. As income expands, aggregate spending expands until both _____ and _____ are equal.

5. When an autonomous injection of spending is introduced into the economy, its effect is _____ so that equilibrium income actually increases _____ than the autonomous injection. This effect is the result of a concept referred to as the _____, and is defined by the ratio of the change in income to the change in _____. The simple spending multiplier is also defined to be equal to _____ or _____.

6. The paradox of thrift suggests that when people collectively desire to save more, they actually end up saving _____. When the economy is slipping into a recession, people generally attempt to save more, _____ the likelihood a recession will occur.

Unlimited Multiple Choice

There Are From Zero To Four Correct Answers For Each Question.

___ 1. Macroeconomic equilibrium occurs in the simple Keynesian model whenever:
   a. actual investment is equal to actual saving.
   b. unplanned changes in inventories are zero.
   c. planned investment equals planned saving.
   d. the dollar value of desired expenditures equal the dollar value of goods produced.

___ 2. Unintended inventory changes help:
   a. balance the macroeconomy.
   b. consumers balance their budgets.
   c. resolve any differences between planned saving and investment.
   d. guarantee that planned investment and planned saving will be equal at all levels of income.

___ 3. In a simple Keynesian model of the economy characterized by autonomous investment and no government, the autonomous spending multiplier is given by:
   a. 1/MPS.
   b. 1/(1-MPC).
   c. 1/MPC.
   d. 1/(MPC + MPS).

Problem 5

Use the figure below to answer the following questions:

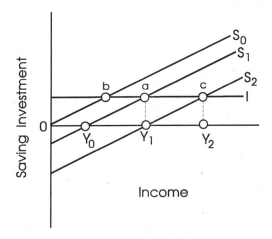

a. Using saving and investment schedules S_2 and I, answer the following (use letters):

    1. Equilibrium income is? _____

    2. The MPC is equal to? _____

    3. Saving when income is Y_1 is? _____

b. Starting with S_1, which curve shows increases in desired saving by the public? _____

c. If consumers actually desire to save less, will they end up saving less? _____

d. The multiplier is equal to? _____

Problem 6

To answer this question you may want to review the optional material included at the end of the chapter. Given below are equations for the components of Aggregate Expenditures (C + I). Use these equations to answer the following questions:

$$C = 250 + .75Y$$
$$I = 100$$

a. Graph C, I, and Aggregate Expenditures (AE) on the figure.

b. Equilibrium income is? _____

c. The autonomous spending multiplier equals? _____

d. Equilibrium consumption is? _____

e. Equilibrium saving is? _____

f. Write the equation for the saving function. _____

g. Assuming that full employment income is 1700, the recessionary gap is? _____ The GDP gap is? _____

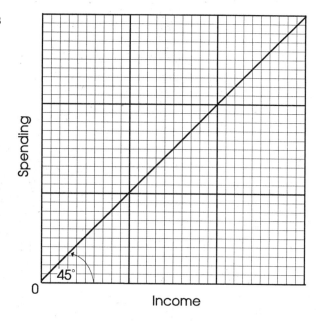

h. Assume that autonomous consumption expenditures increase from 250 to 400. What is the effect on equilibrium income? _____ On equilibrium saving? _____ Show these changes on the figure and label the new Keynesian Aggregate Expenditures curve AE_1 and the new consumption schedule C_1.

Problem 7

To answer this question you may want to review the optional material included at the end of the chapter. Given below are the equations for desired investment and saving. Use the equations to answer the following questions:

$$S = -300 + .20Y$$
$$I = 200$$

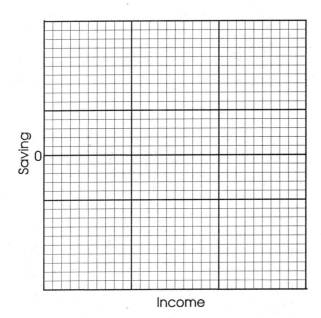

a. Graph the saving and investment schedules on the figure.

b. Equilibrium income is? _____

c. The autonomous spending multiplier is?_____

d. Write the equation for the consumption function. _____

e. At an income level of 1500, planned saving is equal to? _____ Planned investment is equal to? _____ Is the economy in equilibrium? _____

Problem 8

Use this figure to answer the following questions.

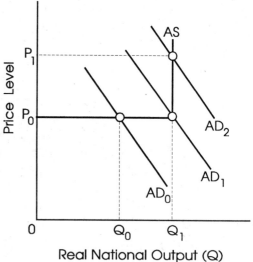

a. Output level Q_1 represents _____

b. If Aggregate Demand were to fall from AD_1 to AD_0 what would be the impacts on price and quantity?_____

c. At Aggregate Demand level AD_0 the economy would most likely be in a _____

d. Using Keynesian policy tools, the move from AD_0 to AD_1 might be accomplished by

_____

e. If Aggregate Demand overshoots the AD_1 level and instead proceeds to AD_2, what would be the effect on price and quantity? _____

f. The range of the Aggregate Supply curve that corresponds to our simple Keynesian income-expenditure model is _____

g. The classical school assumed that market forces always maintained full employment. Based on that logic, what would an Aggregate Supply curve look like for a classical macroeconomic model?_____

ANSWERS

Matching	True/False	Multiple Choice		Unlimited Multiple Choice
1. d	1. F	1. d	7. c	1. bcd
2. h	2. T	2. e	8. a	2. abc
3. b	3. F	3. a	9. b	3. ab
4. f	4. T	4. a	10. c	4. bc
5. i	5. F	5. a	11. d	5. ad
6. g	6. F	6. d	12. b	
7. j	7. T			
8. c	8. F			
9. e	9. T			
10. a	10. T			

Chapter Review (Fill-In Questions)

1. short run; capacity
2. Aggregate Supply; disequilibrium
3. National Income; inventories
4. quantity; inventories; increase; employment; National Income; Keynesian Aggregate Expenditures
5. multiplied; more; multiplier; autonomous spending; 1/(1 - MPC); 1/MPS
6. less, increasing

Problem 1

MPC	MPS	k
1/2	1/2	2
3/5	2/5	2.5
2/3	1/3	3
3/4	1/4	4
4/5	1/5	5
5/6	1/6	6
6/7	1/7	7
7/8	1/8	8
8/9	1/9	9
9/10	1/10	10

Problem 2

AE	Y	C	I	S	APC	APS	MPC	MPS
$300	$0	$200	$100	-$200	---	---	---	---
700	500	600	100	-100	1.20	-.20	.80	.20
1,100	1,000	1,000	100	0	1.00	0	.80	.20
1,500	1,500	1,400	100	100	.93	.07	.80	.20
1,900	2,000	1,800	100	200	.90	.10	.80	.20
2,300	2,500	2,200	100	300	.88	.12	.80	.20
2,700	3,000	2,600	100	400	.87	.13	.80	.20

a. See table and figure.
b. $1,500
c. 5
d. $200; see figure; $1000; the multiplier

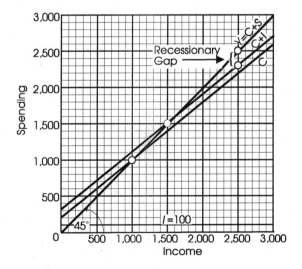

Problem 3

a. See figure.
b. $500
c. $40
d. $40
e. $460
f. 5
g. (1) See figure.
   (2) $600
   (3) $45
   (4) $45
   (5) 6.7 when S is positive
h. (1) $400
   (2) $360
   (3) $40
   (4) .8
   (5) no
   (6) It has declined. Increases in desired saving reduced both equilibrium income and consumption.

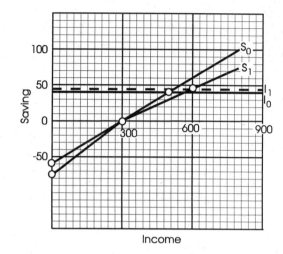

Problem 4

a. $0Y_1$
b. bf or de or A_0A_1
c. cd or A_1A_2
d. Y_0Y_1/bf or Y_2Y_1/cd or $0Y_1/0A_1$ or $0Y_0/0A_0$ or $0Y_2/0A_2$

Problem 5

a. (1) Y_2
   (2) $1 - cY_2/Y_1Y_2$
   (3) 0
b. S_0
c. no
d. Y_2Y_1/cY_2 or $Y_1Y_0/aY_1 = 1/MPS$

Problem 6

a. See figure.

b. $Y = C + I$
$Y = 250 + .75Y + 100$
$Y = 350 + .75Y$
$Y - .75Y = 350$
$.25Y = 350$
$Y = 350/.25 = 1400$

c. $k = 1/(1-MPC)$
$= 1/(1-.75)$
$= 1/.25$
$= 4$

d. $C = 250 + .75(1400)$
$= 250 + 1050$
$= 1300$

e. 100

f. $S = Y - C$
$= Y - (250 + .75Y)$
$= Y - 250 - .75Y$
$= -250 + .25Y$

g. 75; 300

h. increases by 600; stays the same; See figure.

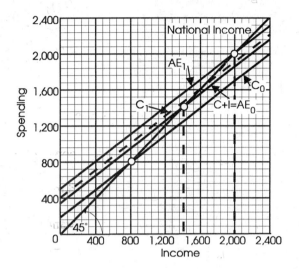

Problem 7

a. See figure.

b. Equilibrium occurs when $S = I$
$-300 + .20Y = 200$
$= .20Y = 500$
$= Y = 500/.2$
$= Y = 2500$

c. $k = 1/MPS = 1/.20 = 5$

d. $C = Y - S$
$= Y - (-300 + .20Y)$
$= Y + 300 - .20Y$
$= 300 + .8Y$

e. 0; 200; no

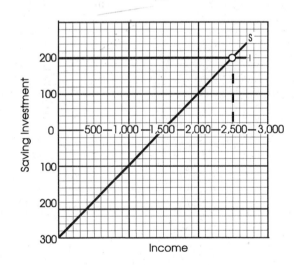

Problem 8

a. Output Q_1 represents full employment or full utilization of resources. It can also be viewed as a point on the production possibility frontier.

b. Under the assumptions of the Keynesian model as depicted here, price would not fall below P_0 but quantity would fall from Q_1 to Q_0.

c. Recession or depression.

d. New government expenditures. It could also be accomplished by increases in any of the other components of autonomous Aggregate Expenditures, such as consumption, investment or net exports.

e. Beyond AD_1 demand increases are converted into price level increases as there are no additional resources to put into the production process. Output stays at Q_1 but the price level rises from P_0 to P_1.

f. The horizontal portion where no price level changes occur.

g. Since Q_1 represents the fully employed level of economic activity, it would be reasonable to assume that a classical AS curve would be vertical at that level of output. Under these conditions, all Aggregate Demand changes are translated into price level changes.

Chapter 11
Government Taxing And Spending

Chapter Objectives

After you have read and studied this chapter you should be able to differentiate between discretionary automatic fiscal policy; explain how the autonomous spending, tax, and balanced-budget multipliers operate; distinguish between structural and cyclical deficits; and identify differences between Keynesian and new classical economic fiscal policies.

Chapter Review: Key Points

1. *Keynesian fiscal policy* is the use of federal spending and tax policies to stimulate or contract Aggregate Spending and economic activity to offset cyclical fluctuations. *Classical (supply-side) fiscal policies* rely on low tax rates and minimal government spending to allow Aggregate Supply to grow.

2. *Discretionary fiscal policy* consists of deliberate changes in federal government spending and taxation for stabilization purposes. Without congressional action *automatic stabilizers* such as corporate and personal income taxes and various transfer programs cause changes in spending and taxation as economic conditions change.

3. Increases in *government spending* increase Aggregate Expenditure and National Income through the multiplier process in the same way as changes in investment or autonomous consumer spending.

4. Changes in *net tax revenues* (tax revenues minus transfer payments) affect Aggregate Spending differently than changes in government spending. Changes in net taxes directly affect disposable income and, therefore, saving. These effects are transmitted into spending through the *autonomous tax multiplier* ($\Delta Y/\Delta T = 1 - 1/mps$), which is weaker than the spending multiplier.

5. In a Keynesian depression, the *balanced-budget multiplier* equals one, suggesting that equal increases (*decreases*) in government spending and taxes will increase (*decrease*) Aggregate Spending and equilibrium income by an equal amount. This result follows from the fact that the autonomous tax multiplier is one minus the autonomous spending multiplier.

6. *Automatic stabilizers* tend to cushion the economy. When income falls, automatic stabilizers keep the level of disposable income from falling as rapidly as income. Our progressive income tax causes tax collections to fall proportionally faster when income is falling and to increase proportionally faster when income is rising.

7. Built-in stabilizers can pose the problem of *fiscal drag*. When potential income is rising, automatic stabilizers brake the economy and slow the rate of growth.

8. The *structural deficit* is an estimate of the deficit that would be generated at full employment under existing tax and expenditure structures. This is a way to estimate the expansionary or contractionary influence of any tax and expenditure mix.

9. The *cyclical deficit* is attributable to business conditions. As unemployment grows, the cyclical deficit grows, and vice versa.

10. The *Laffer curve* indicates that high tax rates may impose such large disincentives to productive effort that Aggregate Supply and tax revenues are both restricted.

11. *Marginal tax rates* are the percentage taxes applied to small gains in additional income.

Matching Key Terms And Concepts

____ 1. fiscal policy

____ 2. fiscal drag

____ 3. automatic stabilizers

____ 4. balanced budget multiplier

____ 5. discretionary fiscal policy

____ 6. Laffer curve

____ 7. high tax rates

____ 8. government spending and transfers

____ 9. structural deficit

____10. autonomous tax multiplier

____11. cyclical deficit

a. Deliberate changes in spending and taxes for stabilization policy.

b. Retards growth in Aggregate Expenditures.

c. Examples of nondiscretionary fiscal policy.

d. Always equals one.

e. The use of government spending and tax policies to stimulate or contract economic activity to offset cyclical fluctuations.

f. Higher tax rates may either raise or lower government revenues.

g. Keynesians see as dampening spending, while new classical economists emphasize the destructive effects on production incentives.

h. $-(MPC/MPS)$.

i. Keynesians perceive as bolstering spending, but new classical economists worry about disincentive effects on production.

j. Occurs if the economy has excessive idle capacity.

k. Tax revenues minus government outlays if the economy were producing at its capacity.

True/False Questions

___ 1. If tax rates are increased to pay increased interest on public debt, incentives to work and invest might be diminished.

___ 2. The biggest sources of federal tax revenues are social security, personal, and corporate income taxes.

___ 3. Fiscal drag refers to the retarding effect that decreased government expenditures have on the economy.

___ 4. Discretionary variations in spending and taxes are the only governmental mechanisms to control unemployment and inflation.

___ 5. Automatic stabilizers are the mechanisms inherent in the economy to automatically dampen swings in economic activity.

___ 6. Given the unpredictable nature of economic activity, an inflexible commitment to annually balancing the budget could prove disastrous, especially during recessionary periods.

___ 7. In the classical model, an increase in desired Aggregate Expenditures will always induce greater production.

___ 8. In the classical model, a decrease in desired Aggregate Expenditures is followed by a decrease in equilibrium for real production and real income.

___ 9. Changes in government spending change Keynesian Aggregate Expenditures and National Income through the multiplier process in the same manner as changes in investment or autonomous consumer spending.

___ 10. Because government outlays involve both spending for goods and services and transfer payments, the balanced budget multiplier is only slightly bigger than one.

___ 11. Automatic stabilizers are also known as discretionary fiscal policy.

___ 12. The tax increase of 1932 probably contributed to the severity of the Great Depression.

___ 13. New classical economists and Keynesians agree that big government spending programs will boost the economy out of a slump.

___ 14. Massive supply-side tax cuts quickly eliminated huge federal deficits in the early 1980s.

___ 15. Cutting tax rates will tend to cure both fiscal drag and disincentives for production.

Standard Multiple Choice

There Is One Best Answer For Each Question.

___ 1. Which of the following is NOT an automatic stabilizer?
   a. Social Security payments.
   b. Unemployment compensation.
   c. An anti-inflationary tax increase.
   d. Progressive personal income tax rates.
   e. The corporate income tax.

___ 2. Using a simple Keynesian model where the mpc = .75 and government outlays and taxes are equal to $250 billion, the multiplier is equal to:
   a. 4.
   b. 1.
   c. 3.
   d. 2.
   e. 5.

___ 3. The autonomous tax multiplier equals:
   a. -MPC/MPS.
   b. 1/mps.
   c. four.
   d. three.
   e. 1/mpc.

___ 4. When built-in (automatic) stabilizers retard growth in Aggregate Spending, the problem is known as:
   a. stagflation.
   b. fiscal drag.
   c. excessive retardation.
   d. frictional inflation and unemployment.
   e. crowding-out.

___ 5. The balanced budget multiplier is:
   a. one.
   b. 1/mpc.
   c. 1/mps.
   d. 1/(1-mpc).
   e. -mpc/mps.

___ 6. Equal increases in the amount of government expenditures and taxes:
   a. have no effect on equilibrium income.
   b. cause equilibrium income to fall.
   c. cause equilibrium expenditures to increase by the same amount.
   d. cause prices to fall.
   e. cause proportional increases in the price level and unemployment.

___ 7. According to new classical economics, increases in which of the following would NOT pose disincentives for production?
   a. Marginal tax rates on wage and salary incomes.
   b. Corporate income tax rates.
   c. Tax deductions and exemptions.
   d. Government transfer programs.
   e. Government purchases of goods and services.

___ 8. The Laffer curve suggests a tradeoff between:
   a. unemployment and inflation.
   b. high tax rates and high tax revenues.
   c. consumption and investment.
   d. production and consumption.
   e. tax deductions or exemptions and a balanced budget.

9. Which of the following is smallest in absolute size?
   a. The autonomous spending multiplier.
   b. The marginal propensity to save.
   c. The balanced budget multiplier.
   d. The autonomous tax multiplier.
   e. The marginal propensity to consume.

10. Keynesians and new classical economists would be most likely to agree on which of the following as a cure for a severe recession?
    a. substantial increases in government 'public works' projects.
    b. deep cuts in government transfer programs.
    c. slashes in government purchases but hikes in transfer programs.
    d. the need to balance the federal budget.
    e. cuts in tax rates.

11. President Reagan's 1981-83 tax cuts were most in tune with ideas from:
    a. modern supply-siders.
    b. Keynesians.
    c. advocates of laws requiring annually balanced budgets.
    d. Friedrich Nietzsche.
    e. Paul Reubens.

12. Huge government budgets cause problems, according to supply-siders, for ALL of the following reasons EXCEPT:
    a. fiscal drag discourages spending.
    b. high taxes causing disincentives for work and investment.
    c. transfer payments discouraging work effort.
    d. government provisions of goods causing people who don't work to enjoy life without labor.
    e. All of these cause problems, according to supply-siders.

Chapter Review (Fill-In Questions)

1. Fiscal policy is the use of government spending and _____ policies to stimulate or contract economic activity to offset _____ fluctuations.

2. Discretionary fiscal policy is the intentional changes in government spending and taxation for the purpose of economic stabilization; whereas _____ fiscal policies are changes in spending or taxing which take place _____ (without congressional action) as economic conditions change.

3. Because all changes in injections are subject to the multiplier principle, _____ in government spending will change Aggregate Expenditures by an amount equal to the changes in autonomous injections times the multiplier. At equilibrium, injections must equal withdrawals, so when both government spending and taxation are introduced, the new equilibrium condition becomes _____. The payment of taxes will come from both consumption and _____.

4. An old idea that hikes in very high tax rates may actually lower total tax _____ is depicted by a device called the _____ curve.

5. Although Keynesians and new classical economists agree that cuts in _____ are stimulative, Keynesians view hikes in government _____ or _____ payments as stimulants for spending, while new classical economists view these outlays as retarding _____.

6. A law requiring annually balancing the budget would place policymakers in a dilemma. If declines in Aggregate Spending cause rising unemployment, balancing the budget requires that either tax revenues must be _____ or government outlays _____. Unfortunately, it is ambiguous as to whether higher tax _____ will yield more tax _____.

Unlimited Multiple Choice

There Are From Zero To Four Correct Answers For Each Question.

___ 1. New classical economists and Keynesians would probably agree that:
   a. tax rate hikes reduce equilibrium income.
   b. cuts in government spending reduce national income.
   c. cuts in government transfer payments increase real income.
   d. expanding taxes and spending equally results in equivalent growth of our national income.

___ 2. Incorporating autonomous taxes (T_a) into simple Keynesian models:
   a. shifts the withdrawal schedule upward by MPC x T_a.
   b. shifts the investment schedule downward by the same amount as tax revenue.
   c. shifts the government expenditure function upward.
   d. shifts the Aggregate Expenditures schedule downward by an amount exceeding tax revenues.

___ 3. Macroeconomic equilibrium occurs:
   a. when planned injections are greater than planned withdrawals.
   b. at the point where autonomous taxes equal autonomous government expenditures, assuming a balanced budget fiscal policy, and no induced government expenditure or induced taxation.
   c. when autonomous consumption equals autonomous saving.
   d. only at full employment income in the Keynesian model.

___ 4. An autonomous spending multiplier of 4 implies:
   a. that an increase in autonomous consumption of $10 billion will cause income to increase by $40 billion.
   b. that a decrease in autonomous investment of $40 billion will cause income to fall by $160 billion.
   c. that a simultaneous increase in both autonomous government expenditures and autonomous taxes of $20 billion will cause income to increase by $20 billion, all else equal.
   d. an MPC of .80, assuming consumption to be the only induced type of expenditure.

___ 5. A Constitutional amendment requiring annual balance of the federal budget:
   a. may be self-defeating if tax hikes and spending cuts are used in attempts to cure deficits occurring during a deep recession.
   b. would have been an excellent cure for the Great Depression.
   c. might result in inflationary policies if the economy was at full employment and the full employment budget yields a large surplus.
   d. would result in much lower tax burdens throughout the remainder of this century.

Problems

Problem 1

Complete this table by calculating the autonomous spending multiplier, tax multiplier, and balanced budget multiplier associated with each of the following values for the marginal propensity to consume (mpc).

MPC	Spending Multiplier	Tax Multiplier	Balanced Budget Multiplier
1/2			
3/5			
2/3			
3/4			
4/5			
5/6			
6/7			
7/8			
8/9			
9/10			

Problem 2

Use this table to answer the following questions:

a. On graph A plot the schedules for consumption and Keynesian Aggregate Expenditures (C + I + G). On graph B plot the saving (S), investment (I), and government (G) spending schedules.

b. Equilibrium income without government spending is _____

c. Equilibrium saving without government spending is _____

d. With government spending of $40, equilibrium income is _____

e. With government spending, equilibrium saving rises by _____

Y	S	I	G
0	-60	40	40
100	-40	40	40
200	-20	40	40
300	0	40	40
400	20	40	40
500	40	40	40
600	60	40	40
700	80	40	40
800	100	40	40
900	120	40	40
1,000	140	40	40
1,100	160	40	40
1,200	180	40	40

Graph A

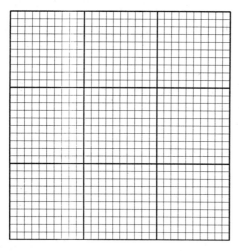

Graph B

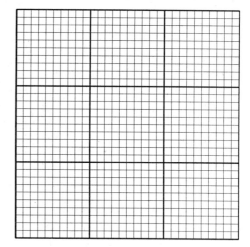

Problem 3

Use this figure to answer the following T/F questions. Assume that $1,200 billion represents full employment national income and that the autonomous spending multiplier is 4.

____ a. A recessionary gap exists when the economy produces an income of $1,400 billion.

____ b. Desired autonomous expenditures corresponding to Keynesian Aggregate Expenditure schedule AE_0 is $300 billion.

____ c. An inflationary gap exists when the economy produces an income of $1,200 billion.

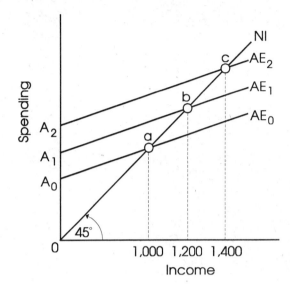

____ d. As the economy moves along the nominal income line from a to b, real output increases.

____ e. As the economy moves from b to c, real output increases, and the absolute price level remains unchanged.

____ f. A recessionary gap of $50 billion exists when the economy produces an income of $1,000 billion.

____ g. An inflationary gap of $50 billion exists when the economy produces an income of $1,400 billion.

____ h. The movement from b to c ultimately yields only pure price inflation.

____ i. If the economy was in equilibrium at point a, the government could exactly eliminate the recessionary gap by increasing its spending by $200 billion.

____ j. If the economy was in equilibrium at point c, full employment (without inflation) could be restored by decreasing both government spending and taxes by 200.

Problem 4

Use this table to answer the following questions:

Before Government				After Government						
Y	C	S	I	G	T	Y-T	C_1	S_1	S_1+T	I+G
0	400		100	200	200					
200	500		100	200	200					
400	600		100	200	200					
600	700		100	200	200					
800	800		100	200	200					
1,000	900		100	200	200					
1,200	1,000		100	200	200					
1,400	1,100		100	200	200					
1,600	1,200		100	200	200					
1,800	1,300		100	200	200					
2,000	1,400		100	200	200					

a. Complete the column labeled "S."

b. Equilibrium income without government is _____

c. Now assume that government enters the picture and spends 200 without taxing. Equilibrium income would be _____ Equilibrium saving would become _____

d. Now assume that government continues to spend 200, but now levies taxes equal to 200 as well.
(1) Complete the "Y-T" column.
(2) Complete the adjusted consumption schedule (C_1). Remember that only a portion (the MPC) of taxes comes from consumption.
(3) Remember that only a portion (the MPS) of taxes come from savings. Complete the adjusted saving schedule "S_1" and the "S_1 + T" and "I + G" columns.

e. With the balanced budget (G = T = 200), equilibrium income is? _____

f. The increase in income accompanying the balanced budget hike was? _____

g. In the graph below, plot the S, S_1, I, G, T, I+G, and S_1+T schedules. Label the original equilibrium (without government) as "a" and the new equilibrium (budget balanced at 200) as "b."

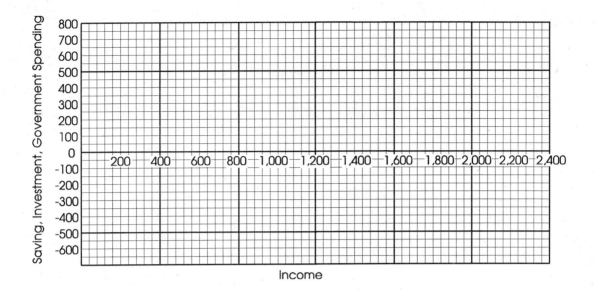

Problem 5

Answering Problems 5, 6, and 7 may require reviewing the Optional Material at the end of chapter. Use this table to answer the following questions:

a. Write an equation for the consumption function without taxes. _____

Y	C	I	G	T
0	300	100	50	50
100	375	100	50	50
200	450	100	50	50
300	525	100	50	50
400	600	100	50	50
500	675	100	50	50
600	750	100	50	50
700	825	100	50	50
800	900	100	50	50
900	975	100	50	50
1,000	1,050	100	50	50

b. Write an equation for the saving function without taxes. _____

c. Write an equation for investment expenditure. _____

d. Write an equation for government expenditure. _____

e. Write an equation for the tax function. _____

f. Write an equation for the consumption function with taxes. _____

g. Write an equation for the saving function with taxes. _____

h. What does equilibrium income (including the government's budget) equal? _____

i. What are the equilibrium values for C?_____ I?_____ G?_____ S?_____ T?_____
j. What kind of fiscal policy is the government pursuing in this example? _____

k. Write the condition for macroeconomic equilibrium when government both spends and taxes._____

l. Assume that $\Delta Ga = \Delta Ta = \$40$ billion, all other things held constant. What does equilibrium output equal? _____

m. Write an equation for the new consumption function with taxes. _____

n. Write an equation for the new saving function with taxes. _____

o. What are the equilibrium values for C?_____ I?_____ G?_____ S?_____ T?_____

p. Show that the balanced-budget multiplier is one. _____

Problem 6

If $G_a = 40$, $I_a = 30$, and $S = -100 + .20\ Y$;

a. What are equilibrium values for C?_____ I?_____ G?_____ Y?_____

b. If full employment national income is 700, is there an inflationary or recessionary gap?_____

c. What is the value of the inflationary or recessionary gap?_____

d. How could a tax change be used to close this gap? _____

e. What are the equilibrium values of C, I, G, and Y after solving question d for: C?_____ I?_____ G?_____ Y?_____

Problem 7

Given that $I_a = 100$, $G_a = 250$, and $C = 400 + .9Y$;

a. What are the equilibrium values of C?_____ I?_____ G?_____ Y?_____

b. If the GNP gap equals 200, is the situation inflationary or recessionary? _____

c. Solve for full employment equilibrium using a balanced budget approach. What are the full employment equilibrium values of C?_____ I?_____ G?_____ Y?_____

ANSWERS

Matching		True/False		Multiple Choice		Unlimited Multiple Choice
1. e	7. g	1. T	9. T	1. c	7. c	1. a
2. b	8. i	2. T	10. F	2. a	8. b	2. a
3. c	9. k	3. F	11. F	3. a	9. b	3. none
4. d	10. h	4. F	12. T	4. b	10. e	4. abc
5. a	11. j	5. T	13. F	5. a	11. a	5. ac
6. f		6. T	14. F	6. c	12. a	
		7. F	15. T			
		8. F				

Chapter Review (Fill-in Questions)

1. tax; cyclical
2. nondiscretionary; automatically
3. changes; I + G = S + T; saving
4. revenues; Laffer
5. tax rates; purchases; transfer; production or Aggregate Supply
6. increased; reduced; rates; revenues

Problem 2

a. See figure.
b. 500
c. 40
d. 700
e. 40

Problem 3

a. F
b. F
c. F
d. T
e. F
f. T
g. T
h. T
i. F
j. T

Problem 1

MPC	Spending Multiplier	Tax Multiplier	Balanced Budget Multiplier
1/2	2	-1	1
3/5	2.5	-1.5	1
2/3	3	-2	1
3/4	4	-3	1
4/5	5	-4	1
5/6	6	-5	1
6/7	7	-6	1
7/8	8	-7	1
8/9	9	-8	1
9/10	10	-9	1

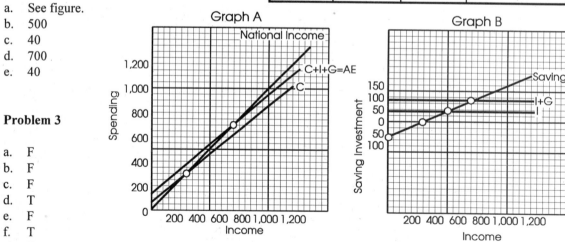

Problem 4

Before Government				After Government						
Y	C	S	I	G	T	Y-T	C_1	S_1	S_1+T	I+G
0	400	-400	100	200	200	-200	300	-500	-300	300
200	500	-300	100	200	200	0	400	-400	-200	300
400	600	-200	100	200	200	200	500	-300	-100	300
600	700	-100	100	200	200	400	600	-200	0	300
800	800	0	100	200	200	600	700	-100	100	300
1,000	900	100	100	200	200	800	800	0	200	300
1,200	1,000	200	100	200	200	1,000	900	100	300	300
1,400	1,100	300	100	200	200	1,200	1,000	200	400	300
1,600	1,200	400	100	200	200	1,400	1,100	300	500	300
1,800	1,300	500	100	200	200	1,600	1,200	400	600	300
2,000	1,400	600	100	200	200	1,800	1,300	500	700	300

a. See table.
b. 1000; saving and investment are equal at Y = 1000 without government
c. 1400; 300; I + G = S when Y = 1,400.
d. See table.
e. 1200
f. 200
g. See figure.

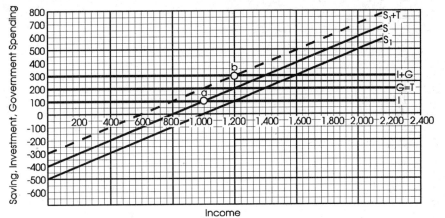

Problem 5

a. C = 300 +.75Y
b. S = -300 +.25Y
c. I = 100
d. G = 50
e. T = 50
f. C = 262.50 +.75Y; the consumption function is shifted down by the MPC x taxes or .75 X 50 = 37.50. Thus, autonomous consumption becomes 262.50 (300 - 37.50).
g. S = -312.50 +.25Y
h. Y = 1,650
   Y = C + I + G
   Y = 262.50 + .75Y + 100 + 50
   Y = 412.50 + .75Y
   Y - .75Y = 412.50
   Y = 412.50 /.25
   Y = 1,650.
i. C = 1,500   I = 100   G = 50   S = 100   T = 50
j. Balanced budget, since G = T

k. $I+G = S+T$

l. 1,690

m. $C = 232.50 + .75Y$

n. $S = -322.50 + .25Y$

o. $C = 1,500$ $I = 100$ $G = 90$ $S = 100$ $T = 90$

p. Balanced budget multiplier = $\Delta Y/(\Delta Ga = \Delta Ta) = 40/(40 = 40) = 1$ or $1/.25 - .75/.25 = 1$

Problem 6

a. (1) $S = I + G$
   $-100 + .2Y = 40 + 30$
   $-100 + .2Y = 70$
   $.2Y = 170$
   $Y = 170/.2 = 850$
   (2) $C = Y - S$
   $C = 850 - (-100 + .2(850))$
   $C = 850 + 100 - .2(850)$
   $C = 850 + 100 - 170$
   $C = 780$
   (3) $I = 30$
   (4) $G = 40$

b. Since we have more than sufficient spending to fully employ the economy we have an inflationary gap.

c. GNP gap = $700 - 850 = 150$; inflationary gap = $-150/5 = -30$, where the multiplier = 5

d. Our objective is to decrease national income by $150, so we must increase taxes. Since the tax multiplier is -4 (= -.8/.2), taxes need to be increased by $150/4 or $37.50.

e. $C = 630$ $I = 30$ $G = 40$ $Y = 700$.

Problem 7

a. $C = 7,150$ $I = 100$ $G = 250$ $Y = 7,500$ Calculated as follows:
   $Y = C + I + G$
   $Y = 400 + .9Y + 100 + 250$
   $Y - .9Y = 750$
   $.1Y = 750$
   $Y = 7,500$
   $C = 400 + .9(7,500) = 7,150$

b. Since the GNP gap is positive we know that there is deficient Aggregate Expenditures; therefore the situation is recessionary.

c. Since the full employment equilibrium equals 7,700, but the economy is currently in equilibrium at 7,500, Aggregate Expenditures must be increased so that the economy will expand by $200. Since the balanced budget multiplier always equals 1, the solution is to increase government expenditures by $200 and increase taxes by $200. The new values for the variables are: $Y = 7,700$ $C = 7,150$ $I = 100$ and $G = 450$. Note that even though total consumption is equal in the before and after situations the breakdown of autonomous and induced consumption is, in fact, different.

Chapter 12
Money And Its Creation

Chapter Objectives

After you have read and studied this chapter you should be able to describe the functions money performs in a market system; differentiate between alternative forms of money and definitions of the money supply; differentiate between potential money multipliers, actual money multipliers, and the monetary base; and explain how the interactions between banks and their customers determine the amount of money in circulation.

Chapter Review: Key Points

1. *Barter* requires a *double coincidence of wants*--trade can only occur if each party has what the other wants and if divisibility poses no problems.

2. *Money* ensures this double coincidence of wants--the seller will accept money because of what it will buy, while the buyer is willing to exchange money (and thus, all else it will buy) for the good or service in question.

3. Money facilitates specialization and exchange by decreasing transaction costs. The more sophisticated the financial system, the greater the level of production and consumption and the higher the standard of living.

4. Money is a *medium of exchange*. It is used for most transactions in monetary economies.

5. Money is a *measure of value*. Used as a standard unit of account, it is the common denominator for pricing goods and services.

6. Money is a *store of value*. It is among the most nominally secure of all assets people can use to hold their wealth.

7. Money is a *standard of deferred payment*. Serving as a link between the past, present, and future, it is used as a measure of *credit* to execute contracts calling for future payments.

8. *Liquidity* is negatively related to the transaction costs incurred in exchanges of assets. *Time, certainty regarding price, and the quality of information in a market* are all dimensions of liquidity. Assets are liquid if transaction costs are low, *illiquid* if transaction costs are high.

9. *Commodity monies* (precious metals, stones, or arrowheads) have values that are independent of what they will buy. *Fiat money* (paper currency) is valuable only because it is money; its use is based on *faith.*

10. The profit governments make from printing money or stamping coins is called *seignorage.*

11. According to Gresham's Law, "Bad money drives out good."

12. The very narrowly defined money supply (*M1*) is the total of: (*a*) *currency* (coins and bills) in the hands of the nonbanking public, plus (*b*) *demand deposits* (checking accounts of private individuals, firms, and nonfederal government units in financial institutions).

13. Some highly liquid assets are viewed as near-monies and are included in broader definitions of the money supply (*M2* and *M3*) by monetary analysts who believe the spending of the public can be predicted better if these assets are included. Examples of such highly liquid assets include short-term *time deposits* (savings accounts) and *certificates of deposit (CDs).* The assets included in "money supplies" defined more broadly than *M1* are judgmental because these assets are not mediums of exchange.

14. Banks "*create*" money through loan-based expansions of demand deposits (checking account money). They make loans based on currency they hold as reserves, and these loans take the form of new demand deposit money.

15. Banks hold *reserves* that are far less than their deposit liabilities. The larger the proportion of deposits held as either excess or required reserves, the smaller are the money multiplier and resulting money supply, given some fixed total amount of reserves.

16. The *potential money multiplier* (m_p) equals $1/rr$, where **rr** is the banking system's planned or legally required reserves as a percentage of deposits. The *actual money multiplier* is much smaller because: (*a*) households and firms hold currency that could be used as a base for the money creation process were this currency held in bank vaults as reserves against deposits; and (*b*) banks hold excess reserves to meet withdrawals of deposits.

17. The *actual money multiplier* (m_a) equals *MS/MB*, where *MS* is the money supply and *MB* is the *monetary base,* or high-powered money. Naturally, $MS = m_a MB$.

18. *Financial institutions* facilitate flows and payments of funds and provide secure places for savers' deposits. Their most important economic function is to channel funds from savers to financial investors and other borrowers through a process called *financial intermediation.* Commercial banks, savings and loan associations, mutual savings banks, credit unions, insurance companies, and stock exchanges are all financial intermediaries.

Matching Key Terms And Concepts

Set I

___ 1. credit

___ 2. money multiplier

___ 3. M1

___ 4. currency

___ 5. Federal Reserve System

___ 6. barter

___ 7. seignorage

___ 8. value of money

___ 9. M2, M3 and L

___ 10. liquidity

a. Created in 1913 to mitigate the impact of financial crises.

b. Extension of money; uses money as a standard of deferred payment.

c. Always equals one in a 100 percent reserve banking system.

d. Broader definitions of the money supply.

e. Currency plus "checkable" deposits.

f. Purchasing power of money.

g. Requires double coincidence of wants.

h. Coins and paper money.

i. Profits made by government when it prints or coins money.

j. Inversely related to the transactions costs incurred when an asset is bought or sold.

Set II

___ 1. measure of value

___ 2. potential money multiplier

___ 3. store of value

___ 4. reserves

___ 5. fiat money

___ 6. Gresham's Law

___ 7. medium of exchange

___ 8. actual money multiplier

___ 9. standard of deferred payment

___ 10. commodity money

a. Money as an asset.

b. Goods trade for money, and money trades for goods.

c. Money that is valuable in itself.

d. Money as a standard of credit.

e. $m_a = MS/MB$.

f. Standard unit of account.

g. "Bad money drives out good."

h. Money valued only for what it buys.

i. 1/(reserve requirement ratio).

j. Cash in bank vaults.

True/False Questions

_____ 1. Currency held in bank vaults is not included in the money supply.

_____ 2. The value of money and the cost of credit are both determined by supply and demand, much as the prices of other economic goods are determined.

_____ 3. Commodity money is valuable only because of its purchasing power, while fiat money has substantial value independently of what it will buy.

_____ 4. The most important service that money provides is that it is used to express the relative prices of goods.

_____ 5. Wealth is the monetary value of all of your assets.

_____ 6. Financial assets are liquid if trading them entails high transaction costs, but financial assets are illiquid if only low transaction costs would be incurred.

_____ 7. The amount of funds held in the vault to meet withdrawals of deposits are called the bank's reserves.

_____ 8. Money as a medium of exchange eliminates the need for a double coincidence of wants that would be required in a barter system before exchange occurred.

_____ 9. Standards of living tend to be very high in money-less economies.

_____ 10. Credit cards are a form of money.

Standard Multiple Choice

There Is One Best Answer For Each Question.

_____ 1. An asset's "liquidity" refers to:
  a. the transaction costs incurred in dealing in the asset.
  b. time it takes to convert it to cash.
  c. "backing" behind a financial asset.
  d. whether it may be bought or sold.
  e. whether the asset is water soluble.

_____ 2. Money is NOT a:
  a. medium of exchange.
  b. measure of value or standard unit of account.
  c. means of interpersonal utility comparison.
  d. store of value.
  e. standard of deferred payment.

_____ 3. "Bad money drives out good" according to:
  a. Gresham's Law.
  b. Say's Law.
  c. Fisher's Law.
  d. Keynes' Law.
  e. Friedman's Corollary.

_____ 4. An appropriate commodity money would NOT be:
  a. durable.
  b. divisible.
  c. optimally scarce.
  d. heterogeneous.
  e. portable.

___ 5. Fiat money has value because it is:
   a. backed by gold or silver.
   b. made of a precious metal.
   c. mandated by government to be accepted for payments.
   d. bereft of value as a commodity.
   e. None of the above.

___ 6. The number of relative prices in an n-good, barter economy is:
   a. n.
   b. n^2.
   c. $(n(n-1))/2$.
   d. 2^n.
   e. np.

___ 7. Relative to barter, money:
   a. facilitates specialization and exchange.
   b. increases the frequency of transactions.
   c. reduces transaction costs.
   d. finesses the "double coincidence of wants" requirement.
   e. All of these.

___ 8. A fractional reserve banking system relies most on:
   a. extensive government regulation.
   b. people keeping most of their money in banks.
   c. a stable money multiplier.
   d. a commodity base for money.
   e. None of these.

___ 9. The profits made by government when it prints/mints money are known as:
   a. exorbitant.
   b. fiat returns.
   c. legal tender.
   d. seignorage.
   e. budgetary revenue.

___10. If no currency exists outside bank vaults, and banks loan exactly 80 percent of total reserves, then there will be:
   a. "runs" on banks.
   b. five times as much money as reserves.
   c. excess liquidity.
   d. inflation.
   e. financial collapse.

___11. The potential value of the money multiplier equals:
   a. 1/mpc.
   b. 1/mps.
   c. 1/rr.
   d. $1/(rr + xr)$.
   e. 10rr.

___12. The actual money multiplier, m_a, is calculated as:
   a. -MPC/MPS.
   b. 1/rr.
   c. 1/(1-mpc).
   d. DM/Drr.
   e. MS/MB.

Chapter Review (Fill-In Questions)

1. In a(n) _____ economy, exchange occurs only when each trader has precisely what the other desires; that is, there must be a(n) _____ of wants.

2. As a _____, money provides a common denominator through which the relative prices of goods may be compared. As a _____, money is exchanged for goods, and goods are exchanged for money. As a _____, money is a relatively riskless way to hold your wealth. As a _____, money binds the past, the present, and the future, making contracts possible that call for future payments for goods delivered now.

3. _____ money has intrinsic value because it is made of something valuable, while _____ money is only valuable because of its purchasing power.

4. In a fractional reserve banking system, the ready cash in bank vaults, called _____, is far less than bank liabilities, or _____.

5. The money creation process occurs when banks receive new _____, which they then _____ to their customers.

6. The factor by which banks can expand a given amount of reserves into new demand deposits is called the _____. Its potential value is _____, where rr stands for the reserve requirement ratio. It reaches this potential value only when banks are _____ loaned-up, and when consumers and businesses hold _____.

7. When only a few banks have outflows of deposits so great that they may not be able to cover all of their liabilities instantly, they can sell _____ to other banks or borrow funds from banks having _____. The banking network facilitating these interbank borrowings is the _____ market. As a last resort, banks can borrow from the federal "bankers' bank," which is known as the _____.

Unlimited Multiple Choice

There May Be From Zero To Four Correct Answers To Each Question.

___ 1. In an economy characterized by barter:
   a. the costs of securing information about potentially profitable transactions are negligible.
   b. goods are exchanged for goods.
   c. transactions can only be carried out when there exists a double coincidence of wants.
   d. few of the advantages of specialization are ever realized.

___ 2. Money serves as a:
   a. medium of exchange.
   b. measure of value.
   c. store of value.
   d. common denominator by which relative prices are expressed.

3. The potential money multiplier:
   a. is always equal to one in a fractional reserve banking system.
   b. equals 1/reserve requirement ratio.
   c. indicates the extent to which demand deposits can be expanded as the result of an initial deposit.
   d. is equal to zero in a 100 percent reserve banking system.

4. Total deposits in any single bank are unlikely to be highly volatile because:
   a. flows of deposits between banks do not affect the total amounts of reserves in the banking system.
   b. the average daily amount in a given account is fairly stable on a month to month basis.

   c. most people have reasonably stable patterns of income and spending, and seldom allow their accounts to drop below some minimum value.
   d. few people use their checking accounts in purchasing goods.

5. Which measures (estimates) of money are correct?
   a. M1 = currency in the hands of the nonbanking public plus funds in "checkable" accounts.
   b. L = the total market value of all assets in an economy.
   c. M2 = M1 plus small time deposits.
   d. M3 = M2 plus gold, silver, and long-term negotiable bonds.

Problems

Problem 1

This table shows the initial T-account for a monopoly bank. Assume that the reserve requirement ratio is 20 percent. Also, assume that all money is held in the bank, and that the monopoly bank is a profit maximizer, which means that it will always expand loans (IOUs) by the maximum amount permitted by law. (Thus, the bank's excess reserves are always zero.)

Assets		Liabilities	
Cash Reserves	$1,000	Demand deposits	$5,000
Loans	$4,000		
	$5,000		$5,000

a. What is the size of the money multiplier? _____

b. Write the formula for the money multiplier. _____

c. Is this a fractional reserve banking system? _____ Why? _____

d. Assume that $2,000 is deposited in the monopoly bank. Balance the bank's T-account.

Assets	Liabilities
Cash Reserves	Demand deposits
Loans	

e. By how much will demand deposits increase? _____

f. By how much have loans increased? _____

g. Explain why the monopoly bank is able to expand its loans by the maximum amount permitted by law._____

h. Why won't this be true for each bank in a multi-bank example? _____.

Problem 2

This table shows the initial T-account for another monopoly bank. Assume a reserve requirement ratio of 10 percent. Also, assume that unless otherwise indicated, all money is held in this bank, which strives to always be fully loaned up. That is, desired excess reserves are always zero.

Assets		Liabilities	
Cash Reserves	$1,000	Demand deposits	$10,000
Loans	$9,000		
	$10,000		$10,000

a. What is the size of the money multiplier? _____

b. Write the formula for the money multiplier. _____

c. Assume that an additional $2,000 is deposited in our monopoly bank. Please balance the bank's T-account. By how much will demand deposits increase? _____

Assets	Liabilities
Cash Reserves	Demand deposits
Loans	

d. By how much will loans increase? _____

e. Assume $1,000 is now withdrawn from our monopoly bank. Balance the bank's T-account.

Assets	Liabilities
Cash Reserves	Demand deposits
Loans	

f. By how much will demand deposits decrease? _____

g. By how much will loans decrease? _____

h. Assume that $500 more is withdrawn. Please balance the bank's T-account.

Assets	Liabilities
Cash Reserves	Demand deposits
Loans	

i. By how much will demand deposits decrease? _____
    Why?_____

j. By how much will loans decrease? _____

k. What are total demand deposits? _____

l. Total cash reserves? _____

m. Total loans?_____

Problem 3

Suppose there are roughly 1,000 banks in our fractional reserve banking system, that the reserve requirement ratio is 20 percent, that each bank holds an extra 5 percent as excess reserves, and that the public holds no cash. Now assume that $2,000 is deposited in the first bank.

a. Show, using the first three banks in the system, how the money supply will increase as each bank expands its loans by the full amount of any reserves greater than 25 percent of deposits.

Bank 1

Assets	Liabilities
Reserves	Demand deposits
Required Reserves	
Excess Reserves	
Loans	

Bank 2

Assets	Liabilities
Reserves	Demand deposits
Required Reserves	
Excess Reserves	
Loans	

Bank 3

Assets	Liabilities
Reserves	Demand deposits
Required Reserves	
Excess Reserves	
Loans	

b. What is the size of the money multiplier? _____

c. By how much will demand deposits increase for the system as a whole? _____

d. By how much will loans increase for the system as a whole? _____

e. Why is money creation in a multi-bank world a cumulative process? _____

f. Why should each bank limit loans to only reserves in excess of 25% of deposits? _____

Problem 4

Assume (a) a required reserve ratio is 20%, (b) each bank quickly lends out any excess reserves, and (c) the non-banking public keeps all cash in banks. Consider an initial $2,000 cash deposit by a patron of bank "A." The bank retains the required reserve and loans out the excess reserve. Complete the table below for banks "B" through "H" and then sum the columns indicated as if this transaction had passed through 1,000 or more banks in the system.

Bank	Total Reserves	Required Reserves	Excess Reserves	Loan/Money Expansion
A	2,000.00	400.00	1,600.00	1,600.00
B	1,600.00			
C				
D				
E				
F				
G				
H		xxx	xxx	xxx
Entire System	xxx		xxx	

Problem 5

This problem is designed to help you practice the various values that a money multiplier might take. In order to complete the table assume that there is a large banking system (1,000 or more banks). Additionally assume that the banks always hold enough reserves to exceed the required reserve ratio by 5%. For example, if the required reserve ratio were 25% the banks would, in reality, hold 30%. Assume that the non-banking public holds no cash reserves.

Deposit	Required Reserve Ratio	Actual Money Multiplier	Single Bank Expansion	Total Expansion By All Banks
2,000	.20			
1,000	.15			
5,000	.1166			
3,500	.05			
500	.075			

Problem 6

Required Reserve Ratio	Potential Money Multiplier	Potential Money Supply	Actual Money Multiplier	Actual Money Supply
1/10				
1/9				
1/8				
1/7				
1/6				
1/5				
1/4				

a. Fill in the potential money multiplier column.

b. Fill in the potential money supply column if there are $1 million in bank reserves (no loans have been made yet), and $1 million in currency held by the public.

c. Fill in the actual money multiplier column if banks hold ten percent (.10) in excess reserves.

d. Fill in the actual money supply column, using the information you just calculated about the actual money multiplier, and assuming that $1 million in reserves sits in banks, and that the public holds $1 million in currency.

ANSWERS

	Matching		True/False	Multiple	Unlimited	Fill-In
	Set I	Set II				

<table>
<tr><td colspan="2">Matching</td><td>True/False</td><td>Multiple</td><td>Unlimited</td><td>Fill-In</td></tr>
<tr><td>Set I</td><td>Set II</td><td></td><td></td><td></td><td></td></tr>
<tr><td>1. b</td><td>1. f</td><td>1. T</td><td>1. a</td><td>1. bcd</td><td>1. barter; double</td></tr>
<tr><td>2. c</td><td>2. i</td><td>2. T</td><td>2. c</td><td>2. abcd</td><td>coincidence</td></tr>
<tr><td>3. e</td><td>3. a</td><td>3. F</td><td>3. a</td><td>3. bc</td><td>2. standard unit of account;</td></tr>
<tr><td>4. h</td><td>4. j</td><td>4. F</td><td>4. d</td><td>4. bc</td><td>medium of exchange;</td></tr>
<tr><td>5. a</td><td>5. h</td><td>5. F</td><td>5. c</td><td>5. ac</td><td>store of value; standard</td></tr>
<tr><td>6. g</td><td>6. g</td><td>6. F</td><td>6. c</td><td></td><td>of deferred payment</td></tr>
<tr><td>7. i</td><td>7. b</td><td>7. T</td><td>7. e</td><td></td><td>3. commodity; fiat</td></tr>
<tr><td>8. f</td><td>8. e</td><td>8. T</td><td>8. b</td><td></td><td>4. reserves; deposits</td></tr>
<tr><td>9. d</td><td>9. d</td><td>9. F</td><td>9. d</td><td></td><td>5. deposits; loan</td></tr>
<tr><td>10. j</td><td>10. c</td><td>10. F</td><td>10. b</td><td></td><td>6. money multiplier; 1/rr;</td></tr>
<tr><td></td><td></td><td></td><td>11. c</td><td></td><td>fully; no cash</td></tr>
<tr><td></td><td></td><td></td><td>12. e</td><td></td><td>7. loans; excess reserves;</td></tr>
<tr><td></td><td></td><td></td><td></td><td></td><td>federal funds; FED</td></tr>
</table>

Problem 1

a. 5
b. $m_p = 1/rr = 1/.20 = 5$.
c. Yes; bank holds less than 100% against deposit liabilities.
d. See table
e. $10,000
f. $8,000
g. Monopolist doesn't have to worry about withdrawn money not returning.
h. Flows between banks in multi-bank systems prevent each from making maximum loans.

Assets		Liabilities	
Cash Reserves	$3,000	Demand deposits	$15,000
Loans	$12,000		
	$15,000		$15,000

Problem 2

a. 10
b. $m_p = 1/rr = 1/.10 = 10$
c. See table; $20,000
d. $18,000
e. See table
f. $10,000
g. $9,000
h. See table
i. $5,000; the bank rebuilds reserves by not renewing old loans or offering new ones as old ones are repaid.
j. $4,500   l. $1,500
k. $15,000   m. $13,500

Assets		Liabilities	
Cash Reserves	$3,000	Demand deposits	$30,000
Loans	$27,000		
	$30,000		$30,000

Assets		Liabilities	
Cash Reserves	$2,000	Demand deposits	$20,000
Loans	$18,000		
	$20,000		$20,000

Assets		Liabilities	
Cash Reserves	$1,500	Demand deposits	$15,000
Loans	$13,500		
	$15,000		$15,000

a. See table
b. 4
c. Demand deposits = $8,000
d. Loans = $6,000
e. Each bank loans a portion ((1-(rr + xr)) of its demand deposits, which in turn become demand deposits in another bank. These "new" deposits then form the basis for more lending, which continues the money creation process.
f. Each bank needs to hold on to reserves in order to meet withdrawals by customers.

Bank 1			
Assets		Liabilities	
Reserves	$500	Demand deposits	$2,000
Required Reserves	$400		
Excess Reserves	$100		
Loans	$1,500		

Bank 2			
Assets		Liabilities	
Reserves	$375	Demand deposits	$1,500
Required Reserves	$300		
Excess Reserves	$75		
Loans	$1,125		

Bank 3			
Assets		Liabilities	
Reserves	$281.25	Demand deposits	$1,125
Required Reserves	$225		
Excess Reserves	$56.25		
Loans	$843.75		

Problem 4

Bank	Total Reserves	Required Reserves	Excess Reserves	Loan/Money Expansion
A	2,000.00	400.00	1,600.00	1,600.00
B	1,600.00	320.00	1,280.00	1,280.00
C	1,280.00	256.00	1,024.00	1,024.00
D	1,024.00	204.80	819.20	819.20
E	819.20	163.84	655.36	655.36
F	655.36	131.07	524.29	524.29
G	524.29	104.86	419.43	419.43
H	419.43	xxx	xxx	xxx
Entire System	xxx	2,000.00	xxx	10,000.00

Problem 5

Deposit	Required Reserve Ratio	Actual Money Multiplier	Single Bank Expansion	Total Expansion By All Banks
2,000	.20	4	1,500.00	8,000
1,000	.15	5	800.00	5,000
5,000	.1166	6	4,166.66	30,000
3,500	.05	10	3,150.00	35,000
500	.075	8	437.50	4,000

Problem 6

Required Reserve Ratio	Potential Money Multiplier	Potential Money Supply	Actual Money Multiplier	Actual Money Supply
1/10	10	$11 mil.	5	$6.0 mil.
1/9	9	$10 mil.	4.7	$5.7 mil.
1/8	8	$9 mil.	4.4	$5.4 mil.
1/7	7	$8 mil.	4.1	$5.1 mil.
1/6	6	$7 mil.	3.8	$4.8 mil.
1/5	5	$6 mil.	3.3	$4.3 mil.
1/4	4	$5 mil.	2.9	$3.9 mil.

Chapter 13
The Federal Reserve System

Chapter Objectives

After you have read and studied this chapter you should be able to describe the purposes of a central bank such as the Federal Reserve System (FED); discuss the FED's primary and secondary tools and how these tools may be used; evaluate the effects of various regulations on the efficiency of the financial sector, and distinguish various types of financial intermediaries.

Chapter Review: Key Points

1. Because fractional reserve banking makes it impossible for all banks to pay all demand deposits simultaneously, government action may help resolve monetary crises. The *central bank* of a country: (a) controls the volume of money in circulation, (b) performs the government's banking functions, (c) serves as a "bankers' bank," and (d) regulates banks and other financial institutions. The central bank of the United States is the *Federal Reserve System*, or *FED*.

2. The value of the potential money multiplier (m_p) is the reciprocal of the *reserve-requirement ratio (1/rr)*. Excess reserves in the financial system and cash holdings by the public are drains on the potential multiplier. The actual multiplier (m_a) equals the *monetary base* (*MB*) -- the currency and bank reserves issued by the FED divided into the money supply (*MS*):

$$m_a = MS/MB.$$

3. The *FED's* most powerful but least used tool is its control of reserve requirements (*rr*). Raising *rr* reduces money multipliers and the money supply, and vice versa.

4. The most useful tool of the FED is *open-market operations (OMO)*. After all adjustments, open-market operations affect the monetary base, not the money multiplier. When the FED sells bonds, both bank reserves and the money supply decline. FED purchases of bonds increase bank reserves and the money supply.

5. The *discount rate (d)* is the interest rate the FED charges member banks. When the discount rate is low relative to market interest, banks hold fewer excess reserves and borrow from the FED. Consequently, the money supply grows. High discount rates relative to market interest rates cause banks to borrow less from the FED and to hold more excess reserves. The actual money multiplier and total bank reserves fall, and the money supply falls.

Matching Key Terms And Concepts

___ 1. moral suasion

___ 2. reserve requirements

___ 3. discount rate

___ 4. excess reserves

___ 5. open market operations

___ 6. margin requirements

___ 7. financial efficiency

___ 8. Federal Open Market Committee

___ 9. federal funds market

___ 10. central bank

a. The FED's most powerful tool.

b. Legal reserves minus required reserves.

c. Minimum differences between interest rates charged and received.

d. Interest rate banks have to pay the FED.

e. Sets policies for trading in U.S. bonds to vary the money supply.

f. The FED's most useful tool.

g. Sets "down payments" on purchases of stock.

h. Exercising persuasive powers to induce changed behavior.

i. Interbank lending of excess reserves.

j. Government's bank and "lender of last resort."

True/False Questions

___ 1. Independently of FED policies, banks influence the money supply through variations in their holdings of excess reserves.

___ 2. If the FED buys more bonds than it sells, total bank reserves are increased and the money supply grows.

___ 3. Banks will generally want to hold the same percent of excess reserves against demand deposits regardless of the reserve requirement ratio, since the percentage fluctuations of bank deposits depend on people's behavior rather than on the Federal Reserve System's reserve requirements.

___ 4. The Federal Reserve System's Open Market Committee has no influence over the total amount of currency in circulation.

___ 5. Banks and other financial intermediaries are less closely supervised than auto makers.

___ 6. The reserve requirement ratio is the FED's most powerful tool.

___ 7. If the FED decided to reduce the money supply, it could buy bonds from commercial banks.

___ 8. In the 1920's, you could purchase stock "on margin" with a down payment of as little as 10 percent.

___ 9. The Chairman of the Board of Governors is the real power in the FED.

___ 10. Lowering the discount rate encourages banks to borrow money from the FED.

Standard Multiple Choice

There Is One Best Answer For Each Question.

___ 1. If the FED sells bonds to banks:
    a. total bank reserves increase.
    b. the money supply decreases.
    c. the money supply increases.
    d. it offsets such policies by cutting reserve requirements.
    e. All of the above.

___ 2. The most powerful tool at the FED's disposal is:
    a. the ability to set reserve requirements.
    b. the discount rate.
    c. open market operations.
    d. moral suasion.
    e. margin requirements.

___ 3. If bankers want to retain reserves of 25 percent against all deposits, if the FED issues $100 billion in currency, and if private individuals keep all money in banks, then, once banks are "fully loaned-up" the money supply will be comprised of:
    a. $400 billion in demand deposits.
    b. $100 billion in currency + $300 billion in DDs.
    c. no additional loans could be made if the FED printed more currency.
    d. $2,500 billion in cash and DDs.
    e. None of the above.

___ 4. The most effective and efficient tool of the FED is:
    a. the reserve requirement.
    b. discount operations.
    c. margin requirements.
    d. open market operations.
    e. moral suasion.

___ 5. The FED attempts to control stock speculation through:
    a. reserve requirements.
    b. margin requirements.
    c. discount operations.
    d. moral suasion.
    e. open market operations.

___ 6. The FED's reserve requirement ratio:
    a. is its most powerful monetary tool.
    b. aids in stabilizing the money multiplier.
    c. reduces the value of the money multiplier.
    d. reduces the money supply relative to the monetary base.
    e. All of these.

___ 7. The FED's "margin requirements" refer to:
    a. down payments on stock.
    b. bank capitalization requirements.
    c. interest rate ceilings.
    d. credit controls.
    e. buying U.S. government bonds.

___ 8. A major purpose of the FED is to:
    a. print money to cover all government spending not covered by tax revenues.
    b. set interest rate ceilings as low as possible.
    c. act as a "lender of last resort."
    d. ensure the profitability of commercial banks.
    e. ensure the liquidity of social assets.

9. The most powerful entity in the Federal Reserve system is the:
   a. Director of Open Market Operations.
   b. President of the New York Federal Reserve Bank.
   c. Chairman of the FED.
   d. Unified District Bank Presidents.
   e. Reserve Requirements Regulator.

10. The Federal Reserve System is:
    a. privately owned and operated.
    b. extremely profitable for its investors.
    c. the tax collector for all government agencies.
    d. the central bank of the United States.
    e. the core of the International Monetary Fund (IMF).

Chapter Review (Fill-In Questions)

1. Although it is not especially useful, the FED's most powerful tool is its ability to set _____. By lowering this tool, the FED initially causes banks to have _____.

2. When the FED reduces the required reserve ratio, banks extend new loans, the _____ grows, and the _____ expands.

3. In the long run, however, changing the required reserve ratio does not affect total legal reserves, nor is the division between excess reserves and required reserves affected. Thus, changes in reserve requirements operate primarily by causing changes in the _____. Hikes in the reserve requirements ratio would cause a _____ in the money supply.

4. The FED may also change its policies about extending loans to banks, a tool known as _____. The interest rate the FED charges banks is called the _____ rate.

5. The FED's most useful tool, _____ _____ operations, is utilized when the FED, through the "open market" trading desk in New York, sells some of the U.S. Treasury bonds in its portfolio. Banks expand their holdings of bonds, but _____ in the banking system decline. Consequently, the money supply falls when banks reduce _____.

Unlimited Multiple Choice

There Are From Zero To Four Correct Answers For Each Question.

____ 1. When commercial banks:
   a. are faced with higher discount rates, they lend more money to the FED, shrinking their excess reserves and expanding the money supply.
   b. receive higher margin requirements, they increase lending.
   c. confront lower reserve requirements ratios, they create more money from a given monetary base.
   d. buy bonds from the FED, bank reserves are decreased, and the banking system will decrease loan-based demand deposits.

____ 2. Open market operations:
   a. involve the buying and selling of government bonds.
   b. are a secondary tool of the FED.
   c. enable the FED to increase or decrease the money supply.
   d. are used when other FED tools fail.

____ 3. Central banks commonly:
   a. act as "lenders of last resort."
   b. control monetary policies where they operate.
   c. collect taxes like the Internal Revenue Service under their direct control.
   d. determine tax rates and collect revenues for governments.

____ 4. The discount rate:
   a. represents the most powerful tool wielded by the FED to control the money supply.
   b. is seldom changed.
   c. is generally changed to reflect changes in market interest rates and the federal funds rate.
   d. is a secondary tool which is seldom used.

____ 5. When the required reserve ratio is lowered:
   a. the potential money multiplier decreases.
   b. the actual money multiplier decreases.
   c. banks tend to decrease loans.
   d. the monetary base increases.

Problems

Problem 1

In each box of this table indicate how the variable would change based on the events described in a through d. Write "increase," "decrease," "unchanged," or "indeterminate" as appropriate.

	Total Bank Reserves	Monetary Base	Potential Money Multiplier	Actual Money Multiplier	Money Supply
a					
b					
c					
d					

a.   The long-run effect if the FED sells bonds.

b.   The long-run effect if the FED raises the discount rate.

c.   The long-run effect if the FED raises reserve requirements.

d.   The long-run effect if the public wants more currency relative to deposits.

Problem 2

Without looking at your responses to Problem 1, fill in this table according to questions a-d. Write the word increase, decrease, unchanged, or indeterminate in the box as appropriate.

	Total Bank Reserves	Monetary Base	Potential Money Multiplier	Actual Money Multiplier	Money Supply
a					
b					
c					
d					

a.   The long-run effect if the FED buys bonds.

b.   The long-run effect if the FED lowers the discount rate.

c.   The long-run effect if the FED decreases reserve requirements.

d.   The long-run effect if the public wants less currency relative to deposits.

Problem 3

In the T-account provided, illustrate the balance sheet of the Federal Reserve Bank and a Member Bank when the Federal Reserve Bank sells $2,000 in securities to the Member Bank.

Federal Reserve Bank		Member Bank	
Assets	Liabilities	Assets	Liabilities
_____ Treasury Bonds	_____ Reserves	_____ Loanable _____ Treasury	

Problem 4

Use the knowledge you have acquired in this chapter to fill in the table.

	Monetary Base	Reserve Requirement Ratio	Potential Money Multiplier	Potential Money Supply
a	$1 billion	1/6		
b	$8 billion		5	
c		1/7		$700 billion
d			6	$100 billion

ANSWERS

Matching	True/False	Multiple Choice	Unlimited MC	Fill-In
1. h	1. T	1. b	1. cd	1. reserve requirements; excess reserves
2. a	2. T	2. a	2. ac	2. money multiplier; money supply
3. d	3. T	3. a	3. ab	3. money multiplier; reduction
4. b	4. F	4. d	4. c	4. discounting operations; discount
5. f	5. F	5. b	5. none	5. open market; reserves; loans
6. g	6. T	6. e		
7. c	7. F	7. a		
8. e	8. T	8. c		
9. i	9. T	9. c		
10. j	10. T	10. d		

Problem 1

	Total Bank Reserves	Monetary Base	Potential Money Multiplier	Actual Money Multiplier	Money Supply
a	decrease	decrease	unchanged	unchanged	decrease
b	decrease	decrease	unchanged	decrease	decrease
c	unchanged	unchanged	decrease	decrease	decrease
d	decrease	unchanged	unchanged	decrease	decrease

Problem 2

	Total Bank Reserves	Monetary Base	Potential Money Multiplier	Actual Money Multiplier	Money Supply
a	increase	increase	unchanged	unchanged	increase
b	increase	increase	unchanged	increase	increase
c	unchanged	unchanged	increase	increase	increase
d	increase	unchanged	unchanged	increase	increase

Problem 3

Federal Reserve Bank		Member Bank	
Assets	Liabilities	Assets	Liabilities
-$2,000 Treasury	-$2,000 Reserves held	-$2,000 Loanable +$2,000 Treasury bonds	

Problem 4

	Monetary Base	Reserve Requirement Ratio	Potential Money Multiplier	Potential Money Supply
a	$1 billion	1/6	6	$6 billion
b	$8 billion	1/5	5	$40 billion
c	$100 billion	1/7	7	$700 billion
d	$16.67 billion	1/6	6	$100 billion

Chapter 14
Monetary Theory and Policy

Chapter Objectives

After you have read and studied this chapter, you should be able to differentiate between the classical, Keynesian, and modern monetarist approaches to the demand for money; explain how variations in the quantity of money might influence macroeconomic activity, given various states of the economy; and explain why interest rates and bond prices are inversely related.

Chapter Review: Key Points

1. You increase your *spending* when you have "too much" money; your rate of *saving* increases when you have "too little" money.

2. People hold money for predictable spending (*transactions demands*) with a cushion for uncertain outlays or income receipts (*precautionary demands*). People also have *asset demands* for money because: (*a*) money is relatively riskless, (*b*) transaction costs associated with less liquid assets may exceed expected returns, or (*c*) people speculate by holding money when they expect the prices of alternative assets (e.g., stocks, bonds, or real estate) to fall.

3. According to classical monetary theory, the sole rational motive for holding money is *to consummate transactions.*

4. Interest rates and bond prices are *inversely related.* Bond prices fall if interest rates rise, and vice versa.

5. The costs of holding nominal amounts of money are: (*a*) *the reciprocal of the price level (1/P)* if the choice is between saving money or buying consumer goods; or (*b*) *the interest rate*, if money is viewed as an asset substitutable for some highly liquid income-generating asset, say a bond. *Inflation* also imposes costs on holdings of money.

6. The *income velocity* (*V*) of money equals GDP (or $P \times Q$) divided by the money supply (*M*).

7. The *equation of exchange,* a truism, is written $MV = PQ$. Therefore, the percentage change in the money supply plus the percentage change in velocity roughly equals the percentage change in the price level plus the percentage change in real output:

$$\frac{\Delta M}{M} + \frac{\Delta V}{V} = \frac{\Delta P}{P} + \frac{\Delta Q}{Q}$$

8. Classical economics assumes that *velocity* (*V*) and *output (Q)* are reasonably constant and independent of the money supply (*M*) and the price level (*P*). Classical economists believe that changes in the money supply result in proportional changes in the price level and expressed this belief in early versions of the *quantity theory of money.* The quantity theory of money is more accurately a *monetary theory of the price level.*

9. Keynes's attack on the quantity theory disputes the assumptions that: (*a*) the natural state of the economy is full employment, (*b*) the velocity of money is inherently stable, and (*c*) the only rational motive for holding money is for transactions purposes.

10. Modern monetarists perceive a direct link between the money supply and national income. Since the demand for money is relatively stable, monetary growth puts excess money balances in the hands of consumers and investors who, in turn, spend this surplus money on output. Monetary growth may temporarily expand output, but monetarists conclude that in the long run, higher prices will result.

11. Advocates of eliminating *discretionary policy* and relying on *monetary growth rules* would replace the FED's Open-Market Committee with unimaginative but reliable clerks who would increase the money supply at a fixed small (3 percent?) amount annually, with the federal budget being set to balance at full employment.

Matching Key Terms And Concepts

____ 1. hoarding

____ 2. crude quantity theory of money

____ 3. transaction demand

____ 4. precautionary demand

____ 5. asset demand

____ 6. real money balances

____ 7. liquidity trap

____ 8. income velocity of money

____ 9. opportunity cost of money

____ 10. equation of exchange

a. Causes income velocity of money to decrease.
b. Arises because of transaction costs, risk aversion, and speculation that interest rates might rise soon.
c. Horizontal money demand curve; might occur if people expected currently low interest rates to rise sharply and very soon.
d. Varies directly with income and inversely with the frequency with which people receive income.
e. Positively related both to income and to uncertainty about future purchases.
f. Assumes $\Delta Q/Q = \Delta V/V = 0$, so that the price level is proportional to the nominal money supply.
g. The interest rate if the alternative to holding money is buying bonds; 1/CPI if the next best alternative is consumption.
h. GDP/M.
i. MV = PQ.
j. M/P.

True/False Questions

___ 1. According to classical theory, any changes in the money supply will be reflected in proportional changes in the price level.

___ 2. In classical theory, the interest rate determines the level of saving, while in Keynesian theory, the interest rate determines the composition of an income-determined level of saving.

___ 3. Variations in the money supply affect investment similarly in the classical and Keynesian theoretical models.

___ 4. Keynesian and classical economists agree that equilibrium investment occurs when the rates of return on investment projects are equal to the prevailing market rate of interest.

___ 5. According to John Maynard Keynes, expansionary monetary policy propels an economy out of a depression.

___ 6. Keynesian economists believe investors' expectations about rates of return to be quite stable, and explain wide swings in investment as responses to small changes in interest rates.

___ 7. Classical economic models allow the possibility that a market economy could be in equilibrium at less than full employment.

___ 8. Milton Friedman argues that the demand for money varies inversely with the interest rate on bonds, the rate of return on physical capital, and the expected rate of inflation.

___ 9. Most Keynesian models ignore the institutional mechanisms used to create money.

___10. The Monetarist prescription for a healthy economy is active federal management of Aggregate Demand.

Standard Multiple Choice

There Is One Best Answer To Each Question.

___ 1. The total demand for money does not include:
   a. transactions demands.
   b. stocks and bonds.
   c. asset demands.
   d. precautionary demands.
   e. Any of these.

___ 2. The crude "Quantity Theory of Money" did NOT:
   a. assume full employment.
   b. assume velocity was erratic.
   c. predict money and the price level to be proportional.
   d. blame inflation on too much monetary growth.
   e. rely heavily on the transactions demand for money.

___ 3. Precautionary demands originate in:
   a. people's desires to "cushion" against the unexpected.
   b. fear that interest rates will rise.
   c. fear that prices will rise.
   d. expectations of economic booms.
   e. fears of stock market crashes.

___ 4. People will hold more money if they expect:
   a. the average price level to rise.
   b. interest rates on bonds to fall.
   c. interest rates on bonds to rise.
   d. tremendous economic growth.
   e. to be paid more frequently.

___ 5. The person most responsible for the reemergence of monetarism during the past quarter century is:
   a. Paul Samuelson.
   b. John Maynard Keynes.
   c. John Kenneth Galbraith.
   d. Milton Friedman.
   e. Irving Fisher.

___ 6. We can infer that you have too little money if you:
   a. are a typical college student.
   b. must spend money as quickly as you receive it.
   c. wear rags and eat cheap food.
   d. increase the amount of cash you save from each paycheck.
   e. use credit cards extensively.

___ 7. People's money-holdings tend to grow if there are increases in:
   a. the expected rate of inflation.
   b. interest rates paid on money.
   c. interest rates on bonds.
   d. the average purchasing power of each dollar (1/CPI).
   e. access to easy credit.

___ 8. The asset demand for money will increase if:
   a. for a given expected return, the risk of holding other assets rises.
   b. people desire increased liquidity.
   c. the interest rate is expected to rise.
   d. bond prices are expected to fall.
   e. All of the above.

___ 9. The transaction demand for money is most closely related to its use as a:
   a. medium of exchange.
   b. standard unit of account.
   c. measure of value.
   d. store of value.
   e. standard of deferred payment.

___ 10. Keynesian monetary theory assumes that the cost of holding money is:
   a. 1/CPI.
   b. CPI.
   c. the interest rates on bonds.
   d. the interest banks pay to owners of demand deposits.
   e. the realized rate of inflation.

___ 11. The Equation of Exchange is written:
   a. $MQ = PV$.
   b. $M = QVP$.
   c. $MV = PQ$.
   d. $V = PQ/M$.
   e. $\Delta M/M + \Delta V/V = \Delta P/P + \Delta Q/Q$.

___ 12. In a "liquidity trap," expansionary monetary policies:
   a. rapidly cure inflationary pressures.
   b. primarily affect people's money holdings.
   c. cut interest rates and boost investment and thus, Aggregate Demand.
   d. quickly pull a sluggish economy out of the doldrums.
   e. create new inflationary pressures.

Chapter Review (Fill-In Questions)

1. Why do people want to hold money? Perhaps the most important motive is the _____ demand for money, which arises because people expect that they will make certain outlays of money in the near future.

2. Uncertainty about future expenditures creates a _____ demand for money. Finally, uncertainty about the future values of potential investments generates the _____ demand for money.

3. Part of this last source of the demand for money is fear that _____ will rise. _____ fall when interest rates rise, so bondholders lose. Keynes identified this part of the asset demand for money as the _____ demand for money.

4. Aversion to _____ and _____ costs are other foundations of the asset demand for money.

5. Classical economists had focused on the _____ demand for money, which is directly related to _____ and negatively related to the frequencies of receipts and payments.

6. Irving Fisher helped formalize classical monetary theory by developing the Equation of _____, which is written _____.

7. Keynes introduced the _____ motive for holding money, which is reasonably compatible with classical theory, and the _____ demand for money, which raised the possibility that even huge increases in the money supply might be _____ rather than spent if the economy were caught in a _____.

8. Keynes argued that _____ is much influenced by the "animal spirits of investors" and relatively insensitive to variations in _____.

9. According to the Keynesian _____, expansion of the money supply only influences autonomous spending by reducing interest slightly, which stimulates _____ slightly, which then, through the multiplier principle, increases Aggregate Expenditures somewhat.

Unlimited Multiple Choice

There Are From Zero To Four Correct Answers For Each Question.

___ 1. Classical economists contend that the:
a. income velocity of money is reasonably constant.
b. quantity of money demanded varies inversely with the interest rate.
c. investment demand is highly sensitive to changes in the expectations of firms.
d. market system is inherently unstable.

___ 2. Modern Monetarists believe that the:
a. demand for money is a positive function of income.
b. demand for money varies inversely with the amount of human capital as a percentage of total wealth.
c. expected rate of inflation does not influence the demand for money.
d. basic cause of instability in a market economy is erratic governmental policy.

___ 3. The crude quantity theory of money:
a. posits that market economies never deviate much from full-employment levels of output.
b. assumes that velocity is reasonably constant.
c. treats velocity as unaffected by the price level, by the level of real output, and by the nominal money supply.
d. posits that people hold money only to consummate transactions.

___ 4. According to the Keynesian monetary transmission mechanism:
a. an increase in the nominal money supply makes people feel wealthier, and they eliminate their excess holdings of money by spending more on goods immediately.
b. an increase in the money supply causes the interest rate to decrease, resulting in an increase in investment and then income.
c. changes in the money supply will affect consumer spending directly.
d. money's effect on interest rates induce changes in aggregate spending.

___ 5. Both Keynesian and classical writers:
a. agree that very high rates of investment lead to somewhat lower rates of return, but disagree about how fast this occurs.
b. believe that investment will occur as long as the expected rate of return to investment at least equals the interest rate.
c. believe that interest rates are determined in the money market.
d. view economic transactors as confronted by much uncertainty.

Problems

Problem 1

Fill in the blanks for interest rates, annual payments, bond prices, etc., so that the following statements are true.

a. An interest rate equaling _____ percent would make perpetual annual payments of $5,000 worth $100,000 today.

b. A perpetual bond would be worth _____ if the interest rate were 12.5 percent annually and the bond paid $2,000 each year.

c. A perpetual bond would need to yield annual payments of roughly _____ to be worth $10,000 if the interest rate were 16.67 percent.

d. If a perpetual bond is priced at $70,000 and pays $10,500 annually, the interest rate yielded is _____ percent.

e. An annual after-tax rental value of a parcel of property equaling $30,000 combined with a current interest rate of 10 percent would make its present value _____.

f. A National Football League franchise costing $12 million is worth buying if the current interest rate is 12 percent and it is forecast to generate _____ million annually after all other expenses.

Problem 2

Use the equation of exchange to answer the following questions.

a. Suppose the money supply grows by 12% and real output grows by 3%, but the income velocity of money is constant. What happens to the price level? _____

b. If potential output grows by 2% while velocity falls by 3%, what rate of monetary growth should keep the price level stable? _____

c. If average prices are rising 20% annually while monetary growth is 12% in a stagnant economy, what is happening to velocity? _____

d. If both velocity and the price level fall by 8% while real output drops 15%, what must be happening to the money supply? _____

Problem 3

Illustrate the Keynesian transmission mechanism in these graphs. Note the steep slope of the investment demand function. Use primes (') to illustrate an expansionary monetary policy.

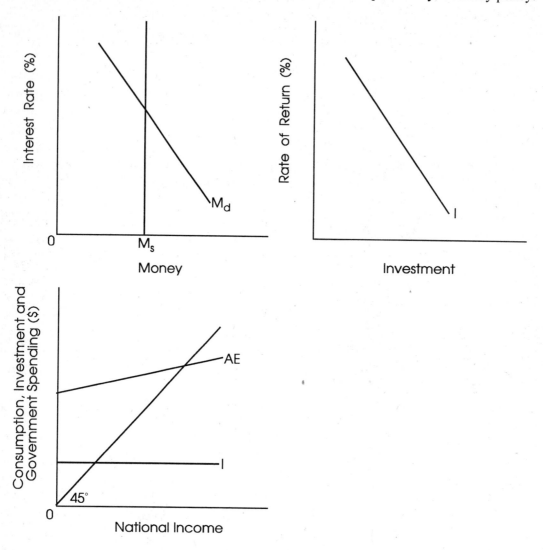

Problem 4

Now that you have developed this Keynesian linkage perhaps a numerical example would be helpful. Suppose that the FED buys $5 million in treasury bonds from the banking system. If the required reserve ratio is 10%, all the banks are fully loaned up, and the non-banking public holds no cash;

a. What is the actual money supply expansion? _____

b. Assume that the money demand curve is linear over the relevant range. If an increase of $20 million in the money supply decreases the interest by 1%, how much will the interest rate decrease? _____

c. Suppose the investment demand curve is linear and that a 1% decrease in the interest rate increases investment by $1 million. How much will investment increase? _____

d. If the MPC = .8, how much will equilibrium income increase? _____

ANSWERS

Matching	True/False	Multiple Choice	Unlimited MC	Fill-In
1. a	1. T	1. b	1. a	1. transactions
2. f	2. T	2. b	2. ad	2. precautionary; asset
3. d	3. F	3. a	3. abcd	3. interest rates; bond prices;
4. e	4. T	4. c	4. bd	speculative
5. b	5. F	5. d	5. ab	4. risk; transactions
6. j	6. F	6. d		5. transactions; income
7. c	7. F	7. b		6. Exchange; MV = PQ
8. h	8. T	8. e		7. precautionary; asset;
9. g	9. F	9. a		hoarded; liquidity trap
10. i	10. F	10. c		8. investment; interest rates
		11. c		9. monetary transmission
		12. b		investment

Problem 1

a. 5
b. $16,000
c. $1,667
d. 15
e. $300,000
f. $1.44

Problem 2

a. P increases by 9%.
b. M equals 5% to stabilize the price level.
c. V increases by 8%.
d. M decreases by 15%.

Problem 3

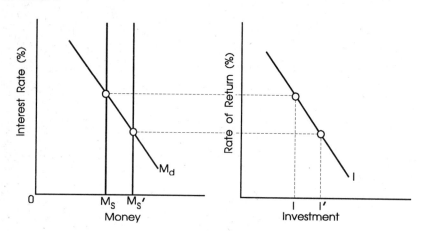

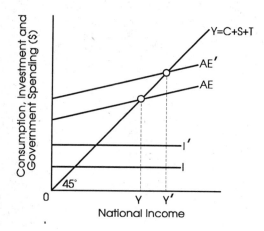

Problem 4

a. $50 million
b. 2.5%
c. $2.5 million
d. $12.5 million

Chapter 15
Budget Deficits and Public Debt

Chapter Objectives

After reading and studying this chapter you should be able to describe problems encountered in balancing the budget; discuss the `crowding out' hypothesis; differentiate between government and private budget constraints; and evaluate the impact of national debt on future generations.

Chapter Review: Key Points

1. The *budget deficit* equals annual government outlays minus receipts. The *public debt* is total federal indebtedness resulting from current and past deficits.

2. *Balancing the budget annually* might result in incorrect fiscal actions to combat either inflation or recession. Some have suggested balancing the budget *over the business cycle*. This would entail running deficits during recessions and surpluses over the boom. Unfortunately, business cycles are not symmetric, and the budget may not be easy to balance over the cycle without hampering prosperity. Advocates of *functional finance* believe that the size of the public debt is unimportant. They suggest that we ignore the problem of balancing the budget and focus on balancing the economy instead.

3. The federal government can finance *public spending* by collecting taxes (T), creating additional monetary base (ΔMB), selling government securities (ΔB), or through confiscation. All of these techniques are drains on *gross private saving* (production minus private consumption) that can crowd out private economic activities. The notion called *Ricardian equivalence* suggests that whether government spending is financed by taxes or borrowing is irrelevant.

4. The *crowding-out hypothesis* states that increases in government purchases inevitably reduces private consumption, investment, or leisure.

5. Federal deficits can be financed by increasing domestic saving, securing the savings of foreigners, or by reducing domestic investment or exports. All else constant, a growing budget deficit will cause growth of a trade deficit.

6. Some government spending is *uncontrollable* (now estimated at 75%). These programs are long-range or are committed by law each and every year. Reducing such outlays may be impossible.

7. A major difference between private and public debt is that *private debt* is owed to persons *external* to the issuing institution, while the bulk of *public debt* is *internal*, being owed to ourselves. Private debt has grown faster than public debt since the 1950s and is currently over twice as large.

8. The *real burden of the national debt* stems from the federal government "crowding out" private investment as it drives interest rates up when competing with the private sector for loanable funds. As a result, future generations may inherit a smaller capital stock and a smaller production-possibilities frontier.

9. Among the major benefits of the public debt are its use as a *stabilization instrument* and as a *risk-free asset* for savers.

Matching Key Terms And Concepts

____ 1. confiscation

____ 2. Ricardian Equivalence

____ 3. uncontrollable spending

____ 4. crowding-out hypothesis

____ 5. government budget constraint

____ 6. external debt

____ 7. roll over

____ 8. internal debt

____ 9. functional finance

____ 10. national debt

a. IOUs the repayment of which entail no loss of purchasing power.

b. The best way to finance government outlays depends on the least costly policies available.

c. Long term programs like Social Security.

d. Repaying old debts by taking out new loans.

e. The cumulation of all budget deficits through history.

f. Eminent domain and the military draft are examples.

g. The idea that governmental growth entails opportunity costs.

h. $G = T + \Delta B + \Delta MB$.

i. How government debt is financed is irrelevant.

j. Purchasing power is lost when this is repaid.

True/False Questions

_____ 1. Selling assets or borrowing to secure resources are methods used by both private and governmental decisionmakers.

_____ 2. Consumption by households is financed by sales of assets, by current income, and by borrowing against current assets or expected income.

_____ 3. The distribution of the opportunity costs associated with government among the public is not a crucial consideration in determining who really pays for government.

_____ 4. Private debt is primarily internally held while public debt is primarily externally held.

_____ 5. The 1993 Budget Reduction Act calls for a balanced budget every fiscal year.

_____ 6. The military draft covers the opportunity costs of labor resources through taxing, borrowing, and printing new money.

_____ 7. Crowding-out does not need to be considered if there are many idle resources during a deep recession.

_____ 8. When the government issues bonds to cover a budget deficit, interest rates tend to rise and crowd-out investment.

_____ 9. Taxes have been used almost exclusively to finance most of the wars in which the United States has been involved.

_____10. Government outlays for Medicare are an example of uncontrollable spending.

_____11. Budget deficits were dramatically reduced during the 1980s.

_____12. Our government is forbidden by the Constitution from acquiring resources from their owners unless the owners voluntarily agree by contract to surrender their assets.

Multiple Choice

There Is A Single Best Answer For Each Of These Questions.

___ 1. The public debt:
    a. results from cumulative budgetary deficits.
    b. is a stabilization instrument.
    c. provides a relatively riskless investment.
    d. is held primarily by U.S. citizens and institutions.
    e. All of the above.

___ 2. Which has grown fastest since World War II?
    a. National debt.
    b. State and local debt.
    c. Private debt.
    d. Gross Domestic Product.
    e. Unemployment.

___ 3. "Crowding-out" is most significant:
    a. at full employment.
    b. during inflation.
    c. during recession.
    d. during war time.
    e. during stagflation.

___ 4. "Crowding-out" refers to:
    a. cuts in private activities caused when government grows.
    b. TINSTAAFL.
    c. the public burdens of increased private purchases.
    d. the decline in unemployment forced by more rapid inflation.
    e. All of the above.

___ 5. Major differences between private and public debt are:
    a. private debt is a risk free asset.
    b. the private debt is almost entirely owned by external persons.
    c. the public debt is entirely owned by external persons.
    d. all public debt is held by Americans.
    e. None of the above.

___ 6. Government cannot secure extra resources by:
    a. collecting taxes.
    b. backing the dollar with gold.
    c. printing money.
    d. selling government securities.
    e. issuing bonds.

___ 7. If private owners are compelled to sell when the government buys land for public use, it is applying its:
    a. right of eminent domain.
    b. law of economic efficiency.
    c. political right of tax preferences.
    d. rights of economic expansion.
    e. unconstitutional powers that the Supreme Court will overturn.

___ 8. Most of the U.S. federal debt consists of U.S. Treasury bonds owned by:
    a. other federal government agencies.
    b. the Federal Reserve System.
    c. foreign governments.
    d. U.S. citizens and corporations.
    e. individual foreigners.

9. "The mix that works best should be used" best describes:
   a. the growth of public of debt.
   b. Ricardian Equivalence.
   c. government's eminent domain.
   d. the functional finance approach.
   e. a chocolate chip cookie recipe.

10. "Uncontrollable" spending includes:
    a. increasing annual budget deficits.
    b. increased imports of crude oil.
    c. local construction of a new park.
    d. a $50,000 binge at Bloomingdale's.
    e. federal outlays for postal service.

11. Robert Barro's theory that bonds and taxes are equivalent is based upon:
    a. the notion of Functional Finance.
    b. the relationship specified in the government constraint.
    c. Ricardian Equivalence.
    d. international trade theory.
    e. Keynesian analysis.

12. The amount of money "printed" by the FED when it buys Treasury bonds issued to cover a federal budget deficit:
    a. is new monetary base, and consequently causes the money supply to grow even more through the bank "money creation" process.
    b. somewhat replaces crowding-out that would have been accomplished by higher interest rates with crowding-out through inflation.
    c. reduces the amount of national debt in the public's hands.
    d. results in greater growth of Aggregate Spending than would have occurred without such expansionary open market operations.
    e. All of the above.

Chapter Review (Fill-In Questions)

1. Government can obtain resources through sales of existing _____ or current _____, by _____ from citizens, corporations, foreigners or commercial banks, through _____, _____, or by _____.

2. Recognizing that confiscation is a relatively minor source of government revenues, the governmental budget can be summarized by the equation _____. The idea that increases in outlays by government inevitably cause reductions in private consumption or investment is known as the _____ hypothesis.

3. When increased governmental purchases crowds out private individuals, they lose leisure or purchasing power through _____ or higher _____.

4. Issuance of bonds increases the demand for loanable funds which typically drives up _____ imposing an added burden on potential borrowers and investors. If there is efficient and full employment of all resources and government purchases are increased either _____, _____ or _____ must decline.

5. The major difference between private and public debt is that the latter is primarily _____ held. Because private debt is owned by _____ persons their claim on the real assets of the firm or individual can deplete the net worth of private parties.

6. When the government issues new bonds, the purchasing power sacrificed by American bond-buyers just _____ the government's gain in purchasing power. However, increased debt may impose several burdens on the society. If taxes must be raised to pay the interest on the debt, _____ to work and invest may be reduced. Further, if interest rates rise as more public debt is floated, private borrowing may be _____. This could squelch _____ so that the national debt did impose a burden on future generations by reducing growth in the stock of capital.

Unlimited Multiple Choice

Each Question Has From Zero To Four Correct Responses.

____ 1. The federal government can:
   a. finance a deficit by printing money.
   b. finance a deficit by buying bonds from the public.
   c. retire some public debt when tax revenue exceeds expenditure.
   d. finance a deficit by selling bonds to the public.

____ 2. It is unavoidably true that government budgetary:
   a. deficits cause increases in the national debt.
   b. surpluses permit either a reduction in the monetary base or retirement of part of the public debt.
   c. deficits require retirement of part of the public debt or reduction of the money supply.
   d. surpluses cause increases in national debt or in the money supply.

____ 3. Which of the following is a form of taxation if it is defined as the loss in purchasing power that occurs when government outlays increase?
   a. Extra consumption induced via the Keynesian multiplier process when government spending grows to combat a serious depression.
   b. Confiscation, as when a military draft is used to acquire labor resources for the Department of Defense.
   c. Inflation following an increase in the monetary base caused when the FED `monetizes' a huge deficit.
   d. Jumps in the interest rate caused by an enormous budget deficit.

___ 4. According to the crowding-out hypothesis, increased government:
   a. spending has no impact on the private sector.
   b. outlays must reduce private consumption or investment in a full-employment economy.
   c. borrowing pushes up interest rates and reduces profitable private investment opportunities.
   d. tax rates drive up the interest rate.

___ 5. Which of the following represent possible examples of crowding-out by the government:
   a. losses of leisure by previously idle workers.
   b. reduced purchasing power of households caused by inflation.
   c. reduced investments caused by higher interest rates.
   d. reduced borrowing by consumers because of higher interest rates.

Problems

Problem 1

Fill in the blank so that it is compatible with the government budget constraint.

a. $G = \$1,200$ billion, $T = \$975$ billion, $\Delta MB = \$0$, $\Delta B =$ _____

b. $G = \$1,250$ billion, $T = \$1,025$ billion, $\Delta MB =$ _____, $\Delta B = \$150$ billion

c. $G = \$1,300$ billion, $T = \$1,375$ billion, $\Delta MB = -\$25$ billion, $\Delta B =$ _____

d. $G = \$1,350$ billion, $T = \$1,400$ billion, $\Delta MB =$ _____, $\Delta B = \$0$

e. Which of the scenarios above will result in a budget deficit? _____

f. Which of the scenarios above will result in a budget surplus? _____

g. Which of the scenarios above will result in an increase of public debt? _____

h. Which of the scenarios above will result in a reduction of public debt? _____

i. Which of the scenarios above will result in inflationary pressures if the economy is at full employment? _____

j. Which of the scenarios above will result in deflationary pressures if the economy is at full employment? _____

Problem 2

On the figures provided, illustrate the concept of "crowding out" caused by the government issuing bonds to cover expenditures.

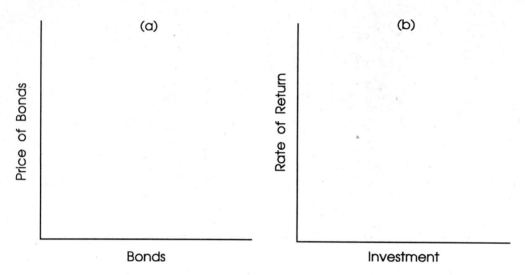

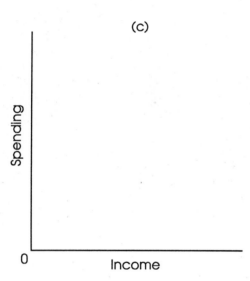

Problem 3

Use this figure to answer the following True/False questions.

_____ a. An increase in government spending from G_0 to G_1 will result in crowding out of the private sector equal to C_2-C_1 in an economy with idle resources.

_____ b. In an economy with idle resources an increase in government spending from G_0 to G_1 might result in induced consumption equal to *b-d*.

_____ c. In a fully employed economy an increase in government spending from G_1 to G_2 will result in a reduction in private spending equal to C_1-C_0.

_____ d. If an increase in government spending from G_0 to G_1 results in movement from point *e* to point *b*, the distance between *b* and *d* is equal to the multiplier times the change in government spending.

_____ e. An increase in government spending from G_1 to G_2 will result in crowding out equal to *d-c* in an economy with idle resources.

_____ f. If the economy is at point *e*, an increase in government spending can enable the economy to move to point *a* through induced consumption.

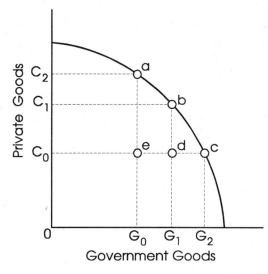

_____ g. If the economy is at point *a* an increase in government spending from G_0 to G_1 will result in a decrease in private spending equal to C_2-C_1.

_____ h. A movement from point *b* to point *a* illustrates crowding out of private activity by government spending.

_____ i. In order to move from point *d* to point *b*, the government will have to increase its outlays and, in the process, crowd out the private sector.

_____ j. A decrease in government spending from G_2 to G_1 must result in a movement from point *c* to point *d*.

Problem 4

Use your knowledge about the government budget constraint to answer the following True/False questions, given the following information:

$$G = \$700 \text{ billion} \qquad T = \$500 \text{ billion}$$

____ a. The government budget is balanced.

____ b. If there is no change in the monetary base, the change in national debt is equal to $200 billion.

____ c. If the change in national debt is equal to $75 billion, the change in the monetary base is equal to $125 billion.

____ d. If taxes are increased to a total of $800 billion, the government can retire $100 billion of the national debt and contract the monetary base.

____ e. If taxes are increased to a total of $750 billion, the government can contract the monetary base by $50 billion if there is no change in the national debt.

____ f. In an open economy (international trade takes place) a $100 billion domestic savings surplus will necessitate a $100 billion trade deficit.

____ g. In an open economy a $300 billion domestic savings surplus will necessitate a $100 billion trade deficit.

____ h. In an open economy a $100 billion trade surplus will necessitate a $300 billion domestic savings surplus.

____ i. In an open economy a $200 billion trade surplus will necessitate a domestic savings surplus equal to zero.

____ j. In an open economy a $200 billion trade deficit will necessitate a domestic savings surplus equal to zero.

Problem 5

Fill in the following blanks concerning foreign trade and the government budget constraint.

a.   G-T = $200 billion, S-I = $120 billion, M-X = _____

b.   G-T = $50 billion, S-I = $90 billion, M-X = _____

c.   G-T = $75 billion, S-I = _____, M-X = $60 billion

d.   G-T = $20 billion, S-I = _____, M-X = -$50 billion

e.   Which of the scenarios above results in a trade deficit? _____

f.   Which of the scenarios above results in a trade surplus? _____

g.   Which of the scenarios above results in a domestic savings surplus? _____

ANSWERS

Matching	True/False	Multiple Choice	Unlimited MC	Fill-In
1. f	1. T	1. e	1. abcd	1. assets; production; borrowing; taxation; confiscation; printing money
2. i	2. T	2. c	2. b	2. G=T+ΔB+ΔMB; crowding out
3. c	3. T	3. a	3. bcd	3. inflation; taxes
4. g	4. F	4. a	4. bc	4. interest rates; consumption; investment; exports
5. h	5. F	5. b	5. abcd	5. internally; external
6. j	6. F	6. b		6. equals; incentives; crowded out; investment
7. d	7. F	7. a		
8. a	8. T	8. d		
9. b	9. F	9. d		
10. e	10. T	10. e		
	11. F	11. c		
	12. F	12. e		

Problem 1	Problem 2	Problem 3	Problem 4	Problem 5
a. $225 billion	a. See figure below	a. F	a. F	a. $80 billion
b. $75 billion		b. T	b. T	b. -$40 billion
c. -$50 billion		c. T	c. T	c. $15 billion
d. -$50 billion		d. T	d. F	d. $70 billion
e. a, b		e. F	e. T	e. a, c
f. c, d		f. F	f. T	f. b, d
g. a, b		g. T	g. F	g. a, b, c, d
h. c		h. F	h. T	
i. b		i. F	i. F	
j. c, d		j. F	j. T	

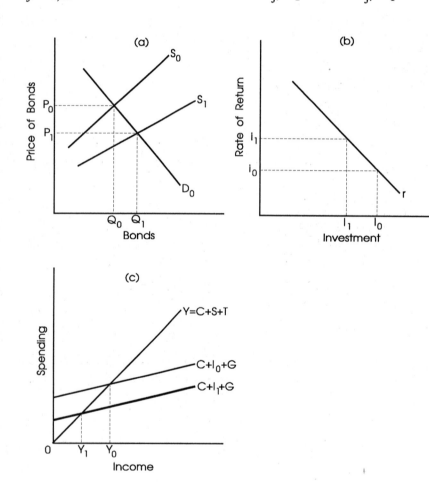

Chapter 16
Microfoundations of Macroeconomic Policy

Chapter Objectives

After you have read and studied this chapter you should be able to explain the foundations of Aggregate Supply and Demand curves and how changes in their major determinants cause these curves to shift; discuss the processes of supply-side and demand-side inflation; and describe patterns of employment and unemployment across different types of business cycles.

Chapter Review: Key Points

1. Most economists, whether classically-oriented or Keynesians, now agree that, in the long run, Aggregate Supply curves are vertical. However, the new Keynesians contend that *wage and price stickiness* can make the short run Aggregate Supply curve positively-sloped for lengthy periods, and thus short run targets may be most appropriate for macroeconomic policymaking.

2. Long-term *labor contracts* (whether implicit or explicit), *efficiency wages*, and *dual labor markets* all provide microfoundations to help explain wage stickiness and involuntary unemployment in an Aggregate Demand/Aggregate Supply framework.

3. Declines in the Aggregate Supply curve trigger *supply-side inflation* and reduces real income and output. *Demand-side inflation* results from rapid increases in the Aggregate Demand curve, and is usually preceded by higher income and output.

4. If Aggregate Demand grows excessively in a fully employed economy, the first phase of the *demand-side cycle* entails rising prices, outputs, employment, and incomes. In the second phase, supply-side adjustments to the demand-originated disturbances drive up prices further, but total employment, production, and income fall. *Demand-side* inflation induces a path of *counterclockwise adjustment* of real output versus inflation. If the economy starts at less than full employment, only the first phase necessarily occurs when Aggregate Demand is increased.

5. Supply-side inflation generates a *clockwise adjustment* pattern. In the first phase of a *supply-side* (cost-push) *cycle,* prices rise while real output and incomes fall. If the government attempts to correct for the resulting inflationary recession by increasing Aggregate Demand, the second phase occurs--prices continue to rise, but real output and income rise as well.

6. *Stagflation,* a contraction of the terms *stagnation* and *inflation,* is the simultaneous occurrence of high rates of both unemployment and inflation.

7. Mild demand-side inflation accompanied the prosperity of the 1960s. From the mid-1970s into the early 1980s, stagflation took over. Whether this stagflation was the supply-adjustment phase of the earlier demand-pull cycle or originated from supply-related shocks cannot be established conclusively. It seems likely, however, that even if the economy had been stable when the *supply shocks* listed previously emerged, considerable supply-side inflation would have plagued the American economy from 1973 to 1980.

8. *Disinflation* is a significant reduction in the rate of inflation. Most people adjust their behavior if they expect inflation. Their expectations cause disinflation to entail losses in real income before it restores the economy to a relatively stable growth path. Thus, the 1981-83 recession was especially severe.

9. In recent decades, accelerating technological advances and the internationalization of economic activity have increased the speed of structural economic change. A massive wave of corporate mergers in the 1980s and 1990s has lead to significant corporate *down-sizing*, with reduced job security for many workers who had intended to be career employees at large firms.

Matching Key Terms And Concepts

____ 1. wealth effect

____ 2. stagflation

____ 3. demand-side inflation

____ 4. money (inflation) illusion

____ 5. incomes policies

____ 6. supply-side inflation

____ 7. efficiency wages

____ 8. labor contracts

____ 9. interest rate effect

____10. dual labor markets

a. The labor market consists of primary and secondary sectors.

b. Can exist in the short run, but not in the long run.

c. Employment rises in the initial stage.

d. Reduces investment when the price level rises.

e. Purchasing power of assets falls when prices rise.

f. Generates a clockwise adjustment path of the price level versus real output.

g. Intended to raise the cost of dismissal and reduce shirking by employees.

h. Attempts to curb inflation without cutting Aggregate Demand.

i. Explains in part why wages adjust slowly.

j. Inflationary recession.

True/False Questions

____ 1. If no one suffers from money illusion, demand-pull inflation will yield both higher employment and higher prices.

____ 2. Both monetary and fiscal policies can boost the Aggregate Demand.

____ 3. Increasing Aggregate Supply can be done quite quickly.

____ 4. Aggregate Supply curves are shifted by changes in monetary or fiscal policies and changes in consumption or investment expenditures.

____ 5. External shocks that raise resource- or other production costs will shift the economy's demand curve leftward.

____ 6. New regulations that facilitate efficiency cause the Aggregate Supply curve to shift to the right.

____ 7. Labor supplies are partly determined by individual preferences for work versus leisure.

____ 8. Hikes in money wage rates imposed by powerful labor unions tend to shift the Aggregate Supply curve leftward.

____ 9. Labor contracts are easily renegotiated when inflation accelerates slightly.

____10. Money wages can be raised at rates equal to growth rates of labor productivity without causing price inflation.

____11. Efficiency wages are below market-clearing wages, so they encourage moves of less productive workers into their areas of comparative advantage.

____12. Corporate down-sizing has decreased the average length of unemployment.

Standard Multiple Choice

There Is One Best Answer For Each Question.

___ 1. Rightward shifts of the Aggregate
Supply curve cause:
a. stagflation.
b. high unemployment.
c. cost-push inflation.
d. high interest rates.
e. deflationary pressure.

___ 2. Aggregate Supply might grow because
of:
a. reductions in the bargaining
strength of organized labor.
b. enhanced unemployment
compensation programs.
c. increased inflationary expectations
by labor.
d. increased preference for leisure by
labor.
e. All of the above.

___ 3. Which of the following actions would
cause a shift to the right in the
Aggregate Demand curve?
a. Congress decides to terminate all
highway and water projects.
b. The President's call for a
permanent tax decrease is
approved.
c. The FED changes the reserve
requirement from 17% to 20%.
d. Sales of U.S. bonds to commercial
banks by the FED are increased.
e. Welfare spending is slashed.

___ 4. A leftward shift in the Aggregate
Supply curve will initiate _____
inflation, while a shift of the
Aggregate Demand curve to the right
will initiate _____ inflation:
a. cost-pull; demand-push.
b. demand-push; cost-pull.
c. demand-pull; cost-push.
d. cost-push; demand-pull.
e. deflationary; recessionary.

___ 5. Rapid technological advances tend to
shift the economy's:
a. supply of capital leftward.
b. labor supply curve leftward.
c. Aggregate Expenditures curve
rightward.
d. Aggregate Supply curve rightward.
e. price level upward.

___ 6. Stagflation is a contraction of _____
and _____:
a. stagnant; deflation.
b. stable; defoliation.
c. stagnation; inflation.
d. stabilization; repugnant.
e. staggered; contraction.

___ 7. Stagflation involves simultaneous high
rates of:
a. unemployment and interest.
b. interest and inflation.
c. unemployment and inflation.
d. economic growth and inflation.
e. stagnation and degeneracy.

8. Which of the following is NOT a reason why Aggregate Supply curves are positively sloped?
   a. Costs adjust less quickly than prices do to changes in demand.
   b. Price changes trigger wealth effects.
   c. Diminishing returns causes it to become ever more difficult to expand output as the economy approaches its capacity.
   d. Higher prices are needed to cover rising production costs as larger amounts of output are demanded.
   e. Expanding production causes more intense competition for resources when the economy nears full employment.

9. Which of the following would be the LEAST likely to cause demand-pull inflation?
   a. A tax cut.
   b. An increase in government spending.
   c. A hike in the discount rate.
   d. A cut in reserve requirements.
   e. The FED buys bonds from banks.

10. Stagflation occurs when Aggregate:
   a. Demand and Aggregate Supply shift right.
   b. Demand shifts right.
   c. Demand shifts left.
   d. Supply shifts right.
   e. Supply shifts left.

11. Cost-push inflation is a likely result if the:
   a. money supply grows faster than our productive capacity.
   b. Aggregate Demand shifts right.
   c. Aggregate Supply curve shifts left.
   d. federal government runs a huge deficit.
   e. Congress repeals all inefficient regulations.

12. A supply-side inflationary cycle follows a _____ path.
   a. clockwise.
   b. counterclockwise.
   c. cyclical.
   d. countercyclical.
   e. sinusoidal.

13. Compared to market clearing wages, efficiency wages tend to:
   a. be higher.
   b. increase unemployment.
   c. raise the costs of being fired.
   d. reduce shirking.
   e. All of the above.

14. The segmentation of the national labor market into primary and secondary sectors is known as the:
   a. foreign sector substitution effect.
   b. interest rate effect.
   c. dual labor market.
   d. wealth effect.
   e. efficiency wages effect.

15. One reason wages fail to adjust as fast as prices do is the existence of:
   a. efficiency wages.
   b. labor contracts.
   c. dual labor markets.
   d. the wealth effect.
   e. supply-side inflation.

Chapter Review (Fill-In Questions)

1. The short run Aggregate Demand curve is negative sloped in part because the stock of money is assumed constant. This means that _____ will rise when the price level increases, shrinking consumer spending on durable goods, spending by state and local governments, and _____ spending by business firms.

2. In sum, the main determinants of Aggregate Supply are the quantities and costs of _____, production _____, _____ about inflation or deflation, and governmental _____.

3. _____ keep nominal wages from constantly changing, and help to explain the "stickiness" of wages. Increased unemployment over time is explained in part by _____ markets, where workers in the _____ sector are paid better wages and benefits than those in the secondary sector. Unemployment is also exacerbated when firms pay _____ wages in order to reduce the amount of shirking by employees.

4. Price hikes may initially "fool" workers through a process called _____, so that firms' _____ do not rise as fast as prices. During such a period, the _____ rate tends to fall and output grows. Eventually, however, workers adjust their inflationary expectations. Real wages will tend to _____ and output fall because, even though prices continue to rise, nominal _____ will grow even faster. A complete demand-side inflationary cycle follows a _____ path.

5. A supply-side inflationary cycle originates from an initial shift of the Aggregate Supply curve to the left. This drives up both the rates of _____ and _____. Policymakers commonly try to combat the recessionary trend with _____ demand management policies. As a result, the longer-term equilibration path for a supply-side inflationary cycle is _____.

6. The empirical evidence of actual equilibration paths suggests that the inflation of the 1960s was primarily _____, while the inflation of the 1970s was essentially _____. The very high rates of unemployment and inflation that plagued the early 1980s might be interpreted as the latter phases of a _____ inflationary cycle, or as the beginnings of a _____ inflationary cycle.

Unlimited Multiple Choice

Each Question Has From Zero To Four Correct Answers.

___ 1. Workers are said to suffer from money illusion when:
   a. they make their work decisions after adjusting prevailing money wage rates for expected inflation.
   b. they anticipate real wage rates that are not realized.
   c. they work more but realize only decreased real wages because of inflation.
   d. their expected rate of inflation equals realized inflation.

___ 2. Incomes policies:
   a. include various measures intended to dampen inflationary pressures but not Aggregate Demand.
   b. may reduce labor's inflationary expectations.
   c. include such measures as wage and price controls.
   d. may worsen inflationary pressures if their inefficiencies cause the Aggregate Supply curve to shift inward and to the left.

___ 3. During the initial stage of a demand-side inflation:
   a. business firms offer higher money wages for more labor to produce more output at higher prices.
   b. the demand for labor schedule shifts to the left.
   c. the supply schedule of labor will shift leftward, assuming that labor suffers from money illusion.
   d. workers suffering from money illusion offer more labor services at a reduced real wage rate.

___ 4. The Aggregate Supply curve:
   a. would be nearly vertical if workers quickly secured increases in money wage rates offsetting any increases in the price level.
   b. would be nearly vertical if workers' expected rates of inflation were much less than the actual rates of inflation.
   c. shifts rightward as workers revise their inflationary expectations upward.
   d. shifts leftward as business firms lower the prices they charge for goods.

___ 5. Inflationary recession occurs during the:
   a. initial stage of a demand-side inflation.
   b. initial stage of a supply-side inflation.
   c. latter stage of a demand-side inflation as workers adjust their inflationary expectations to agree with actual inflation.
   d. latter stage of a supply-side inflation as government resorts to demand-management policies to restore full-employment.

Problems

Problem 1

Use information drawn from the Aggregate Supply and Demand curves depicted to answer the following True/False questions.

___ a. Full employment occurs at output level Q_2.

___ b. The shift of the Aggregate Demand curve from AD_0 to AD_1 could be accomplished by increased government expenditures.

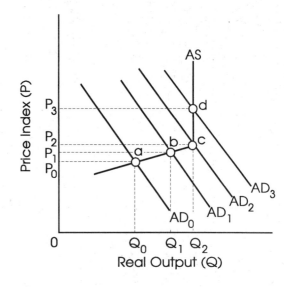

___ c. The price level is stable as the economy moves from a to b.

___ d. As the economy moves from c to d, the percentage increase in the money wage rate equals the percentage increase in the absolute price level.

___ e. Assuming a constant money wage rate, as the economy moves from b to c, the real wage rate increases, causing firms to hire less labor.

___ f. A technological advance could shift the Aggregate Supply curve outward and to the right.

___ g. The Aggregate Supply curve depicted is composed of both a Keynesian segment and a Classical segment.

___ h. As the economy moves up along the Keynesian segment of its supply curve, the real wage rate remains unchanged.

___ i. The movement from c to d represents pure price inflation.

___ j. An increase in the money wage rate would shift the Keynesian portion of the supply curve upward and to the left.

___ k. An increase in autonomous saving might shift the Aggregate Demand curve from AD_1 to AD_2.

___ l. The demand curve for labor services corresponding to the Keynesian portion of the supply curve is a horizontal line.

Problem 2

Output Q_e is at full employment, with original Aggregate Supply (AS_0) and Demand (AD_0).

_____ a. The original equilibrium would be at full employment with price level P_e (point a).

_____ b. Increases in federal spending or growth of the money supply could expand Aggregate Demand from AD_0 to AD_1.

_____ c. Workers' real wages rise with a move from point a to point d.

_____ d. Real wages rise during a move from b to c.

_____ e. Realizing that wages have not kept pace with inflation at point d, workers will compensate by reducing their supplies of labor, so that Aggregate Supply shifts from AS_0 to AS_1.

_____ f. Movements such as those from point a to point d to point c are often referred to as Supply-side inflation.

_____ g. Stagflation occurs when the economy moves from a to b.

_____ h. A move from a to b cuts real wages.

_____ i. The real wage at c and at a are equal.

_____ j. Macroeconomic movements from a to b to c are compatible with a Demand-side inflation.

_____ k. Shifts of Aggregate Demand from AD_0 to AD_1 could be induced by a drop in the discount rate.

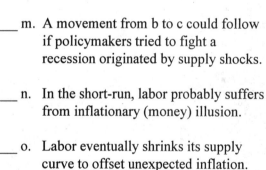

_____ l. Unemployment rates are higher at point a than at point b.

_____ m. A movement from b to c could follow if policymakers tried to fight a recession originated by supply shocks.

_____ n. In the short-run, labor probably suffers from inflationary (money) illusion.

_____ o. Labor eventually shrinks its supply curve to offset unexpected inflation.

_____ p. A shift from AS_1 to AS_0 could follow an increase in the capital gains tax.

_____ q. Policies to reduce monopolistic practices could shift Aggregate Demand from AD_0 to AD_1.

_____ r. A movement from a to b could reflect external supply shocks that induced an inflationary recession.

Problem 3

On the space provided, using Aggregate Supply and Aggregate Demand analysis, illustrate an economy at full employment with a normal amount of frictional unemployment. Label the demand curve AD_0, the supply curve AS_0, and the output level Q_f. Label the equilibrium point a.

a. Illustrate a shift caused by a cut in the discount rate. Label the new curve with subscript 1, and the new equilibrium point b.

b. In the long run workers will react to the illusion created by the situation in "a" above. Illustrate by a shift of the appropriate curve to a new equilibrium point c. Label the new curve with a subscript 1. What is the level of real output after the adjustment? _____

c. What kind of cycle have you illustrated?
    _____

Problem 4

Use Aggregate Demand and Aggregate Supply analysis to illustrate an economy operating at full employment with normal amounts of frictional unemployment. Label the original demand curve AD_0, the original supply curve AS_0, the initial equilibrium point a, and the initial output level Q_f.

a. Lax enforcement of antitrust laws and intense merger activity disturbs the macroeconomic equilibrium. illustrate this shift on your graph by labeling the new curve with a subscript 1. Label the new equilibrium point b, and the new level of output Q_1.

b. The country's leader is alarmed about this situation. She decides to pressure the central bank into lowering the reserve requirement. Illustrate the likely result of this policy on your graph. Label your new curve with a subscript 1. Label the new equilibrium point c. What is the level of real output? _____

c. The situation described above is what kind inflation? _____

Problem 5

Use up arrows (↑), down arrows (↓), zeros (0), or questions marks (?) to indicate how (i) Aggregate Demand and (ii) Aggregate Supply will be shifted by the events described below, and how each will affect (iii) National Income and Output, (iv) employment, (v) unemployment rates, and (vi) the price level. Aggregate Demand and Supply may both be affected in some cases, some reasonable arguments are debatable, and long-run consequences can differ from short-run effects.

a. The FED increases sales of U.S. Treasury bonds to prevent a jump in energy prices from triggering excessive cost-push inflation. i. _____ ii. _____ iii. _____ iv. _____ v. _____ vi. _____

b. Voters blame incumbents for the Depression of 1999-2000. Federal income tax rates are cut by 10% just before the 2000 election. i. _____ ii. _____ iii. _____ iv. _____ v. _____ vi. _____

c. All barriers to free trade between all countries in North and South America are eliminated. i. _____ ii. _____ iii. _____ iv. _____ v. _____ vi. _____

d. An environmental protection law requires all U.S. firms to reduce their pollution per unit of output by 50% before the year 2000. i. _____ ii. _____ iii. _____ iv. _____ v. _____ vi. _____

e. Baby-boomers intent on maintaining standards of living when they retire double the percentages of disposable income they save. i. _____ ii. _____ iii. _____ iv. _____ v. _____ vi. _____

f. The federal budget is balanced by slashing defense spending by $300,000,000,000. i. _____ ii. _____ iii. _____ iv. _____ v. _____ vi. _____

g. The Japanese Parliament eliminates all tariffs and quotas on U.S. agricultural products. i. _____ ii. _____ iii. _____ iv. _____ v. _____ vi. _____

h. Congress relaxes our immigration laws to accommodate a new wave of political refugees. i. _____ ii. _____ iii. _____ iv. _____ v. _____ vi. _____

ANSWERS

Matching	True/False	Multiple Choice	Unlimited MC	Fill-In
1. e	1. F	1. e	1. bc	1. interest rates; investment
2. j	2. T	2. a	2. abcd	2. resources; technology; expectations; regulations
3. c	3. F	3. b	3. ad	3. labor contracts; dual labor; primary; efficiency
4. b	4. F	4. d	4. a	4. money illusion; wage costs; unemployment; rise; wages; counterclockwise
5. h	5. F	5. d	5. bc	5. inflation; unemployment; expansionary; clockwise
6. f	6. T	6. c		6. demand-side; supply-side demand-side; supply-side
7. g	7. T	7. c		
8. i	8. T	8. b		
9. d	9. F	9. c		
10. a	10. T	10. e		
	11. F	11. c		
	12. F	12. a		
		13. e		
		14. c		
		15. b		

Problem 1	Problem 2	Problem 3	Problem 4
a. T	a. T	a. See Figure A	a. See Figure B
b. T	b. T	b. See Figure A; Q_f	b. See Figure B; Q_f
c. F	c. F	c. Demand-side inflation	c. Supply-side inflation
d. T	d. F		
e. F	e. T		
f. T	f. F		
g. T	g. T		
h. F	h. F		
i. T	i. T		
j. T	j. F		
k. F	k. T		
l. F	l. F		
	m. T		
	n. T		
	o. T		
	p. F		
	q. F		
	r. T		

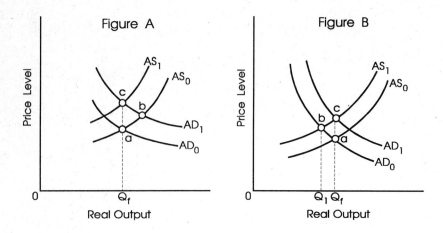

Figure A

Figure B

Problem 5

a.   i. ↓   ii. ↓   iii. ↓   iv. ↓   v. ↑   vi. ?
b.   i. ↑   ii. ↑   iii. ↑   iv. ↑   v. ↓   vi. ?
c.   i. ↑   ii. ↑   iii. ↑   iv. ↑   v. ↓   vi. ?
d.   i. 0   ii. ↓   iii. ↓   iv. ↓   v. ↑   vi. ↑
e.   i. ↓   ii. 0   iii. ↓   iv. ↓   v. ↑   vi. ↓
f.   i. ↓   ii. 0   iii. ↓   iv. ↓   v. ↑   vi. ↓
g.   i. ↑   ii. 0   iii. ↑   iv. ↑   v. ↓   vi. ↑
h.   i. ↑   ii. ↑   iii. ↑   iv. ↑   v. ?   vi. ?

Chapter 17
Active vs. Passive Policymaking

Chapter Objectives

After you have read and studied this chapter you should be able to describe alternative interpretations of the Phillips curve hypothesis that inflation and unemployment are inversely related; discuss the theoretical debate concerning the merits of both active verses passive policymaking; evaluate various policies to fight inflation and stagflation, including the theory of the natural rate of unemployment; describe the natural real rate of interest hypothesis, and the Keynes and Fisher effects; and discuss New Classical Macroeconomic theories such as competitive markets, efficient markets, rational expectations, and real business cycles.

Chapter Review: Key Points

1. The *Phillips curve* depicts a trade-off for policymakers between unemployment and inflation. Lower unemployment rates presumably might be purchased through higher inflation, or vice versa; it is up to policymakers to choose the least harmful mix of evils. The Phillips curve appeared to be relatively stable through the 1960s, but it shifted sharply in the 1970s and early 1980s so that much higher rates of unemployment appeared necessary to dampen inflationary pressures. The reasons for the instability of the Phillips curve are the subject of a continuing debate within the economics profession.

2. Modern Keynesian analysis suggests that several factors in addition to inflationary expectations can cause stagflation and instability in the Phillips curve. Wages and prices are assumed "sticky", especially in downward direction. Unexpected shocks to the supply side, rapid structural changes in demand or output, changes in labor institutions that generate disincentives for work, and changes in public regulatory policies can all shift the Phillips curve. The Keynesian *structuralist* approach emphasizes production "bottlenecks" as foundations for the Phillips curve.

3. The *natural rate theory* of the instability in the Phillips trade-off focuses on worker expectations of inflation. As labor begins to anticipate inflation, greater increases in wages are required for a given level of real output. Thus, accelerating inflation is required if policymakers desire to hold unemployment below its "natural rate," but even this policy will not work forever.

4. If interest rate targets or unemployment rate objectives are set below their "natural rates," expansionary policies may ultimately cause *nominal interest rates* to rise, not fall. *Natural-rate* theorists believe that only temporary reductions in interest rates or unemployment can be obtained through expansionary policies, and even in the short run, only by "fooling" lenders or workers.

5. The *Keynes effect* predicts that monetary growth will decrease interest rates, and vice versa. The *Fisher effect* is the upwards adjustment of nominal interest rates when transactors begin expecting inflation.

6. The *new classical macroeconomics* is based on the model of perfect competition, or *efficient markets,* which suggests that even in the short run, macropolicy only works when the economy is operating inefficiently and that this does not occur.

7. The theory of *rational expectations* suggests that people eventually figure out how a given change in policy affects the economy and learn to predict how policymakers react to swings in economic activity. Thereafter, people will focus on what policymakers are doing and make adjustments that prevent the policies from accomplishing their objectives.

8. *Real business cycle theory* views shocks to Aggregate Supply as permanent, and suggests that attempts by macroeconomic policymakers to "fine-tune" the economy are either self defeating or harmful.

Matching Key Terms And Concepts

_____ 1. rational expectations theory

_____ 2. Keynes effect

_____ 3. demand-side stagflation

_____ 4. Keynesian `shock' and `structuralist' hypotheses

_____ 5. nominal interest rate

_____ 6. Fisher effect

_____ 7. real interest rate

_____ 8. natural rate theory

_____ 9. Phillips curves

_____10. supply-side stagflation

a. The percentage annual monetary premium paid for borrowing.

b. Trade-offs between inflation and unemployment.

c. People learn to anticipate the results of policies.

d. Deviations from normal frictional unemployment are caused by macropolicy.

e. Monetary interest adjusted for inflation.

f. Expanding the money supply unexpectedly initially causes nominal interest rates to fall.

g. Contracting the money supply unexpectedly ultimately causes the nominal interest rate to fall.

h. Workers adjust to anticipated inflation by reducing labor supplies.

i. Falling Aggregate Supply boosts prices and unemployment.

j. Explains Phillips curves by labor market "bottlenecks" and changing intensities of shocks to our economy.

True/False Questions

_____ 1. The nominal rate of interest will be higher than the real rate of interest when the inflation rate is positive.

_____ 2. High unemployment generates political pressures for full employment policies that raise Aggregate Supply.

_____ 3. The stagflation phase of demand-side inflation resembles the initial phase of supply-side inflation.

_____ 4. In the early 1960s, Keynesian policy prescriptions seemed to steer the economy along a prosperous path.

_____ 5. External economic shocks may cause the Aggregate Supply to shift to the right, worsening the tradeoff between unemployment and inflation.

_____ 6. Natural rate theorists believe that long run Phillips curves are vertical at the natural rate of unemployment.

_____ 7. Classical theory suggests that policymakers are faced with a relatively stable Phillips curve tradeoff.

_____ 8. Expansionary fiscal policy reduces frictional unemployment because workers are afraid to change jobs.

___ 9. The Phillips curve for the United States shifted to the left during the 1970s.

___ 10. When Aggregate Demand shifts to the left, the Phillips curve shifts to the left.

___ 11. Aggregate Supply shifts cause Phillips curve shifts.

___ 12. As workers anticipate higher inflation the short-run Phillips relation shifts outward (up and to the right).

___ 13. The particular interest rate paid by a borrower to a lender reflects default risk, length of time to maturity of the note or bond, the anticipated rate of inflation, and legal constraints.

___ 14. The Fisher effect refers to the change in nominal interest rates as borrowers and lenders compensate for expected inflation.

___ 15. Advocates of natural rate theory tend to favor the replacement of rules with discretionary policy making.

Standard Multiple Choice

There Is One Best Answer For Each Question.

___ 1. The Phillips curve posits a tradeoff between:
   a. economic stability and growth.
   b. consumption today vs. tomorrow.
   c. unemployment and inflation.
   d. low interest rates and low taxes.
   e. gasoline service stations and screwdrivers.

___ 2. Second phases of demand-pull inflationary cycles entail:
   a. cost-push inflation.
   b. substantial layoffs of workers.
   c. rising unemployment.
   d. accelerating inflation.
   e. All of the above.

___ 3. The Phillips Curve:
   a. shifted inward during the 1970s.
   b. has been very stable.
   c. shows the tradeoff between balanced budgets and inflation.
   d. demonstrates stable economic growth.
   e. None of these.

___ 4. According to "natural rate" theory, macropolicy can't influence long-run rates of:
   a. inflation and unemployment.
   b. real interest and unemployment.
   c. nominal economic growth.
   d. financial capital accumulation.
   e. All of the above.

___ 5. Hikes in nominal interest rates when people expect higher inflation are examples of the:
   a. Keynes effect.
   b. Fisher effect.
   c. real wealth effect.
   d. Friedman effect.
   e. Kuznets effect.

___ 6. In broad terms, natural rate theory assumes:
   a. balanced budgets at full employment.
   b. stable unemployment/inflation tradeoffs.
   c. inflationary biases in healthy economies.
   d. prices rise more easily than they decline.
   e. independence between monetary and "real" variables.

___ 7. The idea of combating inflation by shrinking Aggregate Demand does NOT involve which of the following theories:
   a. recessions moderate labor's inflationary expectations.
   b. recessions foster inflation that improves political incumbents' reelection prospects.
   c. periods of slack demand aid firms in eliminating "deadwood."
   d. fear of job loss stimulates labor productivity.
   e. recessions dampen the inflationary expectations of workers, investors, business firms, and consumers.

___ 8. The "natural rate" theory of the Phillips curve suggests that expansionary macroeconomic policy may temporarily reduce unemployment with only minor inflation because:
   a. workers are temporarily fooled by higher money wage offers.
   b. workers find long-term jobs easier during business booms.
   c. policymakers are fooled by businessmen into expanding Aggregate Demand.
   d. business decisionmakers are fooled by workers who are lazier than they represent themselves to be.
   e. everyone is happier to work when recessions end.

___ 9. Many modern Keynesians suggest that, for the most part, the stagflation of the 1970s was caused by:
   a. workers being fooled by inflation.
   b. policymakers seeing past the inflation illusion of the 1960s.
   c. business expectations being confronted by reality.
   d. such shocks to the economy as OPEC price hikes and the souring of the Russian Wheat Deal.
   e. All of the above.

___ 10. Overly expansionary monetary and fiscal policies tend to cause:
   a. unemployment to fall temporarily.
   b. rising expectations of inflation.
   c. nominal interest to rise in the long run.
   d. no long-term effect on employment.
   e. All of the above.

_____11. The "supply-side" policies adopted in the early 1980s to counter inflation and stimulate economic growth did not include selective:
   a. increasing the money supply.
   b. increasing government spending.
   c. increasing Aggregate Demand.
   d. decreasing Aggregate Supply.
   e. decreasing Aggregate Demand.

_____12. The explanation of Phillips curves as consequences of labor and product market "bottlenecks" is at the core of the:
   a. modern monetarist approach.
   b. "natural rate" approach.
   c. Keynesian "composition-shift" approach.
   d. Keynesian "structuralist" approach.
   e. classical approach.

Chapter Review (Fill-In Questions)

1. Between the 1960s and 1970s many economists believed that a reasonably _____ inverse relationship existed between unemployment and inflation. This idea is known as the _____ curve tradeoff.

2. Phillips curves are inverse relationships between unemployment and inflation and the _____ curve indicates a positive relation between the level of output (and thus employment) and the price level; thus, the two curves _____ each other.

3. One Keynesian explanation for the Phillips curve suggests that as _____ is approached, it becomes increasingly costly to produce added output because labor market _____ become increasingly severe.

4. The monetarist explanation for shifts of the Phillips relation focuses on rising _____ expectations of workers and their adjustments that shift Aggregate Supply to the _____.

5. Modern Keynesian explanations for shifts of the Phillips curve emphasize the _____, especially downwards, of wages and prices. Shocks are continually bombarding the economy causing changes in demand for various products. In sectors where demands increase, _____ tend to rise. Where demand declines, workers are reluctant to accept wage _____, so firms commonly cut their production costs through layoffs and _____ in production.

6. Natural rate theory assumes that lenders and borrowers focus on the _____, of interest which is the _____ of interest after adjusting for inflation. In equation form, the real rate of interest equals _____, which implies that the rate of interest lenders will charge equals _____.

7. _____ suggests that economic profits are almost purely the result of luck. A related theory, _____, suggests that people will learn to anticipate any predictable consequence of policy, so that overly expansionary policies will result in high rates of _____ and _____, but nothing else. Instantaneous adjustments eliminate all other effects.

8. _____ theory contend that most fluctuations in real GDP are permanent and the result of _____ shocks. Real business cyclists believe that macropolicy should be _____, since attempts to "fine-tune" the economy will be _____.

Unlimited Multiple Choice

Each Question Has From Zero To Four Right Answers.

___ 1. According to the natural rate hypothesis:
   a. attempts to drive unemployment and real interest rates permanently below their natural rates are futile.
   b. the government can induce a permanent increase in the employment rate by pursuing demand-management policies.
   c. frictional unemployment can only be reduced temporarily.
   d. each Phillips curve exists only for a particular expected rate of inflation.

___ 2. Real interest rates are the annual percentage:
   a. monetary premiums paid to use money.
   b. of real purchasing power paid to a lender by a borrower for the use of money.
   c. of extra goods that can be enjoyed if consumption is deferred.
   d. premiums necessary to induce savers to defer gratification.

___ 3. Markets will operate efficiently if there is:
   a. substantial information about profit making opportunities.
   b. vigorous competition among sellers for profit making opportunities.
   c. federal control of wages and prices.
   d. business collusion to fix prices.

___ 4. According to the rational expectations branch of monetarism:
   a. government can fool the public continually.
   b. policy goals can be predictably achieved in neither the short run nor the long run.
   c. nominal interest rates adjust immediately to expected inflation, if the public knows about past countercyclical policies.
   d. some policy goals might be achievable in the short run only if macroeconomic policies are disguised from the public.

_____ 5. According to natural rate theory, if the
FED pursues an expansionary
monetary policy by buying bonds:
   a. the nominal rate of interest will be
      reduced permanently.
   b. the initial decline in the interest
      rate is called the Fisher effect.
   c. the supply of loanable funds
      initially decreases, causing the
      nominal interest rate to increase.
   d. despite an initial increase in the
      real rate of interest, it will return to
      its natural rate.

Problems

Problem 1

Use your knowledge about interest rates to answer the following questions.

a. If the nominal rate of interest is 8% and the rate of inflation is 8%, then the real rate of
    interest (r) equals _____.

b. If the nominal rate of interest is 12% and the rate of inflation is 15%, then the real rate of
    interest (r) equals _____.

c. If the nominal rate of interest is 2% and the rate of inflation is -10%, then the real rate of
    interest (r) equals _____.

d. If the desired real rate of interest is 8% and inflation is expected to be 8% annually, then the
    nominal interest rate (i) a lender would charge equals _____.

e. If the desired real rate of interest is 5% and inflation is expected to be -3% annually, then the
    nominal interest rate (i) a lender would charge equals _____.

f. If the desired real rate of interest is 6% and inflation is expected to be 18% annually, then the
    nominal interest rate (i) a lender would charge equals _____.

Problem 2

Use this figure to answer the following True/False questions as a "Natural Rate" theorist would.

___ a. The natural rate of unemployment is 6%.

___ b. If workers expect 6% inflation and policymakers expand Aggregate Demand to shrink unemployment to 4%, there would be 12% inflation.

___ c. Eliminating inflation when inflationary expectations are 6% could be accomplished while holding unemployment at 6%.

___ d. Reducing inflationary expectations from 12% to 6% worsens the tradeoff between inflation and unemployment.

___ e. If inflationary expectations are originally 12%, maintaining a 10% unemployment rate would eventually (probably rather quickly) bring the economy back to a point where inflation was negligible.

___ f. The expected annual rate of inflation at a is 6%.

___ g. As the economy moves from a to b, the actual real wage rate falls while the expected real wage rate increases.

___ h. Expected inflation at c is 6%.

___ i. Expected inflation at d is 12%.

___ j. At b, the actual rate of inflation equals the expected rate of price change.

___ k. Money wages are higher at c than at b.

___ l. The employment rate decreases as the economy moves from b to c.

___ m. Expected inflation at f is 12%.

___ n. The expected real wage rate is smaller than the actual real wage rate at f.

___ o. Expected inflation at a is zero.

___ p. As the economy moves from a to b, the money wage rate increases at a rate of 6%.

___ q. The expected real wage rate at b is greater than the expected real wage rate at a.

___ r. As the economy moves from b to c, the actual real wage rate increases, since workers' demands for higher money wage rates are partially met.

___ s. An increase in Aggregate Demand could cause the economy to move from a to b in the short run if workers do not suffer from money illusion.

___ t. Workers suffer from money illusion at c.

_____ u. Workers do not suffer from money illusion at d.

_____ v. Expected inflation along E(p) = 12% is 12%.

_____ w. A buyers' market exists in the labor market with a movement from e to f.

_____ x. According to natural rate theory, there is a permanent trade-off between unemployment and inflation.

_____ y. Unanticipated higher prices can mean more real production

Problem 3

You are the chief economic advisor to the president. She asks you for your policy prescription for the current economic climate which features high unemployment and high price inflation (stagflation). You believe in the Keynesian structuralist approach.

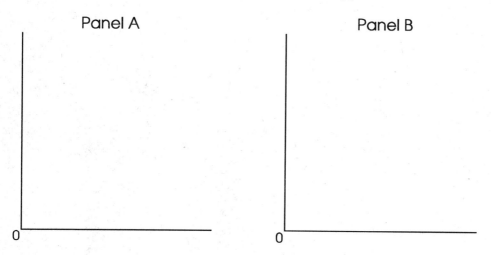

a. Illustrate the present situation using Aggregate Demand and Aggregate Supply analysis in Panel A of the Figure. Label your initial curves with a subscript 1.

b. Illustrate, by movements of the curves in Panel A and corresponding shifts of the Phillips curves in Panel B, what the impact of your program(s) would be. Label your original Phillips curve that corresponds to your initial Aggregate Demand-Aggregate Supply equilibrium PC_1. Label each succeeding curve AS_2, AS_3, PC_2, PC_3.

c. What are some of your proposals to attain this goal? _____

_____

ANSWERS

Matching	True/False	Multiple Choice	Unlimited MC	Fill-In
1. c	1. T	1. c	1. acd	1. stable; Phillips
2. f	2. F	2. e	2. bcd	2. Aggregate Supply; mirror
3. h	3. T	3. e	3. ab	3. full employment; bottlenecks
4. j	4. T	4. b	4. bcd	4. inflationary; left
5. a	5. F	5. b	5. none	5. stickiness; prices and wages; cuts; cutbacks
6. g	6. T	6. e		6. real rate; nominal rate; $i = rd + E(p)$; $r = i - p$
7. e	7. F	7. b		7. efficient markets; rational expectations; interest; inflation
8. d	8. F	8. a		8. Real Business Cycle; supply; passive; self defeating
9. b	9. F	9. d		
10. i	10. F	10. e		
	11. T	11. e		
	12. T	12. d		
	13. T			
	14. T			
	15. F			

Problem 1

a.	0%
b.	-3%
c.	12%
d.	16%
e.	2%
f.	24%

Problem 2

a.	T	n.	T
b.	T	o.	T
c.	F	p.	F
d.	F	q.	T
e.	T	r.	T
f.	F	s.	F
g.	T	t.	F
h.	T	u.	F
i.	F	v.	T
j.	F	w.	T
k.	T	x.	F
l.	T	y.	T
m.	T		

Problem 3

Panel A

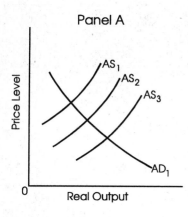

Panel B

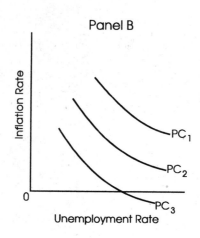

a. See figure.
b. See figure.
c. Any proposals that reduce rigidity and bottlenecks in the economy, will help solve stagflation problems by shifting the Phillips curve to the left and the Aggregate Supply curve to the right. Most of the policies described in the textbook are mentioned under Supply- side economics, but some programs of the 1970s, particularly job training, were designed to increase Aggregate Supply.

Chapter 18
Limitations of Stabilization Policy

Chapter Objectives

After you have read and studied this chapter you should be able to explain the difficulties for macroeconomic policymaking posed by such factors as missed timing, improper dosages of stimulation or contraction, and how private adjustments may frustrate even well intended discretionary policymaking; discuss the ways that policymaking may be misused to introduce "political" business cycles and a long-term trend for growth in government relative to the private sector; discuss incomes policies and their possible effects on the economy; and discuss national economic planning and national industrial policy, and how they apply to the United States.

Chapter Review: Key Points

1. Macroeconomic policymaking is at least as much art as it is a science. A multitude of problems preclude perfect analysis and policy.

2. A *recognition lag* occurs because it takes time to get even a modestly accurate picture of changes in the state of the economy. An *administrative* (implementation) *lag* exists because it takes a while to get the tax and monetary machinery in gear even when policymakers' plans are made. An *impact lag* confounds the proper timing of policy; the economy budges only stubbornly to the prods of the policymakers' tools. These lags, which may be long and variable, may cause discretionary policy to be more destabilizing than stabilizing.

3. Lack of precise knowledge about recessionary gaps, inflationary gaps, and GNP gaps, as well as uncertainty about multipliers and velocity, mean that estimating the correct doses of monetary and fiscal medicine is extremely difficult.

4. Some modern Keynesians challenge the long-term effectiveness of monetary policy, arguing that adjustments in financial technologies will ultimately *insulate financial institutions* and make monetary tools inoperative.

5. Incumbents' re-election prospects improve as per capita disposable income grows immediately prior to elections. There is some evidence that policymakers try to manipulate Aggregate Demand to enhance their positions in the eyes of voters, which induces *political business cycles*.

6. Critics of Keynesian fiscal policies also suggest that the government grows relative to the private sector when policymakers increase spending and cut taxes during downturns policymakers neither cut spending nor restore taxes, however, during periods of prosperity or inflation.

7. *Intentional recessions* can decompress accumulated inflationary pressures and inflationary expectations. However, recessions tend to be very hard on political incumbents, so many politicians favor incomes policies of various sorts.

8. *Incomes policies* (mandatory wage-price freezes or controls, voluntary guidelines, or "jawboning") muzzle the effectiveness of the price system, creating shortages and widespread misallocations of resources.

9. The more involved a country is in international trade and finance, the less will be the impact of any given monetary or fiscal policy because the effects are diffused by foreign markets.

Matching Key Terms And Concepts

___ 1. Incomes Policies

___ 2. Cost-plus pricing

___ 3. Political business cycles

___ 4. Wage and price freezes

___ 5. Overdosing the economy

___ 6. Underdosing the economy

___ 7. Recognition lag

___ 8. Administration lag

___ 9. Impact lag

___ 10. Financial insulation

a. Caused by underestimation of multipliers or overestimation of the economy's capacity.

b. Financial institutions learn to counteract monetary policies.

c. The period between adoption and effect of a change in policy.

d. Most stringent form of incomes policy.

e. Range from jawboning to freezes.

f. The period between an event and the availability of information about it.

g. The money supply grows rapidly in years divisible by 4.

h. Caused by overestimating multipliers or the economy's capacity.

i. The time required to alter the course of policy.

j. Marking up costs by a fixed percentage to set prices.

True/False Questions

___ 1. The recognition lag occurs because it is generally difficult for monetary and fiscal policymakers to determine quickly how much of which policies to use in steering our sluggish economy along a proper course.

___ 2. Since changes in monetary policy can be implemented quickly through the FED's Open Market Committee, administration lags are not much of a problem for monetary policymaking.

___ 3. Wage and price controls have a long history of considerable success at reducing inflation.

___ 4. The impact lag of monetary policy is comparatively regular and short.

___ 5. Critics contend that wage and price controls may actually increase inflationary expectations.

___ 6. The longer that wage and price controls are in force the more difficult it is for economic transactors to distinguish real from artificial price signals.

___ 7. There is little empirical evidence of political business cycles.

___ 8. The Federal Funds Market provides banks with the opportunity to lend or to borrow millions of dollars for one or two days at comparatively low interest rates.

___ 9. Various studies indicate that voters tend to re-elect incumbents more often the faster disposable income grows during the year immediately preceding elections.

___10. Impact lags make it more difficult to cure the economy than simple Keynesian analysis would suggest.

Standard Multiple Choice

There Is One Best Answer For Each Question.

___ 1. Which of the following is an example of financial insulation?
   a. The FED's discount window.
   b. A wage and price freeze.
   c. A wage and price control.
   d. A bank holding on to excess reserves.
   e. The federal funds market.

___ 2. Which lag is longer for fiscal policy than for monetary policy?
   a. Discretionary lag.
   b. Recognition lag.
   c. Administration lag.
   d. Dosage lag.
   e. Impact lag.

___ 3. Which one of the following generalizations about economic theories is not correct?
   a. Keynesians believe that macroeconomic policy works.
   b. New classical macroeconomists believe that macropolicy does not work.
   c. Natural rate theorists believe macropolicy works only temporarily but is harmful in the long run.
   d. Post-Keynesian monetarists believe Keynesian analysis is correct for the very short run but classical assumptions are correct for the long run.
   e. Classical economists believed that macropolicy was effective in both the short and long run.

___ 4. Incomes policies disturb the price system and cause:
   a. efficient usage of resources.
   b. surpluses.
   c. politicians' jawbones to swell.
   d. inflation upon their implementation.
   e. shortages and misallocation of resources.

___ 5. Mandatory price controls are an example of:
   a. monetary policy.
   b. fiscal policy.
   c. automatic stabilizers.
   d. tax policy.
   e. incomes policies.

___ 6. Some new-Keynesians believe that financial technologies change in response to changes in:
   a. the size of the workforce.
   b. monetary policy.
   c. the capital stock.
   d. fiscal policy.
   e. All of these.

___ 7. Assume OPEC hikes the price of oil, and policymakers attempt to offset the resulting tendency for the economy to slide into a recession. Which of the following is NOT a likely consequence of these events?
   a. The "real" price OPEC gets for oil will be less than it expects.
   b. The "real" wages of labor will fall.
   c. "Real" national income will fall because of the OPEC hike.
   d. Our "real" national income will fall solely because of overly expansionary policies.
   e. The price level will rise.

___ 8. Wage and price controls are intended to:
   a. dampen inflationary expectations.
   b. shift the economy's supply curve to the left.
   c. shift the economy's demand curve to the right.
   d. reduce corporate profits.
   e. increase corporate profits.

___ 9. Price ceilings are likely to result in:
   a. shortages.
   b. black markets.
   c. queuing.
   d. rationing by favoritism.
   e. All of the above.

___10. Incumbent policymakers that manipulate macroeconomic policies to obtain reelection may cause:
   a. political business cycles.
   b. stagflation.
   c. excessive unemployment.
   d. countercyclical cycles.
   e. tax rates to rise just before election.

___11. During an election year, incumbents are most likely to support:
   a. tax increases.
   b. reduction of subsidies to all special interest groups.
   c. growth of the money supply.
   d. campaign finance reform.
   e. reduction of the money supply.

___12. Critics of discretionary monetary and fiscal policy point to:
   a. political manipulation of the business cycle.
   b. failures to raise taxes and cut spending during inflation.
   c. problems with lags and incorrect doses.
   d. these policies' reliance on "fooling" people.
   e. All of these.

Chapter Review (Fill-In Questions)

1. Even well-intentioned policymakers suffer from a _____ lag because it takes time and resources to acquire sufficient _____ about the state of the economy to make judgments about the proper course of policy.

2. Once a problem is recognized, there is a(n) _____ lag because it takes time for _____ policymakers to tilt open market directions properly, and even more time for _____ policymakers to change _____ laws or alter appropriations for government outlays.

3. Once a policy is changed, the time it takes for policy to affect economic activity results in a(n) _____ lag. The _____ lag is usually longer for fiscal policy than monetary policy, while the _____ lag is longer for monetary policy if changes in _____ policies are the tools used by fiscal policymakers.

4. Tight money policies may teach financial institutions new ways to conserve on their holdings of reserves. Such changes in financial technology are known as _____, and make repeatedly used monetary policies _____ or useless in their effects on macroeconomic activity.

5. Reluctance in using _____ to combat inflation has channeled many political decisionmakers into experiments with _____ policies. Wage-price curbs have ranged from _____ by the president, to mandatory _____.

6. Opponents point to the wage-price controls of _____ to show that incomes policies do not work. They argue that controls can create expectations that prices will _____ when controls are lifted.

Unlimited Multiple Choice

There Are Four To Zero Answers For Each Question.

___ 1. It may be difficult to design and to implement appropriate countercyclical policies:
   a. because of the timing problems inherent in both monetary and fiscal policies.
   b. because adjustments made by private individuals and firms to certain monetary and fiscal policies can eliminate the desired effects of the countercyclical measures.
   c. because policymakers do not possess current or perfect information about the condition of the economy.
   d. because politicians sometimes base policy on the effects that specific countercyclical measures might have on their prospects for re-election.

___ 2. Mandatory wage and price controls:
   a. have typically been associated with wartime efforts.
   b. were imposed by President Nixon in August of 1971.
   c. are imposed to mitigate recessionary pressures which develop automatically in the economy.
   d. seldom distort relative prices.

___ 3. Wage and price guideposts and guidelines:
   a. assume that rates of price increases can parallel increases in labor productivity without causing upward pressure on wage rates.
   b. have traditionally been mandatory.
   c. are typically tied to a socially accepted level of unemployment.
   d. are very effective in relieving inflationary pressures.

___ 4. Proponents of incomes policies argue that controls:
   a. effectively reduce deflationary expectations.
   b. can reduce inflationary expectations.
   c. distort relative price signals and misallocate resources.
   d. can reconcile the goals of monopolistic industries with the goals of society.

___ 5. Decreasing Aggregate Demand in order to reduce inflation:
   a. is generally favored by politicians.
   b. may cause a recession.
   c. might also 'discipline' a 'slack' labor force.
   d. should increase employment.

Problem

Answer the True/False questions below based on the following scenario:

After moderate sales during the Christmas season of 1995 business pessimism leads to a decline in production in the first part of 1996. Consumers' expectations mirror business' hesitation, and outlays on durable goods are delayed or forgotten. First quarter statistics compiled in mid April indicate that a contraction is taking place. Upon receiving the news, the FED undertakes actions to boost the money supply. In Congress rumors begin to circulate about a possible tax cut to deal with the downturn in business activity.

____ a. The time between January 1996 and mid April 1995 is known as a recognition lag.

____ b. If the FED implements an expansion of the money supply by mid May, the administrative lag (of monetary policy) is approximately one month.

____ c. The impact lag will most likely be longer for a tax cut than for open market operations which expand the money supply.

____ d. The administrative lag will most likely be longer for monetary policy as compared to fiscal policy.

____ e. The recognition lag is longer for fiscal policy than for monetary policy.

____ f. Government purchases to combat declining Aggregate Demand will have a shorter administrative lag than lowering the discount rate.

____ g. The impact lag of open market purchases will be of short duration because money expansion is almost instantaneous.

____ h. If a tax cut is finally passed in November of 1996 and implemented in 1997, there is a chance that the tax cut will help to overheat the economy (cause inflation).

____ i. The impact lag of expansionary monetary policy will increase if banks are reluctant to loan out additionally funds acquired through the sale of government securities to the FED.

____ j. The recognition lag could be decreased by compiling business statistics at intervals of 1 month as opposed to each quarter.

ANSWERS

Matching	True/False	Multiple Choice	Unlimited MC	Fill-In
1. e	1. T	1. e	1. abcd	1. recognition; information
2. j	2. T	2. c	2. ab	2. administration; monetary;
3. g	3. F	3. e	3. none	fiscal; tax
4. d	4. F	4. e	4. bd	3. impact; administration;
5. a	5. T	5. e	5. bc	impact; tax
6. h	6. T	6. b		4. financial insulation;
7. f	7. F	7. d		unpredictable
8. i	8. T	8. a		5. recessions; incomes;
9. c	9. T	9. e		jawboning; wage/price freezes
10. b	10. T	10. a		6. 1971-73; rise
		11. c		
		12. e		

Problem

a. T
b. T
c. F
d. F
e. F
f. F
g. F
h. T
i. T
j. T

Chapter 19
Economic Growth and Development

Chapter Objectives

After you have read and studied this chapter, you should be able to describe the processes of economic growth and development; discuss the special hurdles to development faced in poor countries; and discuss the pros and cons of the "trap of underdevelopment" argument.

Chapter Review: Key Points

1. *Economic growth* refers to quantitative changes in the capacity to produce goods and services in a country. It occurs through expanding capital or labor resources, discoveries of new sources of raw materials, or development of more productive technologies. *Economic development* refers to improving the qualitative aspects of economic growth, including changes in the quality of life.

2. The *Rule of 72* is a rule of thumb for estimating how long it takes for a variable to double in value given some percentage growth rate. Simply divide 72 by the growth rate. For example, if growth in GDP is occurring at 6 percent per year, GDP will double in approximately 12 years (72/6 = 12).

3. *Diminishing returns* because of the fixity of land cause output to grow more slowly, even if labor and capital increase in fixed proportions.

4. Reverend Thomas Malthus and other nineteenth-century economists were convinced that population growth is almost uncontrollable, and theorized that equilibrium is attained only when bare subsistence is common to all.

5. *Population growth* tends to slow as a country develops. The least developed countries of the world tend to have the highest rates of population growth.

6. *Capital formation* requires high saving rates. If *voluntary saving* is used to finance development, greater incomes, higher interest rates paid to savers, and (perhaps) less equal income distributions will lead to higher rates of investment. *Involuntary saving* may be used to free investment resources through confiscation, taxation, or inflation.

7. *Capital widening* occurs when the capital stock and labor force grow at the same rates. *Capital deepening* requires the capital stock to grow faster than the labor force.

8. *Technological advances* occur when given amounts of resources acquire greater productive capacity.

9. Rapid development requires a strong *social infrastructure*--education, communications, transportation, and other networks that facilitate production.

Matching Key Terms And Concepts

Set I

_____ 1. international credit

_____ 2. involuntary saving

_____ 3. Rule of "72"

_____ 4. economic development

_____ 5. economic growth

_____ 6. communism

_____ 7. capital deepening

_____ 8. capital to labor ratio (K/L)

_____ 9. high birth rates

_____ 10. voluntary saving

a. According to Karl Marx, follows the "dictatorship of the proletariat" and then the "withering away of the state."

b. Boosts investment beyond domestic capabilities.

c. Expansion of productive capacity.

d. Individual choice between present and future consumption.

e. Investment is proportionally greater than population growth.

f. A quick way of estimating "doubling" times.

g. Qualitative expansion.

h. Associated with underdevelopment.

i. Accomplished by taxes or inflation.

j. A crucial determinant of labor productivity.

Set II

___ 1. technological advance

___ 2. infrastructure

___ 3. "Trap of underdevelopment"

___ 4. high voluntary saving rate

___ 5. Malthusian equilibrium

___ 6. "takeoff"

___ 7. Labor Force Participation Rate

___ 8. surplus value

___ 9. capital widening

___10. low birth rates

a. Percentage of a population in the work force.

b. A stage in Rostow's growth theory.

c. Net investment and population growth are proportional.

d. A factor temporarily expanding LFPRs.

e. Difference between wage paid and total value produced by a worker.

f. Inhibits Keynesian Aggregate Spending but facilitates economic growth.

g. The edge of starvation.

h. Producing more from given resources.

i. Low income inhibits capital accumulation.

j. An integral part of economic development.

True/False Questions

___ 1. The labor force as a percentage of the population is known as the capital to labor ratio.

___ 2. An important determinant of the size of the labor force relative to the size of the population is the rate of population growth.

___ 3. Increases in the labor force generally result in an increase in potential real output.

___ 4. Net investment represents net new capital formation during a given time period.

___ 5. Capital widening increases real per capita income.

___ 6. A government can rapidly increase potential Aggregate Supply by pursuing appropriate demand-management policies.

___ 7. An increase in the interest rate received by savers increases the price of present consumption relative to future consumption.

___ 8. Widespread poverty inhibits saving and capital accumulation.

___ 9. Higher interest rates charged investors and lower payments to savers will lead to larger capital stocks over time.

___10. Any smoothly functioning economy needs a sophisticated and efficient financial system.

Standard Multiple Choice

There Is One Best Answer For Each Question.

___ 1. The number of years that it takes some variable to double is approximately its annual percentage growth rate divided into:
   a. its current value.
   b. 72.
   c. 76.
   d. 82.
   e. None of the above.

___ 2. Economic development in a primitive society would NOT be fostered by:
   a. an increase in the population growth rate.
   b. expanded investment in capital embodying new technology.
   c. improvements in the education of the work force.
   d. better transportation, communications, and banking networks.
   e. adoption of advanced agricultural technology.

___ 3. Output per capita would probably rise, but output per worker would probably fall if:
   a. capital deepening occurred rapidly.
   b. the labor force participation rate of a given population rose.
   c. technical education of the work force increased.
   d. involuntary saving was increased.
   e. income were distributed equally.

___ 4. In Karl Marx's theory of economic development:
   a. a "takeoff stage" precedes the dictatorship of the proletariat.
   b. feudalism comes just before a "withering away of the state."
   c. communism immediately follows the overthrow of capitalism.
   d. capitalism is succeeded by a dictatorship of the proletariat.
   e. high savings rates launch a takeoff into high mass consumption.

___ 5. Voluntary saving is enhanced by higher:
   a. tax rates and inflation.
   b. surplus values and more central planning.
   c. interest rates and income.
   d. confiscation and inflation.
   e. degrees of equality in the distribution of income.

___ 6. According to Karl Marx, which event immediately precedes pure communism?
   a. The "withering away of the state."
   b. Feudalism.
   c. A "dictatorship of the proletariat."
   d. Distribution "from each according to need, to each according to ability."
   e. A non-sexist, non-racist, non-exploitative Utopia.

___ 7. A problem NOT part of "Trap of Underdevelopment" theory is:
   a. high birth rates.
   b. low per capita income.
   c. a low capital to labor ratio.
   d. low productivity.
   e. high pollution from dirty technology.

___ 8. Voluntary saving will most likely increase if:
   a. tax rates are increased.
   b. income decreases.
   c. interest rates rise.
   d. the distribution of income becomes more unequal.
   e. the rate of inflation increases.

___ 9. An economist who argued that population adjusts to a biological subsistence level given available resources was:
   a. David Ricardo.
   b. Karl Marx.
   c. W. W. Rostow.
   d. Thomas Carlyle.
   e. Rev. Thomas Malthus.

___ 10. Which of the following would NOT tend to cause economic growth?
   a. Improvement in technology.
   b. Increased labor force participation.
   c. Increased training and education.
   d. Increased marginal propensities to consume
   e. An improved social infrastructure.

Chapter Review (Fill-In Questions)

1. Economic _____ occurs when an economy's capacity expands; economic _____ entails qualitative improvements in economic conditions.

2. The time required for doubling any variable is approximated through calculations using the _____. Dividing the percentage annual change in a variable into _____ yields the number of years required for the variable to double its value.

3. Economic growth is the long-run process of expanding the limits to _____. Increased availability of _____ for production is one source of growth.

4. Per capita income tends to rise when the workforce increases through rising _____ rates, although less than proportionally because of declining _____ ratios, assuming investment does not also rise. Productive capacity may also rise if _____ grows, but _____ income is likely to fall because of growing numbers of mouths to feed.

5. Many early economists, accepting the analyses of the Rev. _____, argued that population would always tend towards the maximum sustainable with given resources, so that people would, on the average, live only at _____ levels. This led critics of the day to term economics "the dismal science." Malthus believed population has a natural tendency to grow, in his terms, _____, while food supplies grow only _____.

6. High levels of investment and research and development expenditures create improvements in _____ and/or physical capital resources in a society. Economy-wide technological changes occur with the development of social overhead capital, also known as the _____. This road to economic development entails a well organized _____, efficient _____, and _____ networks, and an educated and disciplined _____.

Unlimited Multiple Choice

Each Question Has From Zero To Four Correct Responses.

___ 1. Economic growth:
   a. is synonymous with economic development.
   b. refers to qualitative change experienced by an economic system.
   c. occurs when an economic system acquires greater productive capacity.
   d. always results in increased real per capita output or income.

___ 2. An increase in the capital to labor ratio:
   a. increases the productive capacity of an economy.
   b. tends to increase real per capita income.
   c. increases labor productivity more in a less developed country than in a developed country.
   d. generally results in economic growth and development.

___ 3. Saving:
   a. enables production of new capital.
   b. is necessary for the accumulation of capital.
   c. is voluntary when individuals decide on their own to defer consumption to some future date.
   d. is determined by national income, according to the classical model.

___ 4. Potential Aggregate Supply is:
   a. determined partially by the state of technology.
   b. potentially increased if government uses highly inflationary policies and secures large tax revenues.
   c. determined strictly by Aggregate Demand.
   d. determined by the qualities and quantities of available resources.

___ 5. Capital deepening:
   a. is an increase in the ratio of labor to capital.
   b. necessarily increases real per capita output or income.
   c. is less likely to be effective in fostering growth in rich countries than in poor countries.
   d. can occur when saving rates are zero.

Problems

Problem 1

This figure shows production possibility frontiers confronting Urbana and Ruritania. A_0 denotes the original production possibility frontiers for both countries and A_1 denotes the new ones. Each economy begins at point a. Use this information to answer the following True/False questions.

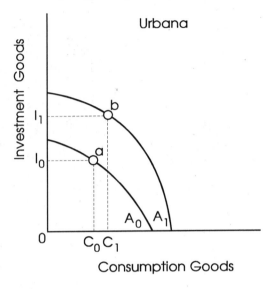

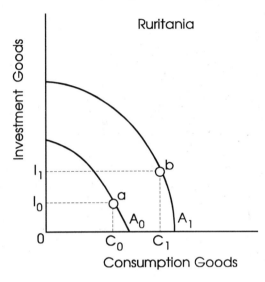

____ a. Rates of capital accumulation in Urbana exceeds those in Ruritania.

____ b. Ruritania has experienced economic growth.

____ c. Urbana must be experiencing economic development.

____ d. Urbana has experienced economic growth.

____ e. The PPF for Ruritania has shifted outward the most because of the relatively large amount of net investment that was made at point a.

____ f. Net additions of real capital in Urbana are probably better suited to produce investment goods than to the production of consumption goods.

____ g. Ruritanian consumers more greatly prefer present consumption over future consumption relative to those in Urbana.

____ h. Consumers in Urbana relatively prefer to defer present consumption to some future date.

____ i. Technological advancement may best explain the relative economic growth that Ruritania has experienced.

____ j. Households in Urbana save more of their incomes than do Ruritanians.

Problem 2

Use the "Rule of 72" to answer the following True/False questions.

___ a. A country's population will double in 72 years if annual population growth is 1 percent.

___ b. Financial investments will double in value in 18 years if the compounded annual interest rate is 4 percent.

___ c. Financial investments will double in 7.2 years if the annual interest rate is 15 percent.

___ d. A population that grows at an annual rate of 7.2 percent will double in 10 years.

___ e. If the annual rate of inflation in consumer prices is 2 percent, it will take 36 years for the CPI to double.

___ f. If an economy experiences an annual increase of 3.6 percent in real output, it will take 20 years for the economy to double its production of output.

___ g. Financial investments will double in 30 years if the annual interest rate is 2.4 percent.

___ h. Financial investments will double in 7 years if the annual interest rate is 10.28 percent.

___ i. A country's population will double in 60 years if population growth is 1.2 percent annually.

___ j. A country's population will double in 40 years if population growth is 1.8 percent annually.

Problem 3

This figure contains the supply and demand curves for the market for financial capital. Assume that the nominal interest rate is pegged below the equilibrium level by the FED at i_0, that it is then raised to i_1; and that i_e is the unattainable equilibrium interest rate. Assume that the rate of price inflation is 10 percent per annum. Use this information to answer the following True/False questions.

____ a. The supply of saving is a positive function of the rate of interest.

____ b. There is a shortage of financial capital at interest rate i_0 this market.

____ c. The capital stock increases as the nominal interest rate increases from i_0 to i_1.

____ d. The real interest rate remains constant as the nominal interest rate increases from i_0 to i_1.

____ e. The quantity demanded of financial capital increases as the real interest rate rises as the economy moves from a to c.

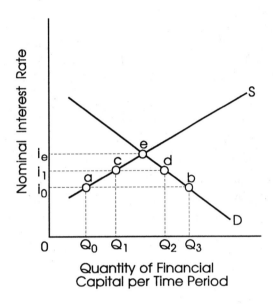

____ f. In this market, the rate of capital accumulation is positively related to the nominal interest rate but negatively related to the real interest rate.

____ g. The relative price of present consumption would rise if the nominal interest rate declined from i_1 to i_0.

____ h. The relative price of future consumption decreases as the nominal interest rate increases from i_0 to i_1.

____ i. The rate of saving is greater at i_1 than it is at i_0

____ j. The rate of present consumption is greater at i_0 than it is at i_1.

Problem 4

You have retained your job as chief economic advisor based on your fine performance in chapter 17. The president, once again, does not seem convinced that you are competent. You have just told him that fixed land and other resource constraints make it impossible to have continual radial expansions of the PPF without diminishing returns. The initial situation involves 2,000 units of labor and 2,000 units of capital and allows the economy to produce up to 100 tons of wheat or 100 military airplanes.

a. Graph this situation in the figure. Label the curve PPF_1.

b. Illustrate an increase of 2,000 units of labor and 2,000 units of capital if there is no diminishing returns. Label this curve PPF_2.

c. Illustrate a scenario where an additional 2,000 units of labor and capital are added to the production process. This time, however, the additional inputs are constrained by the amount of land in the production process. This constraint is particularly severe in the production of grain where you are only able to get half as much grain output per additional unit of input as before. On the defense side you encounter no resource constraint. Label this curve PPF_3.

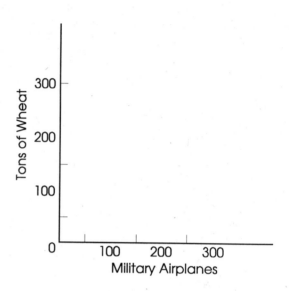

Problem 5

Use the "Rule of 72" to answer the following questions about how long it will take:

a. your savings account to double, if the bank pays annual interest of 4%? _____

b. GDP to double, if economic growth proceeds at 2% annually? _____

c. housing prices to double, if they grow by 6% annually? _____

d. population to double, if the annual population growth rate is 1.5 %? _____

e. for the value of money to fall by one-half if the annual inflation rate is 2%? _____ If it is 12%? _____ If it is 24%? _____

f. for the CPI to move from 100 to 400 if inflation is 1% annually? _____

ANSWERS

Matching		True/False	Multiple Choice	Unlimited MC
Set I	**Set II**			
1. b	1. h	1. F	1. b	1. c
2. i	2. j	2. T	2. a	2. abcd
3. f	3. i	3. T	3. b	3. abc
4. g	4. f	4. T	4. d	4. abd
5. c	5. g	5. F	5. c	5. c
6. a	6. b	6. F	6. c	
7. e	7. a	7. T	7. e	
8. j	8. e	8. T	8. c	
9. h	9. c	9. F	9. e	
10. d	10. d	10. T	10. d	

Chapter Review (Fill-In Questions)

1. growth; development
2. Rule of 72; 72
3. production; resources
4. labor force participation; capital to labor; population; per capita income
5. Thomas Malthus; subsistence; geometrically; arithmetically
6. human; infrastructure; financial system; communications; transportation; labor force

	Problem 1		Problem 2
a.	T	a.	T
b.	T	b.	T
c.	F	c.	F
d.	T	d.	T
e.	F	e.	T
f.	T	f.	T
g.	T	g.	T
h.	T	h.	T
i.	T	i.	T
j.	T	j.	T

Problem 3	Problem 4
a. T	See figure.
b. T	
c. T	
d. F	
e. F	
f. F	
g. F	
h. T	
i. T	
j. T	

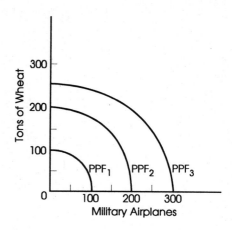

Problem 5

a. 18 years
b. 36 years
c. 12 years
d. 48 years
e. 36 years; 6 years; 3 years.
f. 144 years.

Chapter 20
International Trade

Chapter Objectives

After you have studied this chapter, you should be able to explain why the gains from free trade generally outweigh any losses from free trade; describe the major influences on the composition of a country's imports and exports; and distinguish valid arguments against free trade from arguments that are invalid or abused.

Chapter Review: Key Points

1. *International trade* is important to people throughout the world. The smaller and less diversified an economy is, the greater is the importance of its international trade.

2. The *law of comparative advantage* suggests that there will be net gains to all trading parties whenever their pretrade relative opportunity costs and price structures differ between goods.

3. A country's *consumption possibilities frontier* (*CPF*) expands beyond its production possibilities frontier (*PPF*) with the onset of trade, or with the removal of trade restrictions.

4. The *terms of trade* are the prices of exports relative to the costs of imports. An adverse change in the terms of trade lowers the country's *CPF*, while a favorable change in the terms of trade expands it.

5. Gains from trade arise because international transactions (a) provide *unique* goods that would not otherwise be available, (b) allow highly specialized industries to exploit *economies of scale*, (c) speeds the spread of *technology*, and facilitates *capital accumulation* and *entrepreneurial innovation*, (d) encourages *peaceful international relations*, and (e) facilitates *specialization* according to comparative advantage.

6. Domestic producers of imported goods and domestic consumers of exported goods may suffer short term losses from trade. However, their losses are over-shadowed by the specialization gains to consumers of imports and producers of exports. Gainers could always use parts of their gains to compensate the losers so that, on balance, no one loses. Moreover, *uniqueness, scale, dynamic,* and *political gains from trade* make it unlikely that anyone loses from trade in the long run.

7. Even the most valid of the arguments against free trade are substantially overworked. The arguments that are semi-valid include the ideas that: (a) the income redistributions from trade are undesirable; (b) desirable diversity within a narrow economy is hampered by free trade; (c) national defense requires restrictions to avoid dependence on foreign sources, and (more validly) export restrictions to keep certain technologies out of the hands of potential enemies; and (d) major exporters of a commodity can exercise monopolistic power by restricting exports, while important consuming nations can exercise monopsonistic power through import restrictions.

8. Any exercise of international monopoly/monopsony power invites retaliation and causes worldwide economic inefficiency. Those who lose because of trade restrictions will lose far more than is gained by the "winners."

9. If trade is to be restricted, *tariffs* are preferable to *quotas* because of the higher tax revenues and the smaller incentives for bribery and corruption.

10. *Trade adjustment assistance* is one way that gainers from trade might compensate the losers so that all would gain. However, difficulties in identifying losers and the lack of adequate funding have resulted in mounting pressures for trade restrictions.

Matching Key Terms And Concepts

Set I

_____ 1. arbitrage

_____ 2. law of comparative advantage

_____ 3. terms of trade

_____ 4. specialization gains from trade

_____ 5. political gains from trade

_____ 6. principle of absolute advantage

_____ 7. tariffs and quotas

_____ 8. dumping

_____ 9. dynamic gains

_____10. uniqueness gains

a. Saving and investment fostered by higher real income and transfers of technology.

b. Taxes or fixed limits on imports or exports.

c. Interdependence raises the costs of conflict.

d. (Prices of exports)/(prices of imports).

e. Riskless profit-taking by buying low and selling high.

f. Potential gains from trade among countries exist when relative pretrade costs differ.

g. The expansion of a CPF beyond a PPF that occurs with trade because production costs differ between countries.

h. Arise because some countries lack certain resources.

i. Selling cheaper abroad than domestically.

j. Sell those goods which you produce most, buy those goods which you produce least.

Set II

_____ 1. predatory dumping

_____ 2. infant industry protection

_____ 3. diversification

_____ 4. job destruction

_____ 5. balance of payments deficits

_____ 6. economic power and growth

_____ 7. trade adjustment assistance

_____ 8. national defense

_____ 9. exercising monopoly/ monopsony power

_____10. exploitation doctrine

a. An overused but legitimate argument against trade that is probably more valid as a restraint on exports than imports.

b. Implicitly assumes that trade is a zero-sum game.

c. Generally reduced by protectionist policies.

d. Problems better dealt with by other policies, not protection.

e. Selling below cost to eradicate foreign competitors.

f. Policies to protect emerging industries from mature foreign competition.

g. This argument against trade may apply in smaller countries but not in large ones.

h. Allows gainers from trade to offset hardships on losers.

i. An argument that ignores employment in export industries and assumes that if foreigners don't produce, we will.

j. Policies that may allow a powerful country to gain, but less than the rest of the world will lose.

True/False Questions

___ 1. Terms of trade are prices of exports relative to the costs of imports.

___ 2. Cheap foreign imports tend to increase the problems caused by concentrated monopoly power in an economy.

___ 3. The Trade Adjustment Assistance in federal laws governing trade were intended to provide retraining and financial assistance for workers displaced because of liberalized trade.

___ 4. When imports threaten the survival of an industry, the marketplace is signaling that the industry is extremely efficient.

___ 5. Import restrictions tend to preserve inefficient industries and to retard the growth of efficient industries.

___ 6. Predatory dumping of an industry's exports is a strategy to drive foreign competitors out of their domestic markets.

___ 7. The specialization gains from trade are positively related to differences in pretrade relative costs of production.

___ 8. Imports add to Aggregate Demand.

___ 9. The gains from trade tend to be smallest for the citizens of small, highly specialized countries.

___ 10. Economic efficiency requires all activities to be accomplished at their lowest possible opportunity costs.

___ 11. Trade only requires one of the trading parties to have an expectation of gain.

___ 12. The dynamic, political, and uniqueness losses common from free trade are normally offset by specialization gains from trade.

___ 13. Standards of living in the United States, more than in most countries, depend heavily on international trade.

___ 14. The infant industry argument for trade barriers applies to protection of the U.S. steel, auto, and textile industries.

___ 15. Dynamic gains from trade are generated by technology transfers and the additional saving and investment made possible by higher real income.

___ 16. Interdependence stimulated by trade raises the cost of international conflict and is an incentive for world peace.

___ 17. Import quotas are less flexible than tariffs in allowing adjustments to changes in demand.

___ 18. Trade barriers that make countries independent of foreign suppliers are more capitalistic than socialistic.

___ 19. Imports tend to cause inflation.

___ 20. In the long run, international trade is almost universally beneficial, although some people may be harmed in the short run by competition from foreign buyers or sellers of certain products.

Standard Multiple Choice

Each Question Has A Single Best Answer.

___ 1. Which of the following countries probably gains the most from international trade:
   a. the United States.
   b. Russia.
   c. Australia.
   d. the United Arab Emirates.
   e. Brazil.

___ 2. The Law of Comparative Advantage was first stated by:
   a. Reverend Thomas Malthus.
   b. David Ricardo.
   c. Adam Smith.
   d. Paul Samuelson.
   e. Alfred Marshall.

___ 3. If, in the absence of trade, an English worker can produce either 4 barrels of wine or 16 shirts weekly, while a Portuguese worker can produce either 10 barrels of wine or 20 shirts weekly:
   a. trade allows wine to exchange for between 2 and 4 shirts.
   b. Portugal has absolute advantages in both wine and shirts.
   c. England will export shirts and import wine when trade commences.
   d. England has a comparative advantage in shirtmaking.
   e. All of the above.

___ 4. When, under normal conditions, trade is expanded, the:
   a. gainers could compensate the losers so that all would gain.
   b. transactions costs of exchange inevitably rise.
   c. owners of capital gain, but workers inevitably lose.
   d. large countries gain far more than the small ones.
   e. PPFs for the trading countries shift inward.

___ 5. Arbitragers ultimately reap only normal profits because of:
   a. comparative advantages disappearing as trade commences.
   b. inevitable governmental regulation limiting profits.
   c. competition that causes prices to differ by transactions costs.
   d. competition for the political rights to receive monopoly profits.
   e. All of the above.

___ 6. When trade between two countries commences, the:
   a. consumption possibilities of both countries expand.
   b. gains from trade are shared by everyone.
   c. value of output must fall in one country if it rises in the other.
   d. gains to one trading party are offset by losses to the other.
   e. country with higher opportunity costs benefits the most from trade.

___ 7. If Japan imports American agricultural products and exports cars to the U.S.:
a. American farmers gain from trade, while Japanese farmers lose.
b. U.S. carmakers may lose from trade, but U.S. car buyers gain.
c. Japanese carmakers and food buyers both gain from trade.
d. total gains from trade will almost invariably exceed any losses.
e. All of the above.

___ 8. Dynamic gains from trade include the:
a. growth fostered by exchanges of technologies and the enhanced saving and investment made possible by higher real incomes.
b. conquest of foreign markets from a predatory dumping policy.
c. spread of middle-class values that occurs when primitive cultures absorb more advanced ideas.
d. pressure for international peace that arises from independence.
e. expansions of consumption possibilities frontiers realized strictly because pretrade cost structures differ.

___ 9. When a small country and a large country begin trading, the:
a. costs of imports will fall most in the large country.
b. prices of exports will fall most in the large country.
c. prices of exports will rise most in the large country.
d. gains from trade tend to be greater in the small country.
e. large country's capitalists exploit the small country's workers.

___10. NOT among predictable gains from international trade would be:
a. political gains.
b. specialization gains.
c. uniqueness gains.
d. dynamic gains.
e. capital gains.

___11. An example of a gain from international trade occurs when:
a. El Salvador imposes an import tariff on Guatemalan cigars.
b. Swedish couples drink Brazilian coffee.
c. French bakers bake cream pastries.
d. cheap Taiwanese watches cost Swiss watchmakers their jobs.

___12. A political gain from trade occurs when:
a. wars and conflicts are stimulated by rising real incomes.
b. interdependencies raise the costs of conflicts and so reduce tensions in international relations.
c. political opponents of free trade impose high tariff barriers.
d. countries engage in imperialistic wars in the search for markets.
e. multinational conglomerates exploit cheap foreign labor.

___13. If emerging industries will ultimately
be able to produce at lower cost than
mature foreign competitors can, the:
   a. infant industry protection argument
      is a valid reason for tariff barriers.
   b. consumer losses from protection
      may be offset so that there are net
      gains from such policies when
      prices fall later.
   c. producers will gain more from
      protection than consumers lose.
   d. barriers to foreign trade are both
      inefficient and unnecessary for the
      industry to grow.
   e. government should impose export
      taxes on the emerging industries.

___14. Arguments against free trade that
apply more to small homogeneous
countries than to large heterogeneous
nations focus on:
   a. infant industries.
   b. job destruction.
   c. national defense.
   d. nationalistic or patriotic appeals.
   e. diversification.

___15. Trade barriers imposed in the interest
of national security:
   a. are usually valid when used to
      rationalize import tariffs.
   b. lower the costs of conflict by
      increasing interdependencies.
   c. probably apply more to restrictions
      on exports than on imports.
   d. are always inefficient and cause
      reductions in economic welfare.
   e. raise the costs of conflict by
      increasing independence.

___16. Some people may lose because of
competition from foreign sellers or
buyers of certain goods, but it is
unlikely that the:
   a. specialization gains from trade ever
      exceed the dynamic losses.
   b. net effect of all trade in all goods is
      ever harmful to anyone.
   c. forces of competition will not
      evolve into monopoly power.
   d. trade deficits that harm them can
      last more than 2 or 3 years.
   e. country where they live will allow
      such imports to persist.

___17. Special programs to assist and retrain
people who lose their jobs because of
liberalized international trade are
known as:
   a. Aid to Families Dependent on
      Trade (AFDT).
   b. tariffs and quotas.
   c. Trade Adjustment Assistance.
   d. the Job Corps.
   e. reindustrialization insurance.

___18. Allowing free competition after
imposing tariffs that exactly offset
production cost differences would:
   a. erode the potential gains from
      different comparative advantages.
   b. facilitate efficient diversification.
   c. be incompatible with self-
      sufficiency policies.
   d. be deal to protect infant industries.
   e. immensely profit arbitragers.

___19. Corruption of the officials in charge of the program is most likely for a(n):
a. scientific tariff.
b. import quota.
c. import tariff.
d. tariff on exports.
e. infant industry protection policy.

___20. A voluntary export restriction on cars from Japan will be most beneficial to:
a. U.S. consumers.
b. Japanese consumers.
c. U.S. taxpayers.
d. European luxury car makers.
e. Japanese car manufacturers.

Chapter Review (Fill-In Questions)

1. With no trade, a country's sustainable _____ frontier is limited to its _____ frontier. When trade commences, the uniqueness and specialization gains from trade can be illustrated by a shift in the _____, but not the _____.

2. Gainers from trade include sellers of _____ and buyers of _____; losers include buyers of _____ and sellers of _____.

3. Trade is a _____ sum game, so that the _____ can (at least theoretically) compensate the _____ so that all would _____.

4. _____ gains from trade arise because some countries simply do not have certain resources possessed by others. Rising real incomes stimulate saving and investment, a major source of the _____ gains from trade, which also arise through international transfers of _____. Additionally, _____ gains emerge because trade encourages peace due to the interdependencies associated with the higher incomes from trade. The increases in economic welfare that can be realized through international specialization and exchange are qualitatively the same as those that can be achieved through domestic specialization and exchange.

5. Problems of undesirable income _____ from trade can be offset by _____ to those who lose from freer trade. Generally, import _____ pose more problems than do import _____ as barriers to trade because of the inherent incentives for corruption and the reduced flexibility of response to changes in demand.

Unlimited Multiple Choice

Each Question Has From Zero To Four Correct Answers.

___ 1. The consumption possibility frontier:
   a. depicts sustainable consumption possibilities confronting a country.
   b. is the same as the PPF in the absence of international trade.
   c. shifts inward when a country engages in international trade.
   d. is linear for a pretrade situation of constant opportunity costs.

___ 2. Arbitrage:
   a. moves relative prices toward equality in all markets.
   b. can occur when price differentials exceed transaction costs between two markets for a good.
   c. raises demand in the lower-price market, driving up its price, and raises supply in the higher-price market, driving down its price.
   d. entails buying at a higher price in one market and selling at a lower price in another, where the price differential exceeds transaction costs.

___ 3. When two countries engage in international trade:
   a. the equilibrium international price will exceed the original price of the good in the importing country.
   b. domestic production increases for the good being exported.
   c. domestic production decreases for the good being imported.
   d. consumers of the traded good in the exporting country pay a higher price for the good than they paid prior to trade.

___ 4. When international trade occurs:
   a. the net gains are usually positive.
   b. those who own resources that are relatively scarce worldwide realize gains exceeding any short run losses incurred by those whose resources are relatively abundant worldwide.
   c. gross losses generally exceed any gains to the participants.
   d. the prices of domestic inputs that are abundant worldwide fall, while the prices of inputs that are relatively scarce worldwide rise.

___ 5. According to the infant industry argument for the imposition of tariffs:
   a. domestic industries must be protected from more efficient foreign competitors.
   b. industries in their infancy must charge higher prices because of higher per unit costs of production, so more mature foreign firms have an unfair price advantage over unprotected infant industries.
   c. tariffs generate much needed tax revenue which can be meted out to poor families with many infants.
   d. mature industries need protection from foreign competitors to slow regression into senile infant stages.

Problems

Problem 1

This table indicates the numbers of rollerblades and blue jeans that the United States and Russia can produce in 10 days, given their respective resources. Assume that opportunity costs increase rapidly, and that the final terms of trade fall midway between pretrade costs.

a. Can beneficial trade occur?_____
    Why?_____
    Who would gain? _____
    _____

	U.S.	Russia
Rollerblades	80	60
Blue Jeans	40	10

b. What principle explaining international trade is by the table? _____

c. Define this principle. _____

d. What are the pretrade relative prices of rollerblades to jeans in the U.S.? _____ In Russia? _____

e. If international trade commences, the U.S. will export _____, and import _____.

f. If international trade commences, Russia will export _____, and import _____.

g. Assume that the terms of trade are such that the gains from trade are evenly divided between both countries. The terms of trade will be roughly _____ rollerblades for _____ jeans.

h. Draw a production possibility frontier for the U.S. in the figure on the next page. How is it shaped? _____ Why? _____ Draw the post-trade U.S. consumption possibilities frontiers. Now do the same for Russia, emphasizing the relevant differences. What are they? _____

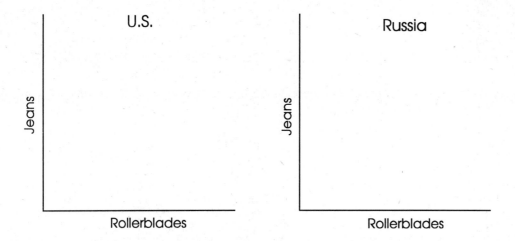

U.S.

Jeans

Rollerblades

Russia

Jeans

Rollerblades

Problem 2

This figure depicts production possibilities curves for Countries Alpha and Beta. The terms of trade are given by the lines TT; points x show consumption and production without trade; points y indicate production combination with trade; points z denote consumption combinations of these goods with trade. Use this information to answer the following true/false questions.

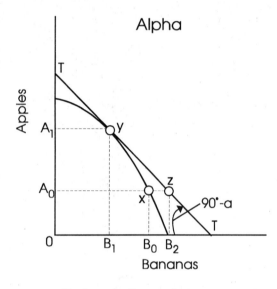

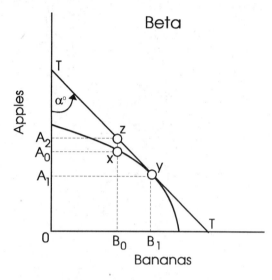

_____ a. Both countries confront constant opportunity costs in the production of both apples and bananas.

_____ b. The slope of both countries' PPFs at points x are consistent with the relative pretrade costs.

_____ c. Once international trade commences, Alpha will produce only apples, while Beta will produce only bananas.

_____ d. In pretrade isolation, each country's PPF also represents its consumption possibility frontier.

_____ e. The pretrade relative costs are the same in both countries.

_____ f. Free trade can enable people in both countries to consume along higher consumption possibility frontiers.

_____ g. Trade cannot yield any net benefits in this example.

_____ h. Once international trade commences, Alpha will produce both commodities.

_____ i. Country Alpha will export bananas and import apples.

_____ j. Country Beta will export apples and import bananas.

_____ k. Before trade, it is cheaper to produce bananas in Alpha than in Beta.

_____ l. The same international terms of trade confront both countries

Problem 3

Suppose workers in Java can produce 10 tons of sugar or 200 shirts per year, while Cubans can each produce either 15 tons of sugar or 45 shirts annually. There are 10 million workers on each island, and assume that costs are constant.

a. Graph the PPF for Java and Cuba in the figure.

b. In Java, what is the opportunity cost of producing 1 ton of sugar? _____ 1 shirt? _____

c. In Cuba, what is the opportunity cost of producing 1 ton of sugar? _____ 1 shirt? _____

d. If Java and Cuba begin to trade with each other, which island will export sugar? _____ Which will export shirts? _____

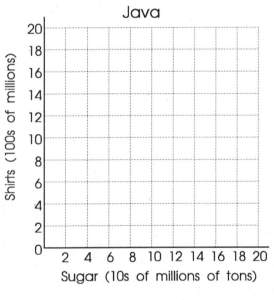
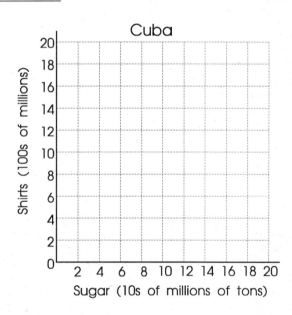

e. Draw each country's CPF on the figure after trade commences, assuming that the terms of trade are halfway between the pretrade relative prices.

f. Which parties gain from the commencement of trade? _____
_____

g. Which parties stand to lose in the short run from trade? _____
_____

Problem 4

Use this figure, which illustrates the U.S. demand and supply of compact disc players, to answer the following questions. Assume that the world price is initially $200 per player.

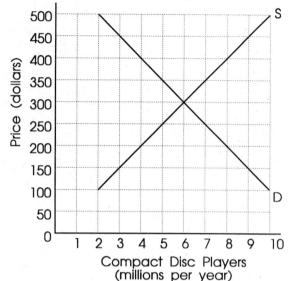

a. How many disc players will the U.S. import? _____

b. How many disc players will the U.S. manufacture? _____

Assume that the U.S. levies a $50 tariff on each compact disc player

c. What price will U.S. consumers pay for a compact disc player? _____

d. How many disc players will the U.S. now manufacture? _____

e. How many disc players will the U.S. import? _____

f. How much in revenues will the government collect from the tariff? _____

Assume the U.S. is currently importing 6 million CD players a year and that there are no tariffs.

g. What is the world price for a CD player? _____

h. How many disc players are manufactured in the U.S.? _____

Assume that the U.S. institutes an import quota of 4 million CD players annually.

i. What is the total number of disc players that will now be purchased annual by U.S. consumers? _____

j. By how many players will U.S. production increase? _____

k. What is the potential total profit to importers as a result of the quota? _____

l. How much revenue will the government collect from the quota? _____

ANSWERS

Chapter Review (Fill-In Questions)

1. consumption possibilities; production possibilities; CPF; PPF
2. exports; imports; exports; imports
3. positive; gainers; losers; gain
4. Uniqueness; dynamic; technology; political
5. redistributions; trade adjustment assistance; quotas; tariffs

Problem 1

a. Yes; differences in pretrade costs; Gainers are American jean makers and rollerblade buyers, and Russian jean buyers and rollerblade makers.
b. Comparative advantage
c. Gains from trade exist when pretrade costs differ
d. 1/2; 1/6
e. jeans; rollerblades
f. rollerblades; jeans
g. 4; 1

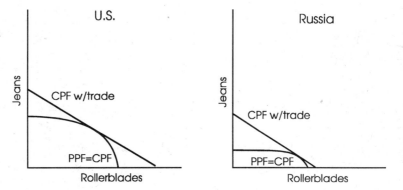

h. See figure; PPF for U.S. is concave to the origin reflecting increasing opportunity costs; PPF of Russia is also concave but skewed towards skates.

Problem 2

a. F
b. T
c. F
d. T
e. F
f. T
g. F
h. T
i. F
j. F
k. F
l. T

Problem 3

a. See figure below.
b. 20 shirts; 1/20 ton of sugar
c. 3 shirts; 1/3 ton of sugar
d. Cuba; Java
e. See figure.
f. Cuban sugar producers, Cuban shirt buyers, Javanese shirt producers, and Javanese sugar buyers.
g. Cuban shirt producers, Cuban sugar buyers, Javanese sugar producers, and Javanese shirt buyers.

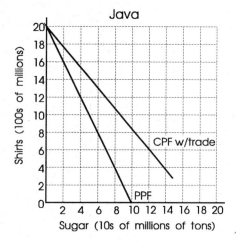

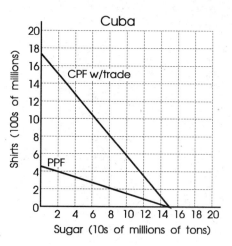

Problem 4

a. 4 million
b. 4 million
c. $250
d. 5 million
e. 2 million
f. $100 million
g. $150
h. 3 million
i. 8 million
j. 1 million
k. $200 million
l. $0

Chapter 21
International Finance

Chapter Objectives

After you have studied this chapter, you should be able to discuss the advantages and disadvantages of fixed and flexible systems of international payments; the problems encountered when currency flows or exchange controls are used to maintain exchange rates at nonequilibrium values; explain the persistence of U.S. balance of payments deficits; and describe some possible reasons for the decline of the dollar from a position of undisputed primacy as the world's medium of exchange.

Chapter Review: Key Points

1. Since we have no world currency, we must establish the value of each national currency in terms of all others. The *exchange rate* is the value of one currency in terms of another.

2. *Balance of payments* accounts record the flows of money into and out of a country and provide information about trade relationships among countries.

3. *Flexible*, or *floating*, systems of *exchange rates* permit the values of currencies to be set by market forces. If a country experiences a balance of payments *surplus* (*deficit*) under such a system, it is an indication that the country's citizens or government (*foreigners*) desire foreign (*domestic*) currencies.

4. A *fixed* exchange rate system imposes price ceilings and floors on currencies, often resulting in persistent disequilibria in balances of payments.

5. Explanations for the decline of the dollar in the 1970s range from relative inflation to expectations of continued inflation and payments deficits to federal budget deficits to the emergence of other strong international currencies to the cartelization of oil to too rapid monetary growth. Opposite trends then strengthened the dollar until 1985. Each of these explanations bears the germ of truth, but none alone is adequate to explain the dance of the dollar.

Matching Key Terms And Concepts

Set I

___ 1. "dirty" float

___ 2. gold standard

___ 3. balance of trade

___ 4. nominal exchange rates

___ 5. appreciation

___ 6. fixed exchange rates

___ 7. depreciation

___ 8. foreign exchange

___ 9. balance of payments

___10. flexible exchange rates

a. Most exchange rates are set by international agreement.
b. Exports minus imports.
c. When the value of one currency rises relative to others.
d. Prices of currencies are set by market forces.
e. Foreign exchange inflows minus funds outflows.
f. Foreign currencies, collectively.
g. Fixed amounts of each currency exchange for given amounts of gold.
h. Government intervention in a flexible exchange system.
i. The prices of currencies relative to one another.
j. When a currency's value falls relative to others.

Set II

___ 1. devaluation

___ 2. dollar surplus

___ 3. relative inflation

___ 4. international portfolio adjustments

___ 5. oil imports

___ 6. exchange controls

___ 7. international supply of dollars

___ 8. exchange risk

___ 9. key currency

___10. real exchange rate

a. Decline of the fixed value of one currency versus others.
b. Governments allocate the foreign exchange available to pay for imports.
c. A currency widely held internationally for transaction, precautionary, and asset reasons.
d. Potential losses to exporters who agree to accept importers' currency, or to importers who must pay in exporters' currency.
e. Relative price of foreign goods in terms of domestic goods.
f. A classic explanation of currency depreciation.
g. "Mirrors" U.S. demands for foreign exchange.
h. Replacing the dollar as the asset of a central bank with some other strong currency.
i. Caused substantial increases in the international supplies of dollars in the 1970s.
j. Identical with a shortage of foreign exchange.

True/False Questions

____ 1. The nominal exchange rate is the value of a currency in terms of itself.

____ 2. If the dollar value of imports exceeds the dollar value of exports, there is a deficit in our balance of trade.

____ 3. An international gold standard would be an example of a fixed exchange rate system.

____ 4. Under a flexible exchange rate system, currencies' relative prices are largely determined by markets.

____ 5. An international gold standard was established by the United Nations at the end of World War I.

____ 6. Foreigners demand dollars only to import U.S. goods or invest in the United States.

____ 7. Unlike other prices, exchange rates seldom change under a system of flexible exchange rates.

____ 8. As is true of markets for virtually all goods, flexible exchange rate systems tend to drive the prices of all currencies to the equilibrium rates at which supply and demand intersect.

____ 9. "Dirty floats" tend to hamper flexible exchange rates so that they change less than they otherwise might.

____ 10. Exchange controls create pressures for government corruption and black markets for foreign currencies.

____ 11. Governments can more independently conduct macroeconomic policies under a flexible than under a fixed exchange rate system.

____ 12. From the end of World War II until 1971, the U.S. dollar was the only major world currency consistently backed by gold, at least for purposes of international trade.

____ 13. The international acceptability of the U.S. dollar has been a major reason why the U.S. has been able to run large and persistent current account deficits from 1981 to the present.

____ 14. The absorption problem prevents countries from running persistent current account surpluses.

____ 15. In 1985, almost all of the dollars held by OPEC countries were exchanged for other currencies.

____ 16. International transactions demands for dollars arise because exporters in many countries view dollars as less prone to exchange risk than the currencies of their customers.

____ 17. International demands for dollars have enabled the United States to offset persistent payments deficits with trade surpluses.

____ 18. Other countries have been far more successful than the United States in reaping seignorage from international financial markets.

___19. Foreign loans by U.S. organizations have accounted for most of the recent surpluses in U.S. balances of payments.

___20. A "dirty float" occurs when foreign central banks buy dollars from international money markets and store the dollars in their vaults.

Standard Multiple Choice

Each Question Has A Single Best Answer.

___ 1. A country that exports more than it imports experiences a:
   a. balance of payments surplus.
   b. deficit in its national budget.
   c. balance of trade deficit.
   d. deficit in its balance of payments.
   e. balance of trade surplus.

___ 2. The major reason for Americans to demand foreign money is to:
   a. add to collections of rare stamps and coins.
   b. pay for imports or foreign investments.
   c. profit from seignorage by printing dollars.
   d. finance tourist visits to foreign countries.
   e. avoid U.S. income tax liabilities.

___ 3. Americans demand foreign currencies by:
   a. exporting capital goods.
   b. supplying dollars.
   c. running balance of trade surpluses.
   d. creating shortages of U.S. currency.
   e. following inflationary policies.

___ 4. A gold standard is an example of a:
   a. fixed exchange rate system.
   b. nondiscretionary "pegged" currency.
   c. flexible exchange rate system.
   d. "dirty float."
   e. "crawling peg" automatic stabilizer.

___ 5. Stocks of foreign currencies that have been received to cover international payments are:
   a. gold coins and bullion.
   b. foreign exchange.
   c. international seignorage.
   d. bills of lading.
   e. international transfer payments.

___ 6. A currency's price in terms of a foreign country's currency is known as the:
   a. nominal exchange rate.
   b. terms of trade.
   c. reciprocal value.
   d. counter price.
   e. par value.

___ 7. Currency revaluation under a gold standard would parallel:
   a. depreciation under a silver standard.
   b. appreciation under a flexible exchange rates.
   c. devaluation under fixed exchange rates.
   d. recycling under an ecological system.
   e. repricing costs in an inflationary system.

___ 8. A balance of payments surplus could result from:
   a. international surpluses of the country's currency.
   b. falling imports and rising exports.
   c. contractionary policies by its trading partners.
   d. shifting from a fixed to a floating exchange rate system.
   e. overseas investments by domestic firms.

___ 9. Reversal of a payments deficit if all countries were on a gold standard might entail:
   a. revaluation of the country's currency relative to other currencies.
   b. depreciation of the currency through normal market processes.
   c. contractionary macroeconomic adjustments.
   d. discoveries of new gold supplies in the deficit country.
   e. decreasing Aggregate Demands in surplus countries.

___ 10. If American balance of payments deficits indicate disequilibrium, the markets for currencies of countries experiencing balance of payments surpluses are characterized by:
   a. shortages.
   b. surpluses.
   c. unusual scarcity.
   d. overproduction.
   e. excessive supply.

___ 11. Appreciation will eliminate a balance of payments surplus most rapidly when:
   a. foreign demands for a country's exports and domestic demands for imports are both extremely inelastic.
   b. foreign demands for exports and domestic demands for imports are both elastic.
   c. domestic exchange controls are rigid.
   d. inflows of foreign exchange are used to pay for all foreign purchases.
   e. none of the above.

___ 12. An American balance of payments deficit would be reduced by:
   a. increased U.S. foreign aid programs.
   b. increased imports by consumers.
   c. greater levels of foreign investment by American corporations.
   d. lower prices for imported goods that are elastically demanded by U.S. consumers.
   e. greater foreign purchases of the bonds of American corporations.

___13. A substantial increase in the national income of a country will:
    a. cause a balance of payments surplus under a fixed exchange rate system.
    b. generate pressure for the country's currency to be revalued upward.
    c. cause its exports to increase dramatically.
    d. cause devaluation under a flexible exchange rate system.
    e. create pressure for the depreciation of the exchange rate of its currency.

___14. Since 1946, relative to the U.S. balance of payments, our balance of trade has:
    a. far more often been in deficit.
    b. often balanced or been in surplus, prior to 1981.
    c. consistently been in deficit.
    d. consistently experienced larger deficits.
    e. None of the above.

___15. The dollar's position as a key international currency has:
    a. allowed Americans to gain through seignorage by issuing international money.
    b. been a major reason for loss of U.S. power and prestige.
    c. stimulated growth of federal deficits.
    d. driven our balance of trade into persistent surpluses.
    e. dampened economic growth internationally.

___16. A hike in international oil prices will cause the dollar to fall more under a flexible exchange rate system if:
    a. foreigners believe that the FED will adapt to these hikes with expansionary monetary policies.
    b. our demands for imports and foreign demands for our exports are both quite inelastic.
    c. foreigners quickly lose faith in the dollar when its exchange rate falls even slightly.
    d. other countries with strong currencies are less dependent on imported oil.
    e. All of the above.

___17. Which of the following has not been offered seriously as an explanation for the 1970s decline of the dollar?
    a. OPEC petroleum price hikes.
    b. expectations of continued relative inflation in the United States.
    c. rapid increases in prices for gold.
    d. overly expansionary U.S. monetary policy.
    e. the increasing stability and acceptability of other currencies.

___18. Until roughly 1970, foreign central bankers could exchange:
    a. $35 to the U.S. Treasury for an ounce of gold.
    b. deficits in their balance of payments for U.S. Treasury bonds.
    c. international loans at a fixed interest rate at the World Bank.
    d. surpluses for silver certificates issued by the International Monetary Fund.
    e. trade surpluses for United Nations payments.

___19. If exporters' currency appreciates, exchange risk losses could be imposed on:
   a. importers who insisted on paying in their own currency.
   b. exporters who insisted on being paid in their own currency.
   c. arbitragers who exploited price differentials between markets.
   d. importers who agreed to pay in the exporters' currency.
   e. speculators who had bought the exporters' currency earlier.

___20. Consistent U.S. balance of payments deficits are partially explained by:
   a. demands in unstable countries for economically stable currencies.
   b. foreign governments bolstering growth by stimulating exports.
   c. habits developed when the dollar was the only currency convertible to gold.
   d. greater foreign demands for dollars than for American goods.
   e. All of the above.

Chapter Review (Fill-In Questions)

1. The price of one currency in terms of another is known as its _____. A country's exports minus its imports is its _____; its inflows of funds minus its outflows is its _____. Currencies received from sales of exports are known as _____.

2. Under a(n) _____ exchange rate system, such as the _____ standard, payments deficits can be met by borrowing or drawing down previously accrued _____, or by _____ controls, under which government allocates the foreign currencies that are available.

3. One problem with _____ exchange rates is that international transactions create exchange risk; if the contract specifies payment in the _____ currency, exchange rate depreciation of that currency will cause the _____ to receive less than expected, while the importer will be forced to pay more than expected if the currency of the _____ is specified and the exchange rate of that currency appreciates. These problems can be finessed, however, if the traders negotiate a contract in either currency and then "buy insurance" against _____ by dealing in the _____ market for foreign exchange.

4. In the past half century, the United States has persistently run _____ in its balance of payments. This has been possible because, internationally, the dollar has been a _____ currency. Foreigners have demanded dollars to facilitate transactions, even when American traders are not involved. Our relative political and economic stability have also caused foreigners to demand dollars for _____ and _____ reasons. The ability of the FED to issue "international money" has allowed Americans to reap _____ because of the huge difference between the _____ of dollars and their value in exchange.

Unlimited Multiple Choice

Each Question Has From Zero To Four Correct Responses.

____ 1. Balance of payments:
   a. deficits occur when a country's receipts of money from foreigners exceed its payments to foreigners.
   b. accounts use double-entry bookkeeping.
   c. record financial flows among countries that trade internationally.
   d. surpluses occur when a country's receipts of money from foreigners exceed its payments of money to foreigners.

____ 2. If there is a fixed exchange rate system and a country's currency is characterized by a:
   a. surplus, then its balance of payments tends to be in surplus.
   b. shortage, then its balance of payments tends to be in surplus.
   c. lower demand by foreigners than it has demand for foreign exchange, then there is an international surplus of its currency.
   d. greater demand by foreigners than it has demand for foreign exchange, then there is an international shortage of its currency.

____ 3. Fixed exchange rates:
   a. respond more quickly than do flexible exchange rates to changes in relative supplies and demands for currencies.
   b. pose no special problems as long as exchange rates reflect the relative supplies and demands for currencies.
   c. distort the true values of all currencies.
   d. cause no problems as long as their values are the same as the values that would exist under flexible exchange rates.

____ 4. The United States has been able to run balance of payments deficits fairly consistently for almost four decades because dollars:
   a. are widely used as an international medium of exchange.
   b. have been viewed as "insurance" in politically unstable countries.
   c. have been supported at artificially high exchange rates by West Germany, Japan, etc., to boost U.S. demands for their exports (or, perhaps, to indirectly pay for U.S. provision of national defense).
   d. create volatility in the exchange rates of monkey currencies.

____ 5. An increased American preference for Japanese goods:
   a. will manifest itself in a decreased American demand for the yen.
   b. will manifest itself in an increased American supply of dollars in foreign exchange markets.
   c. means that American importers of Japanese goods may be forced to pay higher dollar prices.
   d. implies a depreciation of the yen in terms of the dollar.

Problems

Problem 1

Use this figure, which depicts markets for the U.S. dollar and the British pound, to answer the following questions.

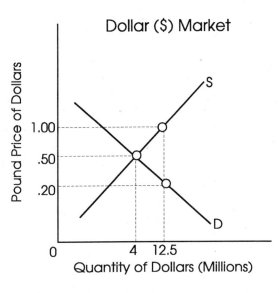

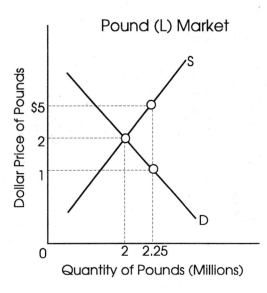

a. What is the equilibrium exchange rate of the dollar? _____

b. What is the equilibrium exchange rate of the pound? _____

c. What is the per unit (pound) price of a dollar? _____

d. What is the per unit price of a U.S. dollar? _____

e. Explain why the U.S. demand for British pounds is downward sloping. _____

f. Explain why the British supply of pounds is upward sloping. _____

g. Suppose Americans purchase British goods valued at $2 million. Americans demand _____ British pounds in equilibrium and supply _____ dollars.

h. Assume the British manifest an increased preference for U.S. goods. Which curves will shift and why? _____ What happens to the British pound? _____ What happens to the dollar? _____ What happens to the pound price of American exports to Britain? _____ What happens to the dollar price of U.S. imports from Britain? _____

i. Assume that the new equilibrium exchange rate is $1 = 1 pound. What is the equilibrium exchange rate of the dollar? _____ Suppose that Britain purchases U.S. goods whose value is $2.5 million. This implies a British demand for dollars of _____ and a British supply of _____.

j. Return to the original equilibrium exchange rate; that is, $.50 = 1 pound. If the exchange rate is pegged artificially high at $1 = 1 pound, what situation would prevail in the U.S. balance of payments? _____ Why? _____

Problem 2

Complete this table to obtain all the possible exchange rates between the six different currencies listed. The first row tells how much foreign currency one U.S. dollar can purchase.

	Dollar	Deutsche Mark	Pound	Franc	Yen
Dollar	1	2	1/2	6	120
Deutsche Mark					
Pound					
Franc					
Yen					

Problem 3

Use this table, which shows the balance of payments for the country of Sata, to answer the following questions

	Receipts	Payments	Balance
Current Account			
Merchandise Exports	+220		
Merchandise Imports		-328	
Trade Balance			
Net Investment Income			
Net Services		-1	
Net Unilateral Transfers		-11	
Current Account Balance			-102
Capital Account			
Capital Outflows			
Capital Inflows	+93		
Statistical Discrepancy	+36		
Official Reserve Transactions Balance			+6
Method of Financing			
Increase in Sata Official Reserve Assets		-9	
Increase in Foreign Official Assets			
Total Financing of Surplus			-6

a. Fill in the missing entries.

b. The trade balance is equal to _____. This indicates a trade (surplus/deficit).

c. The sum of numbers 1 through 10 equals _____. Is this is coincidence? _____

d. The statistical discrepancy accounts for what kinds of transactions? _____

ANSWERS

Matching		True/False		Multiple Choice		Unlimited MC

<table>
<tr><td colspan="2">Matching</td><td colspan="2">True/False</td><td colspan="2">Multiple Choice</td><td>Unlimited MC</td></tr>
<tr><td>Set I</td><td>Set II</td><td></td><td></td><td></td><td></td><td></td></tr>
<tr><td>1. h</td><td>1. a</td><td>1. F</td><td>11. T</td><td>1. e</td><td>11. b</td><td>1. bcd</td></tr>
<tr><td>2. g</td><td>2. j</td><td>2. T</td><td>12. T</td><td>2. b</td><td>12. e</td><td>2. bcd</td></tr>
<tr><td>3. b</td><td>3. f</td><td>3. T</td><td>13. T</td><td>3. b</td><td>13. e</td><td>3. bd</td></tr>
<tr><td>4. i</td><td>4. h</td><td>4. T</td><td>14. F</td><td>4. a</td><td>14. b</td><td>4. abc</td></tr>
<tr><td>5. c</td><td>5. i</td><td>5. F</td><td>15. F</td><td>5. b</td><td>15. a</td><td>5. bc</td></tr>
<tr><td>6. a</td><td>6. b</td><td>6. F</td><td>16. T</td><td>6. a</td><td>16. e</td><td></td></tr>
<tr><td>7. j</td><td>7. g</td><td>7. F</td><td>17. F</td><td>7. b</td><td>17. c</td><td></td></tr>
<tr><td>8. f</td><td>8. d</td><td>8. T</td><td>18. F</td><td>8. b</td><td>18. a</td><td></td></tr>
<tr><td>9. e</td><td>9. c</td><td>9. T</td><td>19. F</td><td>9. c</td><td>19. d</td><td></td></tr>
<tr><td>10. d</td><td>10. e</td><td>10. T</td><td>20. T</td><td>10. a</td><td>20. e</td><td></td></tr>
</table>

Chapter Review (Fill-In Questions)

1. nominal exchange rate; balance of trade; balance of payments; foreign exchange
2. fixed; gold; foreign exchange; exchange
3. flexible; importer's; exporter; exporter; exchange risk; forward
4. deficits; key; precautionary; asset; seignorage; production costs

Problem 1

a. .50 pound
b. $2
c. .50 pound
d. $2
e. law of demand
f. law of supply
g. 1 million; 2 million
h. demand for dollars increases and the supply of pounds increases; depreciates; appreciates; increases; decreases.
i. 1 pound; $2.5 million; 2.5 million pounds
j. deficit; surplus of dollars due to exchange rate imbalance.

Problem 2

	Dollar	Deutsche Mark	Pound	Franc	Yen
Dollar	1	2	1/2	6	120
Deutsche Mark	1/2	1	1/4	3	60
Pound	2	4	1	12	240
Franc	1/6	1/3	1/12	1	20
Yen	1/120	1/60	1/240	1/20	1

Problem 3

Problem 3

	Receipts	Payments	Balance
Current Account			
Merchandise Exports	+220		
Merchandise Imports		-328	
Trade Balance			-108
Net Investment Income	6		
Net Services		-1	
Net Unilateral Transfers		-11	
Current Account Balance			-102
Capital Account			
Capital Outflows		-123	
Capital Inflows	+93		
Statistical Discrepancy	+36		
Official Reserve Transactions Balance			+6
Method of Financing			
Increase in Sata Official Reserve Assets		-9	
Increase in Foreign Official Assets	3		
Total Financing of Surplus			-6

NOTES

NOTES

NOTES

NOTES